Never Go Anywhere Without a Pencil

HARRIET VAN HORNE

Never Go Anywhere Without a Pencil

G. P. Putnam's Sons, New York

Never Go Anywhere Without a Pencil

"Never Go Anywhere Without a Pencil"

Never go anywhere without a pencil
Though what you write may be only a stencil.
Somewhere, somehow, in train or steaming tub,
In subway, street, or accidental pub
There'll be a glory you must annotate
For those who tuned in late.
Given a break, the chance is even to odd
God will catch up with you; or you with God. . . .

—CHRISTOPHER MORLEY,

"The Ballad of New York, New York"

Introduction

"Well, I've had a happy life."

So murmured the great essayist William Hazlitt as he closed his eyes for the last time.

In truth, he'd had nothing of the sort. Hazlitt was a hand-to-mouth journalist who lived in poverty and died in lonely agony. He was a love-hungry man with a fretful nature who contracted two bad marriages and made a public fool of himself over a sluttish servant girl. Rarely, if ever, was he out of debt.

Hazlitt failed as a painter, scholar, husband, father and provider. But that he judged his life a happy one in no way surprises.

For Hazlitt was a working journalist, always at the restless center of life. He wrote about the men, the books, the ideas that gave his world—Regency England—its tone and color. Into all his work Hazlitt put love and anger and truth. He clothed the naked, as he once said of Wordsworth, "with the beauty and grandeur from the stores of his own recollection."

Hazlitt left no one neutral. He was a critic who hymned the beautiful and damned the shoddy. And he did it with such style that John Keats could write, "Hazlitt . . . is our only good damner."

9

Introduction

Dying in cheap Soho lodgings of malignant stomach ulcers, this "good damner" could look back on a life of sorrow and frustration and still declare that his time on earth had been happy. And it *was* happy, I should say, because some vital part of his being had been fulfilled. He enjoyed one satisfaction not granted most men: He was ever able to say what he thought. And people listened. Right there, we may perceive a cup that runneth over.

Not a journalist breathes today who even approaches Hazlitt at his jaunty best. But all of us who live by the word, setting down the brief abstract of our times, have entered into Hazlitt's special joy. He was *involved*. He took sides. Above all, he was a man of his time, and his time could move him to tears of pity and to hot salvos of wrath. So it goes with most of us who toil for the daily press. It is this passionate involvement that makes life bearable, even sweetening the gall at times.

Journalists are a peculiar breed, falling somewhere between ballad singers and unfrocked dons. We write with small hope of getting rich or even attaining ease. Our daily mail brings us cascades of abuse from readers who wish we'd drop dead. Sometimes they even send instructions.

A few years ago, a team of psychologists studied various professions to determine which carried the highest anxiety quotient. Journalism, to the surprise of nobody in my circle, ranked first. There's more worry, more tension, more nagging self-doubt in writing a daily column than in walking a high wire or doing a heart transplant. (No, the psychologists didn't tell me that. I just *know*.)

Anxiety over our prose, our polemics, our deadline is only part of the agony. "Don't you ever get tired of worrying about the state of the world?" readers inquire.

Well, of course I do. I also get tired of paying rent and taxes, of going to the dentist, of sponging Persian cat hair off the dark suits of gentlemen callers. I'm terribly tired right now of deodorant commercials and rock music and jumbo-sized females in hot pants and restaurants where the temperature is kept at a steamy 85° lest the red wine take a chill.

But, in the words of T. S. Eliot that I shall *never* tire of, "There is nothing to be done about it/ There is nothing to be done about anything/ And now it is nearly time for the news."

Since leaving college, I have spent twenty-five underpaid, anxiety-ridden years in the newspaper business. The life is not for the faint of heart. Year before last, at the New York *Post*, I went through my ninth strike. Or maybe it was the tenth. I never picket so I tend to forget. (I never cross the picket line, either.) Strikes, like old love affairs, tend to fade after a time into one big heartbreak.

I have been on strike in the heat of summer and in the bone-chilling cold of winter. Summertime is best. Christmas week is worst. But all strikes break your heart. Next year I daresay there will be another . . . the printers, the engravers, the mailers, the editorial staff. It has become an automatic reflex in the newspaper business. Strikes hastened the death of three New York newspapers. As a weapon against management, it self-destructs.

As any fool can see, the newspaper business, more than ever before, is a great business to get out of. Likely young reporters have a way of quitting the instant they become likely. Some move on to the plusher precincts of public relations, television or advertising. Some write novels or plays. But most of us lack the nerve to quit or the genius to escape. We love newspapers the way a plain woman loves a charming, no-good husband. When the going is good, it's so wonderfully good! When there are secrets known only to the privileged few on the Great Inside, they're the hottest, spiciest secrets in the world.

If I worked each day amid the bustle and clatter of the city room, I'd doubtless be in on more secrets, especially sexy ones. But most columnists work at home.

I work where I live in a luxury slum—that is, I pay twice what I can afford for an apartment that country folk wouldn't live in for half the price. I pay for charm, not convenience. And charm is what I get. But there are certain compensations not mentioned in the lease.

First, I'm in Hip Zip Zone 21, a few steps from Central Park. On a clear day you can smell *earth*. In summer you can see green, growing things. Past my house march children with balloons and starched nannies with English prams. In a city of steel and concrete growing less habitable by the hour, these are agreeable touches.

In Zip 21 we're a short stroll from Bloomingdale's, the BMT and other cultural landmarks. Chic boutiques abound. There's a neighborhood cinema that serves muck-thick espresso while the crowd from the last show gets into its galoshes. And there's a pet shop that shampoos my Persian cat for twelve dollars and sends her home in a bubble-top case smelling like a field of clover.

In terms of architecture, my pad is Blenheim Palace set down among the egg crates. I live in a crumbling relic of New York's gracious past, a survivor of the Edith Wharton era when ceilings were high and rents low. My fireplaces are marble, my floors fine oak. The windows rattle, but the sills are wide enough for plants, books or a basking cat. And there are lots of windows.

My slum walls are as solid as the Bastille, stone between thick boards, stoutly protective. If you can hear a phone ringing or my typewriter pounding through these walls, you're the last of the Mohicans and you also hear twigs snap and pins drop.

My slum pleases me because there are reminders of the gentle, orderly life once led inside these walls. There are swift-sliding paneled doors that disappear into the wall, doors fitted with retractable brass pulls. There's a wall safe behind a bookcase and a master closet big enough for an armoire, a toboggan or a small piano.

The kitchen is the sort that should have an old-fashioned coal range. When our clanging tenement heat goes off, I light the gas oven. A coal fire would be cozier. It glows in the dark and sometimes sparks fly.

Introduction

Though we cook with gas, it's still an old-fashioned kitchen, with wine racks, a cupboard for cookbooks and a lamp-lit corner for reading. It's a kitchen where bread should be forever baking, where Clancy the cop should be dawdling with his coat off, having coffee and a bit of hanky-panky with Nora the cook.

Had I the Dutch thrift I was born with, I'd not, of course, be living in my luxury slum. I'd be making do in a woodchopper's hut and selling my gingerbread at the side of the road. But I'm much too poor to move. Besides, I love all my seedy grandeur. Love it and am warmed, soothed and protected by it—except on the days when nothing, absolutely *nothing* works.

The wiring in my house was installed by somebody who obviously believed oil lamps would shortly be coming back. If you walk heavily past the air conditioner fuses blow. The heat and the hot water always go off together. Sometimes the ceiling leaks and plaster falls in a fine, dandruffy powder. The boiler undergoes repairs several times a year, during which all faucets are shut off. Sometimes we are warned of this calamity and can fill tea kettles and bathtubs. At other times we're reduced to melting ice cubes and washing in bottled water.

The staff problem is touch-and-go in New York apartments today. We have lots of transients. Now and then one of the elevator men gets drunk, insults visitors and bars the door to messengers bearing vital papers. (Newspaper messengers, for example, picking up the copy.)

Today, as I write, the water is off once more and we're brushing our teeth in soda water. The decay of New York's housing is a sin. This old gray stone fortress deserves to be kept in better style. It remembers a time when there were two footmen in the lobby, very smart in their hunter's green livery and white gloves. It remembers topiary trees in fat tubs lining the walk under the porte-cochere.

There was a day when the Thomas Fortune Ryans occupied our penthouse and Peggy Guggenheim kept a *pied-à-terre* on the tenth floor. Now there are sixty doctors in the house. And we've a faded little woman who tells fortunes and takes in $1,000 a week.

And an elderly Southern belle who has partitioned her bedrooms and now takes in distressed young ladies at modest prices. They ride to the basement laundry in the evening with their dirty dainties spilling out of chic shopping bags.

Our dim lobby has marble floors, heavy grillwork doors and a high ceiling. Once upon a time it had a rich, beautiful rug, real plants and handsome sofas. Now the greenery is plastic and we have mock-Spanish chests, straight-backed Jacobean chairs and *art nouveau* lamps with 40-watt bulbs. The effect is rather like the back room of Goodwill Industries. In winter we have cooking odors from six o'clock on. . . .

Our worst problems seem to come in the summer, however. One year the kitchen pipes ruptured in May, leaving a gaping hole in the wall until mid-July. For ten terrible days we had no water, hot or cold, in the kitchen. No water for cooking, washing, filling ice trays, moistening sponges or simply drinking. When the plumbers reached a crucial point in their repairs, there was no water anywhere in the house. It even stopped dripping from the dining-room ceiling.

"What this house needs is a well and a privy," said Catherine, my cherished cleaner. It was a sensible observation, and I passed it on to the landlord.

There are days when life is bleak, even in my fine moated grange. But on those days I can be glad I don't live in a mobile home. I don't live in a split-level ranch house with crab grass. And my luxury slum is not a new high-rise luxury slum. Antiquity may be inconvenient, but it comforts the soul.

It's often lonesome working at home, but there are compensations. A theoretical one is that the writer who writes at home sets his own hours—that is, he rises punctually at 7 A.M., spends the next two hours marking and clipping the *Times* and receiving phone calls from Senators, his stockbroker and various movie stars. Then he reads improving literature for an hour or so, underlining any brilliant thought that strikes his fancy, and hoping it will fit into his next day's essay. Finally, he unsheathes his typewriter and taps out 1,000 words in thirty minutes, every word a jewel.

Maybe this is the way Lord Chesterfield would do it—or William Buckley, Jr., who is frequently under the impression that he *is* Lord Chesterfield. But if one happens to be a deadline writer—and most journalists are—the adrenalin does not flow, nor do the sentences take shape in the mind, until the cold blade of the deadline ax falls on the nape of the neck.

Deadlines smite the conscience and race the mind. They also add to the anxiety quotient and punish the ego. "If only I'd had five more minutes," frets the writer after the copy has been given over to the copy boy, "then I could have polished that last paragraph, put a real stinger in the tail." Or reshaped that lead. Or worked in some statistics on black lung disease. Or quoted something apt from the Book of Revelation. Oh time, oh regret, oh thoughtless copy boy that comes before the Muse dare!

I cannot recall a working night (habit has made me an afterdark writer) when I have not experienced a great quivering pang as the messenger has snatched up the envelope (marked CITY DESK—RUSH) and stepped abruptly back into the elevator. It is at that moment that the rewriting process begins. Sometimes it lasts all night.

But how to rewrite when the copy's gone? Somehow, I always do it. But in my mind's eye, Horatio. Unless one has made some monstrous error, it's not a good idea to ring up the copy desk and say, "Listen, I'd like to dictate four new paragraphs. . . ." What you will hear from the other end of the line could not be printed in the next day's edition.

Down the years, at the old *World-Telegram* and later at the *Post*, I have been blessed with understanding editors. The copy desk and I frequently differ on syntax and spelling. I have learned not to write "had got" because somebody is sure to change it to the vulgar "had gotten." I have learned to write "center in," not "center around." But no copy reader in my experience believes that "loan" must always be a noun, never a verb, that *hoi-polloi* takes no definite article, and that the past participle of "prove" is "proved," never "proven." (Would you say "disapproven"?)

Similarly, the copy desk cannot persuade me that "employee" should have only one *e* and that only affected literary types spell "kidnapped" with two *p*'s.

I learned long ago that deadline writers must suffer the consequences of their haste and carelessness. In general, my job has been brightened by the forbearance of the people with whom I have shared the typos, the strikes and the closing notices.

I am certain there are some wrong guesses in the pieces that follow and there are probably some wrong constructions. One writer's colloquialism is another's barbaric solecism. "Harriet nods," as I have been heard to say. But I hope the pieces that follow project something of the mood and temper, the pain and gusto and folly of the days that closed the '60's and plummeted us, with fear and trembling, into the '70's.

The period surveyed in this book brought agonizing changes to America. We had student demonstrations, prison riots, bombings, shootings, ritual murders and some lovely Earth Days. Our country has been torn, in a terrible way, by such issues as busing for racial balance, by the My Lai massacre and the trial of Lieutenant Calley. We've all formed strong opinions on welfare reform, peace demonstrations, Women's Liberation, organic food that spoiled in a day and Spiro T. Agnew, who, in some eyes, spoiled even quicker.

But as the curtain fell on the 1960's, we discovered some new heroes, stage center. Among them: Ralph Nader, Ramsey Clark, John Gardner, John Kerry and Captain Aubrey Daniel, whose letter of censure to President Nixon will occupy a high place in the history of our time. So will the judges who honored the word and spirit of the First Amendment and allowed the citizenry that has paid so dearly for the Vietnam War to read in the Pentagon Papers how tragically and stupidly their tax dollars had been spent.

If one could choose a time into which to be born, wrote Emerson, would it not be a time of revolution, "when the old

Introduction

and the new stand side by side and admit of being compared"? Certainly that would be my choice. Looking around, it seems I made it.

Comparisons of old and new loom large in the pages that follow. Like Desdemona, I have perceived here a divided duty. By reasons of birth, bias and life-style, I am outside the hairy youth movement. I do not smoke pot, go barefoot, attend pornographic films or devise my days according to the counsel of Tarot cards. I know from scientific evidence that astrology is a fraud and that a macrobiotic diet can kill you.

Though I hardly consider myself doddering, I have taken a decidedly over-thirty stance on the wilder aspects of youth culture.

"Whom the Lord loveth, he chasteneth," as Bible-quoting parents used to tell their young. The hippie movement made me a chastener. But here's where duty divides. If I am outside the long-haired love-in world of the young, I am *totally* removed from the middle-aged, middle-brow Middle America that abhors the "radicalism" of youth.

The dress, the language, the matted hair and the hideous music of the young continue to affront me. But I love the young for their gentleness toward one another, for their stern devotion to peace, to clean air, clean politics and creative craftsmanship. They may yet save us from perdition. But in the meantime, I still wish they'd wash and cut their hair.

There's irony of a personal sort in the time that passes through this book. These, the years I have toiled at the most satisfying job I've ever had, were the years I had once planned to sit out as a contented housewife and occasional scribbler. My husband and I were plotting my resignation from the newspaper business when, quite suddenly in 1965, he died of a heart attack. Emotionally speaking, this was an H-bomb in the walled garden of my private life, and there are still occasional shock waves. When a loved one dies, part of one's self dies. The world never looks the same again.

A few years after losing my husband, I lost my paper. The old *World-Telegram* died of too many strikes, too much penny-pinching and the dead weight of its own mediocrity. Its final years, for all who cared about literary style, honest reporting and decent working relations, were heart-wrenching.

This once fine newspaper's resurrection as the *World-Journal-Tribune* never had a chance. We all tried hard. But we were on the Doomsday Press, and we knew it. New York needed those three papers that sank so pathetically, then surfaced so briefly, before going under for the last time. Many valuable journalists lost their calling, their very sense of identity when that leaky, three-masted tub went down. I was one of the luckier survivors. In three months, quaking with uncertainty, still a grieving widow, I began writing a column for the New York *Post.* A year later the column went into syndication, by grace of the Los Angeles *Times.* Life has been more interesting since then.

Before closing this preface, attention must be paid certain people to whom I am grateful. To my husband, the late David Lowe, whose unseen presence still nags me when I don't feel like writing. To Dorothy Schiff, the publisher of the *Post,* who gave me a job when I needed one. To Paul Sann, the *Post*'s executive editor, who has been kind and fair in every small crisis. To Lois Wallace, my agent, so brisk and tireless, who bound me legally to the contract that left me no choice but to assemble this book. To Marcia Magill, my patient editor, with whom I laughed so much and from whom I learned so much.

And, finally, attention must be paid to Them, my dear readers whose letters, alas, have largely gone unanswered. I must explain this delinquency because it hurts me every day of my life. But when one is poor and works at home keeping hours no secretary would share, a ruthless question must be faced—that is, "Now, do you want to write the column or do you want to write letters all night?" It's a simple matter of either/or. If one writes letters all night, soon there is no column. And shortly after that, no letters.

Since 1968, a few letters—those whose kindness touched me to tears—have been answered. But my conscience still stabs me when I recollect the thousands of letters and clipping requests I have had to put aside.

Letters mean a great deal to a columnist. They're instructive. They reassure. They chasten, they hearten, they sweeten sorry days. I have always felt warm sympathy for Emily Dickinson writing in her narrow spinster room, "Here is my letter to the world/ That never wrote to me. . . ."

To all of you who never got a letter of reply or a requested clipping, I am dreadfully sorry. I'm also grateful. And this book is for you, my letter to the world that always—and mostly with charity—wrote to me.

—HVH

New York City
May, 1972

1968

The Long-Gone Days

. . . Bloody Summer. The year the Democratic Party lost the election in the streets of Chicago. The year we lost Bobby Kennedy and Martin Luther King and sent Richard Nixon and Billy Graham to the White House. The year Spiro Agnew finally became a household word, provided you lived in a permissive household.

It was the year Jackie married Ari and her pedestal began to wobble. It was also the year Julie Nixon and Dwight David Eisenhower II became, in the words of one irreverent reporter, Mr. and Mrs. Howdy Doody.

1968 . . . the year of the Columbia riots, with the New York police coming down like Cossacks on unarmed students and professors. The longest student strike in history got underway at San Francisco State and S. I. Hayakawa became a household word in California. . . . Women's Lib set fires and laid siege to the Miss America pageant in Atlantic City, carrying banners that said THE LIVING BRA—THE DEAD SOLDIER. . . .

Three U.S. astronauts went around the moon ten times during the week before Christmas, singing carols and reading the Bible as they rocketed through the starry night. . . . The young who can't spell learned to spell "sitar" and "guru" as the Beatles flew to India for meditation—and eventually disenchantment. . . .

The *Pueblo* crew came home and a Court of Inquiry prepared to sit. . . . New York City high school students rampaged through the subways for four days, protesting longer school sessions. . . . The Walker Report blamed Chicago police for the "excessive brutality" of the convention riots.

People talked about Biafra and mini-skirts and hippies and student protests . . . and where would it all end?

There's a certain kind of woman who'd rather be rude than right. A woman who'd rather be a screaming shrew at the gates of hell than an angel in paradise.

For this woman there is a certain word—but you're not likely to read it here. We'll simply say she's a bawd, a slattern and a thoroughly unpleasant baggage. But she's the New Woman, shaped by the abrasions of our time, raised to prize rubies—even fake ones—above wisdom. She's not precisely Everywoman, but there are days when I feel she's all over New York.

She sits behind me at the theater in her sixty matched bracelets with the tiny clashing cymbals, complaining loudly that she can't hear the actors. She's at every clearance sale with little spurs on her elbows and a right hand borrowed from Captain Hook. She always—yes, *always*—gets the last decent girdle on the clearance table. Then she ties up the only phone in the ladies' lounge to announce her victory.

Let a group of militant women appear on television, and there's the woman of the hour, Mrs. Bawd. The hostility she has been hoarding all day is suddenly spewed forth as she denounces the mayor, the Board of Education, the police or her landlord. (In the case of her landlord she's probably right, but never mind.) Righteously, she talks of urban renewal, better street lighting, rent control. But her words distil a poison even when she's right.

Mrs. Bawd had the fitting booth next to mine at one of New York's nicest shops last week. I recognized her instantly by the way she suddenly shrieked "Miss!"

"Miss"—who happened to be one of those neat, gray little ladies in basic black who stand all day looking pleasant when their feet hurt and their heart aches—was instantly by her side, all solicitude.

"Just lookit this collar," cried Mrs. Bawd. Calm and courteous, the *vendeuse* asked what was wrong with the collar. "It's *serled!*" came the reply. This was followed by a rush of expletives, including "grimmy."

It was not the accent that grated. Gentleness and courtesy often accompany diction that would send Professor Higgins into a stomping rage. (A rage in which we can again hear his plaintive query, "Why can't a woman be more like a man?")

One reason may be that men are so cowed by these boss ladies that they dare not assert themselves. Men have a lovely way of never creating a deliberate storm, knowing full well that there's a tiny tempest blowing up any minute. H. L. Mencken was on sound ground when he wrote, "Women like men who are docile, well-regarded at the bank and never late for meals."

Well, *that* sort of women like that sort of men. Can there be any doubt that each is getting his ideal mate? Whoever said, "Nature is in earnest when she makes a woman," wasn't jesting.

With all their pretty ways, their historic devotion to love, duty and the little ones, women can be a coarse and ruthless lot. It seems to me awfully lax of nature not to have made more females Just for Fun. It's the lack of a sense of humor in women en masse that makes their character seem worse than it is.

Nobody likes women who try to emulate men, but some women could well emulate men's principles. In the ordinary business of life, men tend to behave more decently. As an example, here's a snatch of party conversation that has always haunted me:

"That's a marvelous dress, dear," says an admiring lady. "Did you have it made?"

"Yes, I've a superb little dressmaker. But I'm not giving anybody her name because she'll suddenly get very busy and very grand and raise her prices."

I've heard this exchange, with variations, a thousand times. It always makes me ashamed of women who keep little dressmakers hidden away in the back streets, safely out of prosperity's way.

I'm also ashamed of women who are rude to hairdressers and waiters, women who use four-letter words in mixed company, women who nag their husbands in public and women who lodge their maids in rooms the size of jail cells and imagine they're having a rich, full life in there with a TV set and a box of chocolates. Ah, the ladies! Why doesn't somebody open a national charm school? We need it.

In one of Anthony Carson's wildly funny books there is a testy old English colonel whom I shall always cherish. "Of course I'm fond of animals," said he. "I used to keep a bee."

Well, I flee from the bee, but I've kept dogs and cats over the years. And I'm a fascinated reader of animal books. On my shelves you'll find Konrad Lorenz, Bernhard Grzimek, Gerald Durrell—yes, even Beatrix Potter with her cheerful, exquisitely detailed drawings of Tom Kitten, Squirrel Nutkin and fat, foolish Mrs. Tiggy Winkle. Humankind, as we've been told, cannot stand very much reality. And there's much to be said, in these menacing times, for old Walt Whitman's line, "I think I could turn and live with the animals; they're so placid and self-contained."

In particular, Whitman admired animals because "they do not sweat and whine about their condition . . . and not one is demented with the mania of owning things."

As the study of animal behavior grows more sophisticated, we are exhorted by scientists to consider the beasts of the field and grow wise. Last year we received the message in Desmond Morris' book *The Naked Ape*. It rose quickly to the best-seller list because it spoke with terrifying bluntness on two subjects: sex and war.

Now we have an equally fascinating—but less ominous—work titled *Signals in the Animal World* edited by a Viennese appropriately named Wolfgang Schleidt. Like Professor Morris, he is filled with awe and respect for animals and their incredible techniques of survival. One begins to feel that the habit we all have of humanizing our pets—anthropomorphism, it's called—should be reversed. With the world in such a state, maybe it's time we began animalizing ourselves.

With the war still raging in Vietnam, with students erupting in violence all over the world, with 10,000,000 Americans literally starving to death because their own species has stopped its ears to the cries of the hungry, one feels a new respect for the pride of lions that kills only to eat, for the great apes which live a complex social life without slaughtering their own kind.

In many ways we all still resemble our simian forebears. Our tensions and hostilities, our need for love and authority, our foolish pride all may be seen in the activities of the higher apes. And I enjoy this parallel every time I read of the ritualistic ballet going on at the peace talks in Paris. The attitudes being struck by both sides are so absurd and yet so fated that we might as well send in two teams of chimpanzees and let them draw up a peace treaty.

Desmond Morris tells us that when animals are attempting to settle a conflict they exhibit "strange and seemingly irrelevant behavior." They find outlet for their energies in ridiculous posturing.

Well, look at the proceedings in Paris. The opening day of the conference was devoted to an Alphonse and Gaston ritual over who should occupy the choice seats under the tapestry. Then came endless debate, with earphone translations, over the seating of minor delegates, the amount of information to be released to the press—all the matters Averell Harriman dismissed as "routine garbage."

27

Never Go Anywhere Without a Pencil

It should comfort the folks back home, especially the doves who want nothing but a cease-fire and permanent peace, to learn that these absurd rituals serve a useful purpose. Both man and beast must perform the "vamp till ready" dance. Only in this way can they evolve a repertory of signals. Wars began in this world when combatants no longer could signal to each other. When the gun replaced the rock and the club, we were on a downward slope. Apes are wiser and luckier. When one combatant is exhausted, he puts out a limp paw. Apes, says Professor Morris, are too smart to murder. We, alas, are the dumb beasts.

Apparently, it isn't enough that our political preferences are being solicited night and day, in cafés, buses and supermarkets, by those tireless poll takers.

Now our social attitudes and emotional responses to the candidates are being studied and coded.

"Narcissistic men and women feel safe only if they vote for a person who reminds them of themselves," a psychiatrist tells readers in a ladies' magazine.

"For many voters, political preferences may better be considered analogous to cultural tastes—in music, literature, dress, ethics, speech, social behavior." This view is from a worthy book *The Degeneration of Our Presidential Elections* by Jules Abels.

After a few weeks of this sort of reading I am thinking of designing a new button that says DON'T ASK ME ANYTHING—I'M THINKING!

And if stating one's political preference rips the veil from one's inner self, a good many people are going to announce their support for James K. Polk. (Well, it's a free country, and you can write him in—in some states.)

Democracy, one begins to suspect, functioned closer to the founding fathers' ideal in the days when you never saw the candidate unless you attended a torchlight parade in his honor. Or sat in your buggy down by the depot as he waved from the rear platform of his chugging campaign special.

Now we learn that a distinguished sociologist, Dr. Paul Lazarsfeld, has compiled an "Index of Political Predispositions." I haven't seen it, but it probably suggests that if you're a rural Nebraska farmer whose parents always voted the straight Republican ticket, why, confound it, you're going to vote the straight Republican ticket, too.

But I wouldn't count on it. In these changing times nothing is certain—particularly in politics. Ask Hubert Humphrey.

There was once a politician who said that Iowa would vote Democratic "the year hell goes Methodist." Well, nobody has polled sectarian preferences in hell this year, but Iowa has gone Democratic many times. And if you went to the trouble, you'd doubtless turn up a Nebraska farmer of pure Republican lineage who voted for Norman Thomas. (If you find more than one, though, hell is certainly going Methodist this year.)

The games people play in an election year are desperate and sometimes foolish. But I'm inclined to agree with some generalities about personality factors influencing voters' decisions. In a book I can't put my hand to at the moment, Professor Clinton Rossiter of Cornell wittily describes the outward differences between a roomful of Democrats and a roomful of Republicans. I've spent considerable time in both, and I find his generalities, for the most part, valid.

The Democrats, wrote Dr. Rossiter, tend to be gregarious, boisterous, good-humored, generous, politically shrewd and not conspicuously elegant. They make a lot of noise, have a good time and occasionally get into some timber-shaking rows. The Republicans, by contrast, are apt to be sedate, well-dressed, efficient, intolerant of dissent, a bit stingy and not so ready to laugh and be merry.

The fact that we have all met stingy, efficient, intolerant Dem-

29

ocrats and some shrewd and boisterous Republicans must be one of those exceptions that proves no rule. All I can tell you with certainty is that the Democratic National Convention—except in 1968—is always a lot more fun than the Republican one.

The conclusion of Mr. Abels' thoughtful book is rather depressing. "Our Presidential election is in trouble," he writes. "If it continues on its present course, it will degenerate into more and more of a burlesque, and the public will increasingly tune out the noise in favor of escapist entertainment."

The fakery, the cheap emotionalism, the backstage fighting, the crude appeals to fear—all must go, Mr. Abels believes. Perhaps in his next book he will tell us how.

What is so rare as a day in June that isn't the anniversary of something?

Oh, I don't mean just your sister's wedding or the Duke of Windsor's birthday. June is the month of Waterloo and the Magna Carta. It's the month a man named Graham made the first trip over Niagara Falls in a barrel and lived to tell it.

June is the month of blueberries and Bloomsday (sacred to all Joyceans) and the month you're asked back to your class reunion. If you're not in your perfect mind, you go. I have not been back since my tenth, which is a testament to my sanity. It's also a confession of vanity. For in that tenth assembly I saw the dreadful signs and portents of the twenty-fifth and fiftieth and resolved never to go again. Ever.

This week two small events, quite unrelated, persuaded me anew that class reunions are to be avoided by all women save those who grow younger, prettier and richer with every passing year.

The Long-Gone Days

My first event was a letter from a dutiful classmate who never misses a tree-planting on the old quad. She loves reunions and has a great gift for describing minutely how age has withered those slender, petal-faced girls of yesteryear.

The letter was the sort that should appear in the *Alumnae News* but never will. Mary X. now looks like a dirigible and talks of nothing but the stock market. Jane Y. (who used to write funny, naughty verses) has had two breakdowns and is so thin she *rattles*, honestly. Somebody else went to India on a Fulbright and caught some hideous, wasting disease and should have been seated with the class of 1909, poor thing.

Well, I read that letter over my coffee and muffins and went straight to the window to look at my skin in a strong light. Then I stepped on the scales and resolved to give up muffins. Also coffee. Up to 101. In college I weighed 95 in my field hockey suit with the Green Bay Packer padding on the knees. But, oh, the ravages of the years, the little laugh lines, the tired eyes. As the French say, it is to cry.

The other aging event in my day was the reading of a book called *The Body* by Anthony Smith. "Nothing quite like this book has been written before," says the jacket. That may be a tiny exaggeration, but wait till you get to the chapter on aging. You may take splendid care of your health, and your death at eighty-five will be attributed to old age. Nonsense! says Dr. Smith. Nobody ever died of old age. You'll die of a fatty heart, hardened arteries, softened spleen, diseased lungs and brain clots. All these horrors will have come upon you so slowly nobody will notice till the autopsy.

I've another book at hand that says we shall be able, in not too many years, to postpone death by hibernation and long-term coma. Well, that's how I'll go to my fiftieth reunion—in a long-term coma. It's the only way.

No doubt there are pleasant aspects to the ritual of class reunions. But "all things that pass are woman's looking glass," as Christina Rossetti rightly wrote. I do not wish to be gathered under the elms with the fallen peach and the withered rose. I prefer to identify with Byron's Laura—wise Laura, "who made the best of time . . . and time returned the compliment."

If the old girls must meet once a year, I would suggest a candlelight reception—with one candelabrum—at some place like Elizabeth Arden's or an out-West beauty ranch. Old pippins may be toothsomest—a highly debatable notion—but not in those sensible shoes and terrible girdles. A few women are slim and chic and sexy at sixty-five (they look, of course, forty-five). But these are the women who abhor reunions. On the rare occasions they attend one they're apt to bring their youngest daughter, a fresh-faced beauty who calls back the lovely April of Mummy's prime. That's another reason for staying away from class reunions. The daughters tell you, with an innocent glance, how old you really are.

Most women—and I mean nice, average women—live in a world of boundless illusion. They imagine that a thorough drenching with French perfume makes them sexy. They believe a deft hand with pineapple upside-down cake binds a husband to the hearth with hoops of steel. And they move serenely through life convinced that any man who strays from the connubial chamber is married to some common slattern who simply doesn't understand the subtle mysteries of a good marriage, such as French perfume and upside-down cake.

Never disparage that old cliché about ignorance being bliss. It is, it is.

Men, bless them, tend to look upon women's little iron whims with benign amusement. Innocence in women can be most endearing, even when it borders on stupidity. Men like cloistered women, unspotted from the world. I used to know a man who rarely let the cocktail hour pass without quoting that funny little woman in one of John van Druten's plays who couldn't remember what a martini was. "Is it," she asked, "the one with the cherry?"

That joke must be thirty years old now. The modern girl can mix martinis, drink martinis and freeze them on a stick for picnics. But in terms of the world, the flesh and the devil, she's still an innocent. And that, I imagine, is why one hears so many gently bred ladies making sly little jokes this summer about that "health club" on New York's Upper East Side that turned out to be the grandest palace of sin the New York cops have raided in years.

The jokes, of course, are laced with disapproval. But there's no disguising their curiosity. Most of us girls, after all, are never likely to see the inside of a genuine, deluxe brothel with marble washstands, sauna bath, leopard-skin laundry hampers and velvet sofas with hair dryers mounted at one end. (There are certain women, we now know, who dry their hair lying down, and never mind why.)

The health club, as the ladies have all read, was raided on a "normal business day." Some customers, understandably rattled by the arrival of the police, fled over the rooftops of Lexington Avenue. One chap left behind a fine English suit containing his wallet and all his credit cards.

The owner of this establishment (who said he believed he had rented it out as a bona fide health club) reported that the young ladies on the staff—"Prettiest damn bunch you ever saw"—were highly educated, some with master's degrees. He didn't say in what.

The ladies who heard this part of the story sniffed in disbelief. One said, "I don't suppose those poor girls ever find a good husband and settle down." All that knowledge, worldly and scholarly, her tone implied, but no little nest for baking and barbecuing and bewitching with clouds of French perfume. If cozily

33

wedded wives envy the ladies of the evening, they keep the envy a secret. I daresay that tells us something proud and lovely about the American wife.

The most memorable comment in the story of Manhattan's plushest brothel came from one of the raiding policemen. "They used to hold Roman orgies here," he told a reporter. The idea clearly struck him as marvelous.

I tried to conjure up a really smashing orgy from antiquity suitable for revival on Lexington Avenue. One Roman scribe tells us of banquets where the guests lay on silken couches, fanned by slaves and besotted by wine made of absinthe and honey. Showers of flowers fell from the ceiling. On the menu were such delights as camel's heels, combs torn from living cocks and bowls of lentils in which lurked pearls and rubies. The host often arrived on a silken cushion, heralded by trumpets. Naked girls emerged from pies in a flutter of thrushes.

At some orgies guests overcome by wine were carried to adjoining bedrooms. On waking up they found themselves staring at lions, tigers and panthers. "Tame, of course," we read, "but some of the guests were stupid enough not to know it and died of fright." Now there, officers, was a *real* orgy. Doubt that you'd even see one like it today, not even on Park Avenue.

In times of trembling uncertainty, I admire people who build houses, breed babies, plant trees and put away precious heirlooms for unborn grandchildren.

With the Vietnam War dragging on, with Red China testing nuclear weapons, it takes courage these days even to take advantage of a Big Money-Saving Five-Year Subscription—to say nothing of building a house or begetting a baby.

The Long-Gone Days

Doing all these things is an affirmation of life. The most valuable people in this world are those who say "Yes!" to life and damn the bombs. Let us salute the gallant ones who, in the face of Vietnam and drug-dotty hippies and assorted Dr. Strangeloves roaming the corridors of power, maintain their sunny optimism about the human condition.

"We know nothing of tomorrow; our business is to be good and happy today." So wrote my favorite nineteenth-century wit, Sydney Smith. In our own private worlds there may be much to be good and happy about, if we can learn to take the short view and cast out fear. It is faith in the ultimate goodness of man that gives us our inner security—more security than you can buy with gold bullion, more than you can build into the snuggest bomb shelter this side of the catacombs.

Americans in recent years have shown themselves susceptible to odd forms of hysteria—hysteria over Communism, over black power, student insurrections, sex and drugs. As a nation we also tend to react with extreme prudence and caution when a threat is posed. There was a man named Hulbert Taft in Ohio who epitomized, to my mind, the prudent man who looketh well his going. He went sky-high while inspecting his costly deluxe model bomb shelter.

It's nice to think that poor Mr. Taft left a message in his mortal dust, for people who fancy salvation can be found underground with tinned fruit juice and a first-aid kit. The message: We are saved, at the last, by hope and faith. Not by nuclear weapons, not by carpeted dugouts with chemical toilets, not by intrigue or low cunning.

The Pentagon view of the Vietnam War can only shock and repel those of us who would like to go on planting trees and putting down fine brandy to age for a golden wedding. From time to time one of those retired generals, blazing with ribbons and wrath, announces that the war could be ended in a week if only our missions over North Vietnam let go with a *real* bomb. It's also likely that many military strategists share General Curtis

LeMay's view that North Vietnam fights on because of "undying Oriental fanaticism."

But while the war goes on and the generals talk of bombing those Oriental fanatics back to the Stone Age, it is good to remember that the rambler roses are blooming in country lanes and golden children are learning to swim in turquoise pools. Old oaken barrooms are dim and cool on July afternoons and young lovers are warm and wanton in hidden coves, as the loveliness of summer ripens toward autumn.

With autumn will come great national decisions. Old rascals turned out, new rascals brought in. The easily affrighted will take flight. The papers will continue to be filled with those ominous initials—ICBM, ABM, FOBS and all the rest. ESCALATION will be back in the headlines. But somewhere people will still be planting trees, exclaiming over a new baby or weeping at a daughter's wedding. The only victories that matter are all there. And the chief duty is still to be busy and happy today.

"June's twice June since I breathed it with her," sang the poet Browning. In June, if ever, come perfect days. But how do you face June when the one who has breathed its beauty with you lies in a fresh grave with a bullet through his head . . . and the glory of June all around?

If you are Ethel Kennedy you face this first June of widowhood as you have always faced life—with pluck and spirit and a convent girl's faith in God. You face it with ten children needing to be soothed and kissed, and another on the way.

So many times lately, as I have stepped forth into the tender glow of another June day, my eyes have suddenly misted, remembering the quick, tawny figure of Ethel Kennedy leaving St. Patrick's, a stranger in her black veils. To say that she is gallant pays tribute to the obvious. She is also beautiful. And shattered, torn, bitter and lost. All widows are.

A woman who enters the state of widowhood enters it alone. Yes, even with ten children beside her. She becomes the sole inhabitant of a world as bleak and vast as the moon. I know. I have been there.

36

Widowhood is a wild, primitive country where even the light and sound are different. Clocks and calendars cease to mean what they once meant. A ghostly face stares at you from mirrors, dumb, swollen, bruised by grief. You cannot bear the morning mail because so much of it is still addressed to him. You cannot open the closet where his clothes hang because *he is there*—warm, familiar, reaching out to life.

After a long time in this shadow world, you begin to see faint patches of life. You notice the weather, you buy a new dress. Someone who loved him now gently removes his clothing, his desk, his toothbrush. You hear yourself promising to do this or that next week, next year. You have begun to feel alive again.

But before you begin saying "Next year . . ." you must cry out for death a thousand times. Every wound must bleed. There are nights when even sleep is torture. Nights when you reach out and start to say, "Darling, I had this awful dream. . . ."

And there are other times when you wake with a start, thinking, "My God, somebody's sobbing." And of course it's you. And it's four o'clock in the morning. And the world ended a week ago. Or a month . . . or six months ago.

Only widows know through what wild nights widows must endure. In that huge Kennedy clan, only Jacqueline could tell Ethel what life will be like in the year to come. But a widow's grief is beyond all telling.

People have told me I am wrong, but it has always seemed to me that death is harder to bear when it comes suddenly. At first the shock numbs all the senses. Then the full horror of it washes over one, a bath of scalding acid. Gone! Not coming back. "Never glad, confident morning again." Never.

My husband died suddenly one evening of a heart attack. It happened at his club. His son, his doctor and his best friend arrived at midnight to tell me the news. Only the doctor believed it. He had signed the death certificate.

A true sense of widowhood did not overtake me until the funeral. Then I was one with the black-cloaked women of the Sudan, the wives waiting in the rain after the mine explosion, the

37

women on the banks of the Ganges watching the flame consume the bone and sinew of love.

Up to a certain point in life, death has no dominion. You expect to live forever. And you expect those you love to live forever, too. You have the talisman—love—to ward off evil. When a loved one dies before his time, before he has run his race, grown old with honors thick upon him, the injustice is bitter, the heart breaks for him.

A number of reporters commented on Ethel Kennedy's dry eyes and good spirits during the long train journey to Washington. In truth, few widows give way to wild weeping with the world looking on. The saddest rites for the dead are the tears shed alone.

Lawrence Whistler, English artist and poet, wrote a beautiful book, *The Initials in the Heart*, when his wife, the actress Jill Furse, died shortly after the birth of their second child. It was then he entered "the hemisphere of loss which has, not a weather of its own, but a whole new climate of weathers flowing forward without end."

In the weeks immediately following his wife's death, Whistler says he "wanted nothing better than to live always in the immediacy of her loss. In the sharpness of it, I felt near to her."

We all shelter inside our agony for a while. But the life-force does finally assert itself. The need to talk to people, to share the bread and the wine, to repay the kindness that saw you through the worst of it begins to put down grief. The people who said, "He'd want you to go on living, to be busy . . . ," at last have the satisfaction of hearing you reply, "That's right. And I'm trying."

With so many children to occupy her attention and so many tributes and acts of public courtesy to acknowledge, one imagines that Mrs. Kennedy will find solace in duty. Many women do. But duty has never yet banished loneliness. The blessing of a good marriage is that it somehow breaks down one's primal isolation. You *become* each other, in so many little ways.

What a woman misses most in her days of mourning is not the

touch of a vanished hand but rather the loving, the sharing, the "doing for." The hardest hour of the day starts at 6:30 P.M. That was when you would sit down, you two, with the whiskey and soda, the cat and the fire, to go over the errors of the day. Who called, what the letter from home said, what happened today at the office. Whoso hath despised the day of small things? Not the old lovers by the fire, sipping their scotch at dusk.

Now, to see night fall outside the window and hear no key in the lock, no cheery whistle . . . that is to know the darkest pain of widowhood. After five years, when I dream of David, it's a homecoming dream. The key turns. Then the whistle, very soft. Then the cold stab of truth. And it's never glad, confident evening again, either.

A man can die in a second. But the image of the man—the being lodged forever in the mind and heart and dreams of the woman who loved him—dies slowly, reluctantly. A breath a day at first.

Elderly people give up their dead more easily. They have known so many who have gone before. "He is with his fathers now," they say. "Judge none blessed before his death," they quote.

The young who mourn cannot patch grief with proverbs. And because they are in the thick of life, they pity the dead and curse whatever gods there be. It is the young who suffer what psychiatrists call survivor guilt. They're ashamed of their rude good health. ("What right have I to go on living?") This, too, ultimately passes.

The customs and trappings of death in our society do not, Mr. Joyboy to the contrary, ease a widow's grief. A belief in the soul's immortality is still the major solace. As she kneels beside the two Kennedy graves in Arlington, the Senator's widow may find comfort in remembering Saul and Jonathan, they who were slain upon the high places. "Lovely and pleasant were they in their lives, and in their death they are not divided."

Like Bottom the Weaver, I've a reasonably good ear in music. And I'm always ready to dance to the tongs and bones.

Except for the hideous dithyrambs of the discothèques and the sound a small child produces by beating a drum, I can listen to anything—anything at all, including very bad sopranos, accordionists in restaurants and bagpipes.

But, please, don't ever come to one of my musical evenings with an Indian sitar. I do not wish to hear a haunting raga about the arrival of a stillborn infant during last year's monsoon. I don't even want to hear the medley of squeaks known as Tuning Up. One wee wail from this idiot instrument and my central nervous system goes bonkers. A fingernail scuttling across a blackboard is, to me, a richer, sweeter sound.

I'm aware that the sitar is very big with the flower children, the tone-deaf and those free spirits who buy Zen perfume at Macy's and hang a beaded curtain at the bathroom door. My musical tastes are eclectic. I love to hear Bach played on a harpsichord. I sing Puccini in my bath. I revere Louis Armstrong. But the sitar—and the whole sick cult of bogus mysticism that goes with it—strikes me as another stride toward the life of total nullity.

Not surprisingly, the hippies have made the shuddery squeaks of the sitar their own sacred music. It's the improvisation that appeals to them. Each raga, it seems, is improvised on the spot and never heard again. The form is free, the raga sufficiently primitive to strike a chord in those simple lads who wear tinkling bells to concerts, setting up a weird counterpoint to the sitar squeaks.

On a recent TV program we were treated to a philosophical dissertation on Indian music and related topics by George Harrison, one of the Beatles. He said nothing particularly striking or original—or even sensible—but I daresay he represents the new wave in music. He's a recent convert to what dabblers in Hindu religion call Being—with a large *B*. Next season he may be a Gymnosophist, large *G*.

I have lately been reading the Beatles' thoughts on yoga, on music, on life, death, serenity and, to be sure, Being. I can only conclude that the movement East is accompanied by the music it deserves.

On one aspect of the hippie style and kindred fads that scorn discipline agreement seems to be solid. They are aesthetically impoverished, all the way. Hippie paintings are ugly daubs. The handicrafts they peddle in the street (reportedly to raise a few pennies for pot or LSD) are slovenly. Their verse is nasty, prurient gibberish. Naturally, they are transported—almost into non-Being—by the high, thin whine of the sitar.

To express these prejudices automatically puts me in a back pew with the squares. I don't appreciate hippie art? Well, obviously my house must be hung with gilt-framed paintings of little girls in sunbonnets feeding geese, or two fat kittens peering out of an old boot. No feeling for the art that expresses communion with the universe. No sense of Being.

The enthusiasm of the Beatles for Maharishi Mahesh Yogi—a bearded swami who meditates on "thoughts without meaning"— inevitably stirred a warm response among the tinkling flower children of London. They are all reading books on yoga and trying to follow Maharishi's instructions on how to arrive at That—with a large *T*.

Asked to define That, this wise man of the East replies, "I am That, you are That, all is That." And that's the kind of a statement that calls for a glissando on the sitar. Small *s*.

In my favorite book of household hints—I say favorite because it's the funniest—there are specific instructions for thawing out the loaf of bread you've left too long in the freezer. Are you ready?

All right, you slice the bread, presumably with the kitchen ax you keep at hand, and then you *press* each slice with the steam iron.

Now, it's a rare steam iron that has a dial setting for *bread.* But in this age of fortified, unsaturated, preservative-added foodstuffs, you really don't need a setting marked "bread." Just move the dial to a point halfway between "cotton" and "dacron." And, *voilà!* you've got the true flavor of store-bought bread.

It's ironic that in this age when anybody who's cut his second molars considers himself a gourmet, the quality of our staple foods is so dreary. I had imagined that only fusspots like me were complaining about the gummy bread, the brackish eggs and the bits of twig and bark that make up an ordinary tea bag. But no, there are hordes of us, all mad, all hungry. Count among them culinary expert Mimi Sheraton whose remarks on food constitute my favorite quote of the week.

"What fascinates me," says Miss Sheraton in *New York* magazine, "is that the more interest there is in gourmet food, the more terrible the food is in the markets. You can't buy an unwaxed cucumber in this country. . . . You can't buy a really fresh egg because they have been washed in hot water so the shells will be clean."

In Miss Sheraton's view, we are the last generation blessed with even "a vague memory of what food is supposed to taste like."

Who is to blame for this sorry state of affairs? Miss Sheraton blames the food editors, endlessly preoccupied with their *quiche lorraine* or *boeuf en daube* and heedless of consumer problems.

Some people blame the corner grocer and the big supermarket. This is not where the trouble begins. We should blame Congress for so adulterating the "truth in packaging" bill a few years ago that food processors continue to get away, if not with murder, then with sneaky practices that deprive us of nourishment. We are also deprived—and this is important—of the rich sensual experience known as Good Eating. When the pleasures of the chase, the game, the boudoir all have gone, the pleasures of the table are left, or should be. It's sad to be making this complaint at this season. For the plenteous time of year is come again. The fruits of autumn are making food counters lovelier than any display in Tiffany's. Who can resist apples polished to a ruby gloss? Or late peaches in their little jackets of topaz suede and jolly pumpkins all in a row? Suddenly the daily marketing chore is a fine, aesthetic experience. Suddenly, too, in the midst of preparing dinner, you are struck by the perfect Flemish still life on the cutting board; the copper bowl, the fruit, the cheese. Nature jogging memory, bowing to art.

But beauty is only a part of this all-cheering plenty. What comforts a housewife even more is the sure knowledge that nature—sweet, old, unpackaged, unrefined nature—isn't cheating her. She need have no nagging worries about false bottoms, slack weight, illegal adulteration or strange foreign bodies.

It's good that we can enjoy the richness of the harvest with an easy mind. True, the commerce committee and the food lobby emasculated the bill envisaged as protecting the hard-pressed consumer from fraud. The egg yolks may sprawl, the bread may be ashes in the mouth and the cucumber redolent of Glo-Coat, but an apple is usually all-apple to the core. And inside each grape there can only be pulp, seeds and the lingering sweetness of September's sun. No certified caramel coloring, no calcium propionate to retard spoilage. Nothing but the wine of life, plucked young and sweet.

Even the squash, the swine's snout among these fruits of paradise, is pure gold within. No fumaric acid, no wax, no wadding, no monosodium glutamate. Just squash.

How to restore the good flavors of the earth to our tables is a major problem. You begin, I expect, by baking your own bread and keeping chickens. Then you can move on to grinding your own curry powder and drying fish on the radiator. No, no!—better write to your Congressman!

The generation gap, from all I've been hearing lately, is becoming a chasm. Parents can't talk to their children, teachers can't get through to the students. It's all terribly sad. And the strain and the silence are leaving older people with a sense of desolation they've never known before.

I've done a bit of reading about the youth movement these past few days. I've been touched by the idealism, the religious zeal of some youngsters. But to the wilder militants with the obscene picket signs, to the Yippies with their idiotic prattle of drugs, I can only say, "Don't come near me, sweet-and-twenty. I've no wish to talk to you."

Those of us who wish to see every youth as ripe for grand exploits and mighty enterprise can be forgiven for seeing the nettles in flower power. And, worse, incipient totalitarianism in the rigidity and elitism of the New Left. It's a square sentiment, but the movement could also do with fewer loonies and layabouts.

I have no doubt that the Youth International—those hairy hooligans called Yippies—have given the entire student protest a bad name. One would like to see the responsible student leaders fastidiously detach themselves from these gibbering exhibitionists.

When Stewart Alsop of *Newsweek* respectfully asked Abbie

Hoffman, a leading torchbearer of the youth revolt, to name the long-range goal of the New Left, he was told, "Abolish pay toilets, man. That's the goal."

Humor and high spirits in youth are always lovely to see. But this is deranged humor. It comes with a sneer that's almost a snarl. Any interview with Abbie Hoffman and his shaggy colleagues must be set against the sorry fact that this is an "outgroup" in the fullest sense. It's out—up, up and away by grace of LSD and other drugs.

The drug culture has done more to estrange the young from their fathers that begat them than any other single custom, including the new sex morality and the draft protests. But in rejecting the "materialism" and the "puritan values" of the older generation, youth lately seems to be rejecting the simple common sense that preserves life and decency. Thus does the gap widen.

A not incidental effect of this widening gap is the estrangement of older people who greatly enjoy involvement in youthful affairs. The youth culture, from fashions in dress to a private patois—an argot of new slang and old obscenities—has immured them in a world parents find as strange as the Arctic tundra.

The day will come, predicts Marya Mannes in her novel *They*, when the young will outnumber the old and the old will be put away in special enclaves. The novel may be a fantasy, but it is chilling all the same.

"I remember the first time in my life I was afraid of the young," says a character called Annie. "I was afraid of them in groups, like when they came out of high school at 3 o'clock, they were so tough and hard and dirty-mouthed. And then . . . I couldn't find any dress to fit me. They were all for little girls."

Though some of Miss Mannes' old folks struck me as gratuitously dirty-mouthed, I was moved by her account of how intellectuals, men and women who'd spent a lifetime in the arts or humanities, found themselves baffled by the "new forms."

"We would read a book that others reviewed as brilliant and find it self-indulgent gibberish. . . . We would go to plays celebrating evil with four-letter words, or uttering nothing, and come

45

away empty. . . . We kept looking for meaning, for standards, for order and were told they were no longer relevant."

Given that kind of world, those concentration camps for people over fifty may become centers of culture and learning. But the sad fact remains: Separation by age groups is a damaging development. We all need one another, men and women, old and young, black and white. Such is the nature of man.

The trouble with women, men used to be fond of saying, is that they just don't know how to be gentlemen.

Men were fond of saying this a good many years ago. Now they're more likely to complain that women—some women—simply don't know how to be ladies. It's the truth, and the world is poorer and nastier because of it.

It probably stunned nobody to read recently that obscene language is becoming commonplace among women. Particularly women of the upper class: college girls, nice young matrons, women whose grandmothers always undressed in the dark and called the piano legs "limbs." Now they're cursing like old sailors—and wondering why a man no longer removes his hat in an elevator and surrenders his bus seat to a member of the weaker sex.

We live in an age of androgyny, as sociologists are busy pointing out. Sex differences are slowly blurring as women take to tweed pants and motorcycles, as men grow long hair and perfume themselves like harem dancers. It's a thoroughly unattractive trend, and God knows where it will end. Meantime, we've got all those rough-tongued girls cursing like fishwives at cocktail parties, at campus rallies and busy intersections. The question in older, gentler minds is Why? Why, when such foul language demeans the user far more than it shocks the hearer?

A New York University psychologist, Professor Ladd Wheeler, suggests that obscene language filtered down to college girls from "female movie stars and the Beautiful People." This seems to me an unlikely theory. If it's true, the so-called Beautiful People must be rather coarse types, newly rich and hiding their insecurity behind scorn and smut.

As for female movie stars, some of them have risen from the meaner streets of show business where harsh oaths are as common as a how-do-you-do on Park Avenue.

Another common fallacy is that the police were moved to lay about with billy clubs because they, being lower class, were so incensed to hear upper-class women casually use words once washed from tenement walls by pious mothers.

I doubt that the police were all that shocked. It has been my experience that the middle class is the most shockable group. The police would do well to bear in mind Groucho Marx's famous quip, "I can't stand rough talk from anybody but a lady."

After many years as a journalist, novel reader and playgoer, I fancy I have heard all the dirty words there are. But I still find obscene language offensive, and particularly so in mixed company. It is, in the final analysis, *hostile* language. The aggression may be veiled, but it is there. That bawdy talk is commonest among the lower classes should hardly surprise us. This is where life is most vile. Aggression—with tongue and fist—is natural, a survival of the primitive.

Throughout history the bored, vacant-minded upper class, including the ladies of the royal court, has sought to give life a rougher edge by adopting the lewd language of beggars and whores. And from time to time, as social customs change, women assume coarse habits in an effort to be "one of the boys."

That the boys worth pleasing despise this crude aping of male prerogatives hasn't occurred to these gross young things. Women never have a stronger hold on men than when they are armed with all their weaknesses and delicacies. One can easily reduce a man to stuttering devotion with a gentle word, a hurt expression. It's not so easy to do it with a stevedore's oath.

As proof of human progress, some pious philosopher has cited the fact that the world "began with a garden and ended with a holy city."

"Some progress!" a gritty-eyed, footsore New Yorker might sniff as he contemplates the uncollected garbage, the sooty skies, the taxi shortage, the children running wild in the streets because all the schoolteachers are out on strike.

Just let any Lord Tennyson whisper, "Come into the garden, Maud!" and I'll be there with a *tour jeté* over the trellis.

Urban blight, urban sprawl, urban nerves—anybody residing in a town big enough to hold three churches and a jail has got them all. City people are dying of city sickness. Even those residing amid the holy relics of Rome and Jerusalem would, I fancy, reverse that aphorism about man's progress from garden to city. Obviously, it's a great piece of philosophy that has come down to us backside to.

Living in New York—except for the very rich who come and go and never get caught in the great maw—is an exercise in fortitude. Almost daily one feels the air and space diminish, the dirt and disorder worsen. The skyline grows ever uglier. And the air over Manhattan now has the consistency of fuzz and a color you might call autumn smog.

There are days when a short stroll will persuade you that the science-fiction nightmare about industrial haze blacking out the sun may yet come to pass. I often think of Robert Herrick's love lyric with its wistful "Oh, to kiss the air that lately kissed thee!"

Kiss that air, dear boy, and you'll get a sweet smack of sulphur dioxide, carbon monoxide, benzopyrene and hardly a whiff of Chanel No. 5. That's what pollution is doing to romance in this town.

Since World War II some 40,000 buildings have been razed in New York. We live amid ruins and cold, steel replacements of ruins. Apartment hunters have been known to ask the real-estate agent showing them about, "Is this view permanent?" In New York it rarely is. Of twentieth-century planners, posterity may one day say, "They found New York brick and left it rubble." And nowhere in sight are there men with sufficient will or taste—or influence—to find it rubble and leave it marble.

Americans live, a visiting Englishmen once wrote, in "a chaos of nonrelation." We have manipulated our environment so badly that it has begun to strike back. Fifty-story buildings are as menacing to decent living as air pollution. They darken the sky, they generate traffic, they dwarf older, smaller buildings and mar their proportions. They please nobody but the construction industry.

What one misses so much in New York are the classic designs —the weathered stone, the fine cornices and diamond panes of European buildings. Yes, and the sudden, tidy little parks set here and there like baskets of greenery. Strolling in this city of sharp angles and cold glare can be hideously oppressing, especially in November. Kate Simon is right in her contention that "solid streets of glass buildings have the secretive, uncomprehending look of people in very thick glasses."

The breakdown of services and amenities in New York is somehow in keeping with the banishment of beauty and style. It is said that New York could not survive a week if the water supply or the electric current were to fail. How long, one wonders, can a city survive when beauty and grace and order fail?

In his book *So Human an Animal*, Dr. Rene Dubos of Rockefeller University writes: "I doubt that mankind will tolerate our absurd way of life much longer without losing what is best in humanness. . . . We shall have to change our technological environment, or it will change us." When, one wonders, shall we start? When the city is a silent, deserted hulk, stark as the landscape of the moon?

Five years ago this gray November we lost the only President of modern times who was touched with romance. The immediate shock and horror of that day in Dallas have now passed from memory. But what still hurts is the realization that in the earth of Arlington are buried the New Frontier, along with an elegance and style that fired our national pride. Under that flickering lamp are the finest dreams of the best young men in the land.

Nothing was the same after John Kennedy passed from the scene. The solemn business of government never again looked exciting. And nobody thought of the White House lights as shining over fair women and great men. Some of us even saw a terrible symbolism in President Johnson's pious ritual of economy—turning off the lights in the White House. They were never turned on again in his time.

It is said that people return home from funerals as good and gentle or as evil and greedy as they went. Only the dead are transfigured. The crank becomes a martyr, the politician a Paladin. Legends rise and grow. And we nourish them as the tribute the living owe the dead.

Time—and historians born too late to share our guilt—eventually redress the balance. Time has not yet dimmed the shine of the Kennedy legend because we have an aching need in these troubled times to hold fast to all our legends. These last years have been downhill much of the time. Our great traditions, our noblest heroes are all of another century.

After President Kennedy's death, Governor John Connally of

The Long-Gone Days

Texas announced that the nation had to escape "the web of violence, bigotry and hate" that was destroying us. We made an effort. We remembered the ancient Greek belief that pity and terror and love—the elements we always meet in tragedy—produced an emotional catharsis that lifted men above their grosser selves. Maybe our effort wasn't good enough, though the pity and terror were certainly there.

In five years we have seen three national leaders murdered in brute hate, then buried with so much love that the eyes still mist in remembrance. Are we, in consequence of such intense tragedy, a wiser, better people? Or are we simply more cynical?

In the five years since Lee Harvey Oswald closed the New Frontier with his skulker's shots we have learned little about making this country a more decent place to live. Millions of us are still too shabby, too hungry, too miserable. Our laws favor the privileged and punish the poor. Our Congress tugs a forelock to lobbies and turns a deaf ear to citizens with honorable grievances.

But if we have learned little about making the world safer for our children, we have learned a great deal about making it tougher for assassins. Laborious studies by psychiatrists and mountains of data fed into the great maw of computers have produced a firm profile of the would-be assassin.

In case you're curious, he will be short, straitlaced, resentful of authority, a failure with women and a chronic outsider. He will have delusions of persecution. He will feel his father let him down. He will be a loner with few minor vices. And he will imagine he's on a divine mission when he takes aim. His sex problems are described as "severe."

You doubt that such prognosis is possible? Dr. David Rothstein, who made a careful study of ten men who had threatened Presidents, found a pattern so consistent he was able to label it the Presidential assassination syndrome. Wherever Presidents visit local police are appraised of this research. But will research prevent another assassination?

51

"The world of fashion passeth away," the Bible consoles us. And the way fashion is running these days, it's a thought to cherish.

Having long held the view that fashion is what one wears oneself, I have an important message today for Paris and New York's Seventh Avenue. And for all those chic boutiques that display Tibetan love beads, voodoo dolls and coyote mittens alongside ladies' herringbone tweed suits with two pairs of pants. The message is: *Those pants have got to go.*

The time has come to tell the light-footed lads in the rag trade to go fly a kite. Having made women boyishly breastless for the past five years, they are now finishing us off by outlawing the skirt. The "in" costume these days is a pair of bell-bottom trousers worn with a matching jacket and a little-boy cap. As mass produced, the pants are wide and woolly, baggy and bulky, graceless and sexless. They are also, in a terribly depressing way, unwholesome.

Why unwholesome? Because they are another step toward what I take to be the desideratum of the fashion world: the total blurring of sex distinctions. Citypants, as they're called, are unwholesome on women the way ruffled organdy shirts and charm bracelets are unwholesome on men. They sin against instinct and nature and womanly dignity. Also, this monstrous role-changing bodes ill for our society. The pants craze, if you look behind the boutique mystique and the peacock pretensions, is sick the way Dorian Gray was sick.

In our costume, at any given moment in history, are summed up our social attitudes, our customs, our values. What girls in pepper-and-salt trouser suits and men in violet lace and beads are telling us about our world I'd really rather not hear. And I honestly don't see what female charms—save possibly a sexy posterior—can be enhanced by the wearing of trousers.

So entrenched is the ladies' trouser craze that all skirts seem to be divided into two parts these days. You can scarcely find a hostess gown, a little black dinner dress or a cottage apron that isn't secretly a culotte. Even Mrs. Amelia Bloomer, the lady who invented short pantaloons, would be shocked by the grotesque extremes that have sprung from her basic—and courageous—design.

I wasn't aware of how insidious this trouser craze had become until I tried on a long satin dress in an elegant boutique the other day and discovered it had a great deal of material left over. "Is this a train?" I asked the dainty young man in charge.

"No, madam," said he patiently, "that's your other leg." It was, too. Being a size 6, I had simply encased myself in one pajama leg of the costume that shouldn't have had legs in the first place.

At the young man's insistence—and in the interests of journalistic research—I tried on the pants suit. It was beige tweed with lots of pockets for pipes and things. But it scratched. The legs, scraping together as I walked, made a noise like wind in the sails of a three-masted schooner. A jaunty little cap went with this outfit. From a distance I would have evoked in world travelers the memory of those sad female street sweepers in Moscow.

"If you are not in fashion you are nobody," wrote that crashing old bore Lord Chesterfield to his son. Well, I intend to be nobody when the newest thing in pants comes to my neighborhood boutique. That would be the "unisex pants," already being cut for spring and summer. *Women's Wear Daily* reports that a company called Happy Legs will be making pants for either sex in sizes 3 to 34. Unisex trousers will be available in linen, cotton, quilted fabrics and floral prints. If you're a traditionalist, you can wear pink if you're a girl, blue if you're a boy. At first, it is believed, women will buy more of these either/or pants than men. After reading that Joe Namath, famed quarterback of the Jets, was wearing a $5,000 mink coat, I'm not so sure. Boys just won't be boys anymore.

This neutering of the sexes is a thoroughly revolting, nasty business. What disturbs me is that we all seem to be acquiescing like sheep. Can't somebody launch a counterrevolution?

Note: All right, so I was wrong about the trouser craze. I sometimes reflect *how* wrong as I slip into my marvelous red jersey pants from Rome, my lime-green pants with the tricky belt, my purple pants suit with the box jacket, my custom *tailleur* with the too-tight seat, my black velvet trousers with the jeweled belt, my chic boutique dungarees. . . . But one touch makes all these pants *mine*. The legs are narrow. With my feet (size 4B) they have to be. The standard wide cuff extends a good four inches beyond my toes. Had I embraced the bell-bottom fad my friends would now be calling me Stumpy.

We were discussing, in the soft tones women employ to muffle the mysteries of pain and death, the news of Robert Taylor's lung cancer.

"How awful," said my friend, "that a public announcement has to be made whenever a famous man is going to die."

"We're all going to die," murmured an older, wiser voice. "Why deny it?"

Indeed, why do we? It's a basic—and often blessed—fact of life.

We deny it, I suspect, because the trappings of death are so chilling. And so heavy with guilt, so tainted by high costs and smooth fraud. Instinctively, we loathe Mr. Joyboy, the mortician, cosseting the mourners with pious chat about the dear departed.

We loathe him because we're all his victims, society having arrived at no kindlier mode of seeing the dead out of this world.

Most of all, we deny death because in our trim American ship "youth is on the prow and pleasure at the helm," precisely as Thomas Gray said. In our youth-oriented society, age has begun to lose its dignity, and death is rapidly becoming obscene.

In denying death we may be losing a certain respect for life, particularly for the decencies, the gentle courtesies that hold society together. The rise of violence in our time has damaged far more than synagogue windows and youthful bones and campus greens. It has bruised the national soul.

I am haunted by the poet Auden's dictum: "We must love one another or die." When we fail to love one another—in the sense of respecting each man's humanity—something warm and good in our native spirit dies.

The American revulsion against death may also be blamed on the slow decay of religion, particularly among the young.

A recent poll by the World Council of Churches brought out the interesting fact that only about half of the Christians on this planet believe in heaven. And virtually nobody believes anymore in hell. Such skepticism may clear the mind of foolish terrors, but it also robs the dying of certain grand expectations.

In England the subject of death has been much in the public mind of late. For weeks a debate raged in the Sunday press on the subject of euthanasia. Elderly people wrote deeply touching letters in its behalf. Some said firmly that euthanasia was more pleasing to contemplate than suicide.

So lively and so protracted has this discussion become that an English physician was moved to observe that death as a subject stands today where sex stood twenty-five years ago. It is creeping out of the closet.

In a recent Sunday supplement devoted entirely to death, a number of celebrated persons stated their feelings with admirable candor. "I have this feeling that death will be friendly . . . that it will be like meeting someone I've known about for a long time. I will be interested," said Odette, one of the most brilliant secret agents in the last war. Having experienced torture at the hands of the Nazis, she added, death can no longer frighten her.

To delay the hour of one's death, to increase the span of productivity is a dream shared by all. Many recipes are offered, but I like best the one set forth by Dr. Donald Gould of London. "Work!" says he. "Let us ban retirement . . . with idleness there's a decrease in the secretion of hormones . . . established diseases worsen . . . new diseases take hold. Quite literally, the rot sets in."

This is the season when Americans, the most hygienic people on earth, conscientiously renounce fresh, clean air in favor of bad colds and flu.

"Close the window, I'm in a draft!" goes the cry. And next time it is said to me I intend to reply, "Splendid! The draft will clear out the germs, sweeten the air and recharge everybody's batteries. Shall we have it a little higher?"

An understanding of the germ theory of disease may be too much to expect in a nation where people take their ailments to a chiropractor and their emotional problems to an astrologer. But it has been firmly established, scientifically and beyond any reasonable doubt, that colds are not caused by drafts. Nor by frostbite, wet feet or falling in a snowbank.

And while this may come as a shock to hothouse types who are forever sniffling, nobody ever caught cold from spending an evening in a room where the temperature was comfortably fixed at 68°.

New York in winter can be bleak and cheerless. The slushy gutters, the cars encrusted with filthy snow, the uncollected litter all depress the spirit. But given a choice, I'd rather spend an evening trudging the snowy streets than sitting in a hot, airless apartment where the stale bouquet of 10,000 dinners hangs overhead like a musty canopy.

Cooking odors, like body odors, are preventable. First, you open a window in the kitchen while food is being prepared. If you've an exhaust fan, you turn it on. You cover every pot and pan, and you close the kitchen doors. For your digestion's sake, to say nothing of keeping that boardinghouse fug out of the halls, you broil, bake or braise the meats uncaring folks fry. After dinner, there should come a fine, bracing moment when you open one window wide and let the cool night rush in to ease the burdened air. Everybody will feel better, smell better and sleep better. And colds and flu will be as rare as smallpox.

Bedtime at my house finds no lady with a lamp making her rounds. Instead there's me with a spray can, whooshing, sloshing and spritzing, insuring that when I rise in the morning everything's coming up lavender.

Lavender will not ward off cold and flu, but the fresh air will. Colds are communicable diseases whose viruses—some 600 varieties—are airborne. Hot, sealed rooms in which no clean, cool air circulates force us all to inhale what others have exhaled. Ergo, the sniffles.

Since I loathe catching a cold, I find myself in the uncomfortable position of delivering brief hygiene lectures to hairdressers, shop clerks and, if I know her well, my hostess. Since I never step into a cab without immediately rolling down the right-hand window about two inches, I have set off some lively dialogue.

"Lady!" goes the wounded cry. "You want me to catch my death?"

Patiently, I explain. I tell the cabbie about the forty-seven healthy men who went out in the January morn wearing only their shorts, who sat in cold rooms and took icy baths, all in the interests of medicine. *Not one caught cold.*

The driver is rarely impressed. He tells me about his bad back, his stiff neck. "Would you rather have Hong Kong flu?" I asked a driver whose cab smelled like a humidor. "I already had it a week," came the hoarse reply.

In my neighborhood we are blessed with a number of very good French and Italian restaurants. But not even the finest food and the most efficient waiters can compensate for the hot, musty air, the lingering traces of long-gone feasts and old mackintoshes. But suggest to a waiter that it might be nice to open the door for a few moments, and the astonished reply is, "But that would put the people at the bar in a draft." And by tomorrow, his tone implies, they'll all be dead of pneumonia.

I am not addicted to cocktail parties in any season, but in winter they put me in mind of Calcutta at high noon. I vividly recall a party last year in a lovely room lit by candles and a crackling fire. The air was dense, drowsy, heavy with all the perfumes of Araby. My host, his collar wilted, his forehead glistening, gave me a handshake like a hot towel. "It would be a marvelous party if somebody would just open a window," I said brightly.

"Oh, I couldn't do that," replied my panting host. "All the people on that side of the room would be in a draft."

"Jolly good," said I.

It doesn't do to cast a cool eye upon Christmas. Certain illusions, like holiday punch, should be kept warm and sweet. Face one unpleasant truth about the jolly yuletide, and a dozen more come snapping at you through the tinsel.

Celebrating Christmas is like being in love. It's a more joyous experience to the pure in heart. At any of life's high moments, one touch of cynicism can still the music and sour the wine.

Still, if wrongs are to be righted, sorry facts must be faced. And the sorriest fact I know today is that between now and Christmas some $700,000,000 worth of merchandise will be stolen from the nation's retailers. Half the thieves will be teen-agers. Others will be store employees, professional thieves and sweet old ladies with wistful smiles.

Clearly, the American Christmas operates on a split level, morally speaking. While choirboys are piping "Joy to the World" and Salvation Army lasses are ringing their bells on windy street corners, several million citizens, products of our comfortable Christian culture, will invade the shops in their "booster bloomers" and coats with twelve inside pockets, all designed for the quick concealment of Christmas loot.

Television showed us some of the shoplifter's equipment the other night. It was complex gear, suggesting that "impulse thievery" is not the general rule. Trick boxes with secret compartments are a great help in stealing clothing. Jewelry thieves go forth wearing special belts fitted with drapery hooks, ideal for hanging a row of bracelets.

Viewed in its totality, the shoplifting picture is shaming to us as a nation. But in some cases of thievery—a penniless boy unable to resist a pretty trifle or a box of sweets—the story is simply pathetic. One also recalls the old adage: Little crooks go to jail; big crooks go to Congress.

A statement that always makes me feel shame for the man who says it (since he is betraying a mean little slice of his own soul) is the tiresome "There's a bit of larceny in everybody." I've never been sure about that. But I am sure that there's far too much of it in too many Americans nowadays. The Christmas season is really not an enormous factor in the annual "inventory shortage." Stealing has become a year-round business.

Consider this: During its first ten months in business the Americana Hotel lost 75,000 finger bowls, 100 Bibles, 18,000 towels and 355 silver coffeepots. Some 500,000 supermarket carts disappear every year. In all, thievery costs merchants well over $2 billion. The merchants, inevitably, pass the cost on to the consumer. If nobody pilfered goodies from the grocers, our food bills would drop by 15 percent. (Well, that's the theory. Whether the grocers would pass along the savings accruing from honest patrons is a moot point. One likes to believe they would.)

With the scent of pine in the winter air and everybody in a warm mince-pie mood, it's sad to be brooding about the incidence of shoplifting. But the question persists: Why do people do it? And why do we tolerate such appalling crime statistics?

In his splendid book *The Crime of Punishment*, Dr. Karl Menninger says—and this will shock the righteous—that we get a vicarious thrill out of crime. "Crime is everybody's temptation," writes this distinguished psychiatrist. That is, we all feel guilty about something; therefore, we need criminals to represent our alter ego, our bad self. And we tolerate filthy, inhuman jails because "we like to see our bad self punished."

Do most shoplifters go unpunished? In 1967 there were over 2,000,000 arrests and uncounted apprehensions. Still, the pilfering goes on, come Christmas or come the constable.

The New York City fuel haulers graciously consented to get back to their hauling just before Christmas, and we all turned off our ovens and started thawing out.

The city's radiators were soon clanging like "The Trolley Song," and hot tubs foamed with a fine, steamy fragrance. We were civilized again. And suddenly we knew how the ancient Britons felt when, after pigging it all those cold, smelly centuries, the Romans finally arrived and turned on the heat and hot water.

The blessings of central heating may be overrated in general, but not by the apartment-dwelling New Yorker. One's whole life-style changes when the heat goes off. We huddle over fires. We retire early with a book because the electric blanket is so cozy. We sip what the seventeenth century called Wound Drinks until we feel, in a word, overrestored.

That last heatless weekend we rediscovered the warming powers of hot coffee with cognac, hot tea with cordial, and mulled wine, the drink Elizabethans stirred with a red-hot poker. I find today's cinnamon stick entirely adequate. But had I been serving a mug of this spicy brew to a striking fuel trucker, I fancy I could have found a red-hot poker somewhere.

In the *Oxford Book of Ballads* there's an ancient lay that begins, "Along about yule, when the wind blew cule, And the round table began. . . ." Some bard should steal that opening line for a ballad about the way we live today in New York. From years of bitter experience we all know that as we draw nigh to yule, and the wind blows cule, the strike season is officially on.

Who can forget the cule yules when the subways stopped at midnight? And the years when the dockers refused to dock and the garbage collectors let the garbage go uncollected?

Have you occasionally doubted Mayor John Lindsay's cheery insistence that New York is a Summer Festival? I have. But I've no doubt whatsoever that New York is a winter disaster.

It's ironic that these wintertime strikes, righteously called by labor leaders who profess to be the true friends of the working class, are most punishing to the poor. To make those three days without fuel bearable, it was necessary to have roaring fireplaces, electric heaters, electric blankets and quantities of good food and drink. Color television and a Christmas tree winking with lights also helped.

Those of us who enjoyed those comforts ought perhaps to feel churlish in complaining about the lack of heat that bitter weekend. Flu sufferers, of course, had a valid grievance. But moving through my cold rooms, with barely strength enough to blow in my mittens, the thought recurred: This is what winter living is like in cold-water flats. This is the chill that lodges in the bones of Harlem and the East Village. And in those bleak lodgings there's no blazing fire, no Persian cat asleep on her downy puff, no cognac in the coffee. Yes, one feels churlish complaining.

But how quickly we'll forget the chill now that the radiators are hissing again. I've resumed opening windows and proclaiming my own formula for comfortable winters: a high hemoglobin and a low thermostat. And I'll again align myself with Queen Victoria who visited Napoleon III and Eugénie during their exile and instead of writing a thank you note sent a servant to announce that her majesty would not visit them again until they aired out their stuffy rooms.

But it's good to remember the rigors of that heatless weekend. Until then I went along with literary critics who claim that the "coldest line" in the English language is Keats' "The hare limped trembling through the frozen grass." I now know a colder one. That's my elevator man saying, "The oil is gone and it's going down to zero tonight."

1969

It Wasn't a Very Good Year

. . . Santa Barbara got its first oil slick. . . . President Eisenhower, his honors thick upon him, passed to his reward. The Sharon Tate murders horrified the nation. . . . Senator Edward Kennedy drove off a rickety bridge in Chappaquiddick, Massachusetts, taking Mary Jo Kopechne and his Presidential hopes with him. . . . Nixon was inaugurated and Lyndon Johnson went home to Texas to let his hair grow long and write his memoirs. . . . Student protests increased, and the *Saturday Evening Post* folded, and President Nixon went to Europe for eight days to show them who's President now.

Congress fought bitterly over the ABM, and the peace movement gained momentum. Scandal in the Green Berets over the killing of a Vietnamese spy. . . . The world lost Everett Dirksen and Ho Chi Minh. . . . The Senate, in a rare demonstration of integrity, rejected Clement Haynsworth and Harrold Carswell for the Supreme Court. . . . Bell-bottom trousers arrived and were snatched up by short, dumpy women who instantly became shorter and dumpier.

1969 was the peace movement's most dramatic year, and the first Moratorium—with 30,000 marchers filing past the White House with lighted candles—was judged a great success.

It was the year of the Chicago Seven, with Abbie Hoffman trading insults with Judge Julius Hoffman. . . . The Court of Appeals reversed the conviction of Dr. Benjamin Spock. . . . Blacks demanded $500,000,000 reparations for past injustices. . . . Troops began to leave Vietnam. . . . The Apollo 11 astronauts landed on the moon and took a short walk while the whole world gasped in wonder.

What I cannot forgive the fanatical, flag-draped patriots is that they make patriotism so embarrassing for the rest of us. Patriotism ought to be a private matter, like saying your prayers or telling your love. A genuine devotion to one's country requires no bumper stickers, no big parades.

It's difficult for many of us to understand Shaw's dictum that "We'll never have a quiet world until we knock patriotism out of the human race." To Americans, such talk is bloody heresy. It offends our peculiar pride in being American. But one can reject Shaw's remark and, with equal fastidiousness, reject the shrill jingoism of those patriots hell-bent on proving each day how patriotic they are.

These rather cross remarks are prompted by a note in the papers stating that hundreds of outraged citizens called CBS the other evening to protest an omission—specifically, the words "under God"—in the Pledge of Allegiance recited on the *Smothers Brothers' Comedy Hour.*

Had viewers called to protest the lewd jests (of which there are too many) or the hideous crashing music, I'd endorse their views completely. But the words "under God" don't belong in the Pledge of Allegiance and they were not there when Francis Bellamy composed it in 1892.

This brief, dignified oath, recited daily by small children with hands on hearts, excluded God because our founding fathers chose not to invoke God's name in matters of state. Patriotism was considered out of place in the pulpit, and the pulpit had no place in the schools, as Jefferson and Madison weighed these matters in 1787.

It may shock some old-time religionists to meet so hard a truth, but some of our founding fathers, including the brilliant Thomas Jefferson, were not even true believers. Rejecting the dogma of the Christian church, they perceived God to be a force of *goodness.* They believed in truth and honor and the sanctity of the human mind. They would have looked with disapproval upon the funda- mentalist mind that demands the words "under God" in any document pertaining to the state.

Embedded in our Constitution are a good many ideas that might strike the "Love It or Leave It" crowd as dangerous, among them the notion that every man is free to worship God or reject God, according to his conscience.

It was during the Fearful Fifties, when Senator Joe McCarthy and the American Legion were wrapping themselves in the flag and muttering pieties about "Americanism," that the words "under God" were added to Bellamy's pledge. The Legion lob- bied hard for this emendation, and anybody who opposed it would have been branded a dirty Commie spy.

And so it came to pass in 1954 that we became one nation, in- divisible, under God, by a joint Congressional resolution, ap- proved by President Eisenhower. Old school books and some al- manacs still omit the words "under God," however.

It's a great pity that those ferocious patriots who scolded the Smothers brothers have so little feeling for the free and open soci- ety that used to exist under our flag. Once upon a time, we were a nation of free thinkers, nonconformists and unrepentant liber- tarians. We trusted our fellow man and tolerated his opinions, however woolly.

In New England, old-timers will tell you, "We always used to have a town drunk, a spoutin' atheist and a few Democrats." There's a lovely, lost America in that hoary joke. As the Fourth Amendment guaranteed the right of all Americans "to be secure in their persons, houses, papers and effects," so does the First Amendment—and the tradition that derives from it—guarantee that the community will tolerate every religion, with each man's God his own design and the state neither favoring nor supporting any religion.

There's something totalitarian—and a little frightening—in the thinking of the superpatriots. The idea that "You must believe in God" and "You must show the flag" to qualify as good Americans is in its basic assumptions insulting. Must a man beat his breast and show an arm tattooed with entwined hearts to prove that he loves his wife? Would a bumper sticker saying GOD BLESS MARY JANE establish beyond doubt his fidelity and passion?

Superpatriots have been described as status-strivers anxious to prove their virtue by a zealous display of patriotism. The late Professor Richard Hofstadter, who devoted two books to the subject, said, "Conformity is a way of guaranteeing and manifesting respectability among those who are not sure they're respectable enough."

The shabbiest enemies of freedom in this country have been the Yankee Doodle zealots, the witch-hunters, the deniers of civil liberties. There are no swords as bloody as the swords of holy wars. And no patriots as unworthy of our flag as the flag-draped superpatriots.

A dreadful thing happened to me this week. I got new glasses. Suddenly, Oh Lord, mine eyes are dazzled. I not only see life clearly and see it whole, I see it in blinding detail. The shock is so great I may never peer through these $35 lenses again. There have been too many changes in the landscape since last I took a long, hard look.

No eye, artists will tell you, can ever exhaust the meaning of an object. This is a profound truth if you happen to be contemplating a bust of Homer or seeing eternity in a grain of sand. But I have been looking at the mean streets, the hard faces, the rasping air of New York. By now my eye has exhausted the meaning of everything.

Some eyes, when beholding the afflicted, suffer the affliction. I claim no such exquisite sensitivity. But this I do know: I'd rather grope and stumble and bang into brick walls than see precisely what—or who—is lying in the gutter. I'd rather pass an old friend unawares than be affronted in every block by the praying mantis eyelashes, the Bride of Dracula makeup that's now besmirching the fresh faces of teen-age girls.

Most of all, I'd rather view the world through a painted veil than look again into the dead eyes of our so-called "alienated youth." Poor lost babes! In my new glasses I cannot escape them. There they are, loitering their lives away in the eerie glare of Times Square's neon. There they are, numb, passive—"stoned," I guess is the word—begging coins outside Greenwich Village coffeehouses. I look away . . . but in one glance I have seen too much.

Rounding a busy corner in London, a novelist ran full tilt into a notorious swindler named Bottomley, newly sprung from prison. "His skin was loose," he wrote, "his eyes dead, like an old elephant."

Those are the eyes I see on the bearded, sandaled young men who stand on street corners, selling underground papers, wilted flowers, leather belts, cheap Mexican jewelry. In times past, my naked eye never once bespied their eyes. But my lensed eyes, alas, see all. And it's all too much.

The world viewed suddenly through new glasses can be as mind-boggling as those first TV photos from the moon. Yesterday I suddenly saw swirls of dust in the air, faint clouds of grit rising from the gutter. "Look thou not down but up!" I reminded myself. But the grit was everywhere. I saw the sulphur dioxide plain.

It matters little to me that I cannot tell a bus from a truck until it's bearing down at me. I've learned to move with extra caution in December, since I have several times confused a

Christmas light with a traffic light. I have also walked into a Chinese restaurant and asked, "What time does the feature go on?" Once I offered a light to a lady at a conference table who happened to be holding a white pencil. But never mind. Did it disturb Matisse that he painted outside the lines? I should hope not.

From the foregoing, you might think these new glasses are my very first pair. Offhand, I'd say they were my twenty-seventh. I have managed to lose, break or retire the other twenty-six, and I expect to do as well with these. Some people never suspect I'm out without my glasses. They think I'm glued into the wrong contact lenses and will be all right in a day or so.

There are elements of paradox in my vision problems. I can read the finest print and thread the tiniest needles *without glasses.* I can scan page one of the morning paper upside down. But until she walks in I have difficulty recognizing my sister. I'll never fall in love with a romantic stranger across a crowded room. The only room I can see across is a closet.

My most threatening problem, however I jest about it, is this inability to make out street signs. Looking back upon this long, cold winter, I always see myself in a high wind, standing forlornly on the corner of DON'T WALK and DON'T WALK wondering which way to go.

Does anybody remember that glorious line—Tennyson, perhaps?—"In each of her eyes there smiled a naked boy"? Well, it struck me one day, standing in confusion amid the WALK and DON'T WALK signs, that in each of my eyes there trembled a little old lady with a white cane and a cup. My eyes began to overflow. I went home and called the oculist. "If it's an emergency," said his nurse, "come straight over." I went and learned it was true grit in my eyes and no mistake. On my second visit I was able to see the eye chart. This, mind you, with one eye covered and a monocle that might have been ground down from Galileo's first telescope! The doctor wrote a prescription for new glasses and said, "Don't ever go out without them."

The first day in new glasses is the worst. Besides giving one a shattering look at the polluted world, new glasses provide another surprise—that is, a shattering look at one's self.

"Out flew the web and floated wide. . . . The mirror cracked from side to side." That's definitely Tennyson, "The Lady of Shalott." It is also any woman over thirty gazing at her face through new prescription lenses for the nearsighted.

The first thing the lady notices is that her little gossamer laugh lines are now *trenches*. The second thing she notices is that the ravaged lady in the looking glass is crying.

Some day soon I must find out if the science of optics is working on a reverse lens. I'd like to place my order early. What I have in mind is a pair of simple rose-colored glasses which will blur everything, thus turning time backward in flight. The blurring, let me add, can start with those little gossamer laugh lines.

When I go forth to do battle with the world tomorrow I shall probably forget my fine new glasses. "Therapeutic forgetting," they call it. Once again the spring air will be hazy and full of whispers. The stately old town houses in my neighborhood—all by Time's fell hand defaced—will resume their remote, enchanted look. No more shall I see the dead eyes of the hippies or the ghastly Fellini masks on the girls of sweet sixteen. Nature, in her infinite wisdom, has bestowed upon me the device photographers employ to touch any contemporary picture with romance. I was born with a soft focus lens in each eye. And the way the world is looking these days, I'm grateful.

Though the event traditionally passes in babble, revel and wine, the emergence of a new year is not without its bracing moments of truth. One of these is the certainty that the human condition isn't going to change very much. No, not even with Richard Nixon in the White House and Catholic bishops endorsing the pill and the flower children folding their petals and vanishing. Social progress, like spring in Vermont, comes slow and cold.

Still, against all present horror, we go on hoping. This could be the year they find a cure for cancer, the common cold and the hangover. And the year hostilities finally cease in Vietnam, and in the ghettos of our blighted cities. And in the corners of all housetops where contention sits, flexing its little adder tongue.

So, I'm asleep in the daisies? Very well. "Tread softly or you'll tread on my dreams."

In this year now aborning we could, if all ladies of fashion will take a vow, banish forever the mini-skirted "little nothing" dress. The dress that betrays melon knees and defames all but the daintiest rumps. The dress that makes pretty girls tawdry and tawdry girls tarts.

I'm clearly an old-fashioned type, but let me dream on. Could this be the year discothèque couples rediscover the bliss of dancing in each other's arms? Maybe in 1969—oh, the peace, the glory of it!—the electric geetar with the 10,000-decibel jolt and the gibberish song in 4/4 time will be discarded as too savage for a civilized society. Gone forever would be the private, catatonic shuffle that now passes as dancing.

How lovely if this were the very last New Year's Eve that saw lemur-eyed girls in tight, sequined sacks dancing that jungle stomp an old-time band leader calls the Alienation Blues. How lovely, but how unlikely!

If we all practice clean living and high thinking—and badger our state legislatures—perhaps the watchman who keepeth the city will end the brutal "uglification" of our great cities. Proud old buildings, weathered by time, must not give way to any more cement boxes with square, unadorned windows. Like some women, good architecture grows lovelier growing old.

The impulse to gaiety is loud and clear on New Year's Eve. Is

72

it relief, I wonder, that we have somehow weathered another one? Or is it to avoid facing the vast unknown of 1969?

But there's one reflective moment I fancy we all share on New Year's Eve, the moment when the sense of time past, time lost forever, suddenly engulfs us. All the fire and beauty the years have stolen from our hearts is suddenly rekindled. We feel fearfully and wonderfully alive. But from somewhere, as yet far off, we hear the iron gates of time begin the slow creak, the first warning that they'll one day click shut.

Never believe that this feeling comes only when the first fine, careless raptures are gone. I distinctly heard those gates at twenty-five. Now, as the wild bells ring out to the wild sky, I hear them again. And as always I remember the words of T. S. Eliot's Prufrock, "I have seen the moment of my greatness flicker, And I have seen the Eternal Footman hold my coat and snicker. . . . And, in short, I was afraid."

It's a mood that passes. It's a comfort to turn back to Tennyson and his wild bells. "Ring out the want, the care, the sin," he wrote at the height of the starchy Victorian era, "Ring in the love of truth and right."

A cry from the heart in 1850, unanswered in 1968—but let us look to the light and hope.

In the two areas that dominate most people's lives—love and money—my instincts are all on the side of excess—that is, of giving, spending, enjoying and heigh-ho for the rainy day after tomorrow.

I've deep pity for the unloving. But the unspending, the piously thrifty put me in a pout. Prudence is a virtue, but penny-pinching is a nasty habit betokening a mean spirit. If ever I turn ribald, it's in the face of those righteous Pecksniffs who remind us that happiness consists not in the abundance of our possessions but in the simplicity of our wants.

Well, my wants aren't the least bit simple. And most days I believe I could be certified as reasonably happy. The reason may be that I do not covet riches. Nor do I fear poverty. If it comes, I'll weather it. Meantime, I enjoy good food and fine wine. I perfume my sheets and purr in my fur. My dark days are made brighter by the paintings on my walls. I aid such causes as I believe worthy. If I cannot travel first class, I don't go. Should my old age be poor, it will be rich in memories.

But profligate as I am, I've lately taken to worrying about the people whose wanton disregard for money easily matches mine but who lack the stern counsel and small—very small—cushion with which I, as a widow, am blessed. Fellow spendthrifts, we are in trouble! This may well be the year when we all take in sail. (Or laundry, if certain rougher predictions come to pass.)

A guest at my dinner table chilled the food on every plate the other night with stories about the increase in bankruptcies across the land. Times are hard. New York City issued a year-end report saying that the standard of living in the metropolitan area, for the first time in several years, had gone down.

My financial expert attributed the current economic chaos to wanton abuse of the credit system. He sees trouble ahead for the not-quite-rich class whose private road to paradise is paved with broadloom and littered with hi-fi sets, color television, sports equipment, costly toys and fake diamonds as big as the Ritz, all with no down payment—easy terms, just sign here.

"WHAT easy terms?" the debt-ridden consumer may well ask. (He should also inquire, "WHAT did I sign?")

There was no exaggeration in the title of a famous TV documentary on our credit problem. It was called "IOU $315 Billion." Yes, that's billions. And it all works out to a debt of $1,600 for every man, woman and child in the land, including some who

74

don't even have a piggy bank. (Now, three years later, the figure has no doubt tripled.)

In a healthy society, the living standard is always rising. But as ours rises, personal debt zooms ahead faster than personal income, personal savings or the gross national product. This is dangerous.

Here are some sorry statistics. Mortgage foreclosures have doubled in the past five years. And such items as TV sets and furniture are repossessed daily, both in slum neighborhoods and in some not so slummy. Suburbia, it is said, lives on meat loaf and great expectations.

Contemplating this sorry problem, we may well ask whatever happened to the old puritan ethic that required payment first, possession later. Well, it seems to be gone, along with evening prayers in the parlor and the framed samplers that warned "Waste not, want not." The consumer society has painted over the old proverbs with "Live now, pay later." The terrible irony of that quip is that it's true. It should be amended to read "and pay and pay and pay." Installment buying, with service charges and interest jacking the price by 50 percent, is no convenience.

Banks are culpable for much of the new despair over making ends meet. Their custom of sending out unsolicited credit cards is making a bad situation worse. One also wishes the FCC would rebuke the radio stations that are forever droning, "Own a human-hair wig for only three dollars a week." Or movie camera or a color TV set. This lures the poor into further troubles.

There are few virtuous women who are not weary of their honor. One of those lovable old French cynics said that in the

75

seventeenth century (presumably on his exit from the chamber of some lovable old abbess). It's a sentiment one could fairly apply today to virtuous American taxpayers. They, too, are weary of their honor. And they're increasingly angry at the conspiracy of dishonor that keeps Congress from reforming—which is to say equalizing and *humanizing*—our disgraceful tax laws.

Last week on television, Representative Wright Patman (D-Tex.) said, in a quavering voice laden with doom, that the nation could not survive the runaway inflation we're now experiencing. We are entering, he predicted, an era of sheriff's sales and foreclosures.

At every hand one hears that private debts are mounting and savings dwindling as Americans spend faster than the nation can produce. The 10 percent surtax, which many Nixon voters expected to see repealed, no doubt will remain.

In New York we have been warned to expect higher sales taxes. Prime interest rates have reached a 100-year peak, and Representative Patman says that's frightening, too. We are told to expect a slower growth rate in the next decade. This is attributed by one economist to such diverse factors as the pill and longer vacations. If Patman's doom machine goes off, nobody will be able to afford the pill, and the longer vacation will be involuntary, as factories close and soup kitchens open. It's odd that we can stabilize a rocket to the moon but still can't stabilize the economy.

To most people, understanding economic theory is a skill on a par with smashing atoms. We know that everything costs more than it should and that rich people are given kindlier tax breaks than poor people. Adam Smith—the original—would not have approved.

I mention the eighteenth-century Adam Smith because his classic rules for honorable taxation are violated every time we pay our tax bills. Taxes should be "certain, not arbitrary," said Smith, and they should be levied according to ability to pay.

Under our present internal revenue code, with its monstrous inequities, the tax rates are most punishing to the salaried worker earning between $3,000 and $10,000 a year. The combination of tax loopholes and preferences to oilmen, mine owners and other privileged citizens loses the U.S. Treasury an estimated *$40 billion a year*. Were these loopholes closed and preferences abolished, the tax rate could be lowered by 50 percent. The total tax revenue would be the same.

Ideally, as Philip M. Stern has pointed out, the rates should range from 11 percent to a maximum of 50 percent. And there should be no Americans with incomes of over $1,000,000 who pay not a cent in income taxes. (There *are* such Americans, Mr. Stern reports, year after year.)

As everyone knows, the greatest tax cheats are the Texas oilmen. They are also among the heaviest contributors to political campaigns. Congressmen—and Presidents—can slip into their thrall one year and never get free. The awful irony of the depletion allowance is that the oil wells are far from depletion. Some are prudently held to 30 percent of capacity.

There are bound to be pious speeches in the months ahead about tightening the loopholes and spreading the burden. The rich will be asked to pay more. The poor may receive some modest tax credits. The rich will roar that the poor get all the breaks.

It brings to mind the law Louis XIV passed conscripting all the silver plate in France—this because the aristocracy flatly refused to pay one more sou to Louis' treasury.

"The nobility had put themselves on porcelain within a week," Saint-Simon tells us in his Versailles journal. But the gesture got to be a bore. A month later the tables of the rich again gleamed with fine silver. And the *very* finest. The canny aristocrats had sent Louis only their cheapest and shoddiest plate. Now they were free to put their best on the table. That's the kind of patriotism a Texas oil tycoon would understand.

Ever planning ahead, Pan American Airways has announced it has a waiting list of 200 for the first commercial round-trip flight to the moon. I'm not surprised. There are people who would sign up for the first weekend tour of the Paris sewers, provided only that it was advertised as Exclusive, Historic and the First Ever.

Of course, veteran travelers know precisely what will happen the minute airlines start shooting regular rockets to the moon. The moon will be overrun by all the wrong people. It won't be a quiet, unspoiled little resort anymore. "Really, it's getting to be just like Acapulco—so common."

Right now the moon sounds exciting and romantic, a lovely place to visit. But wait till somebody opens a tacky string of gift shops. Wait till the Moon Dream Drive-in holds a Star-Trek Festival. Wait till there's a moonburger stand beside the Sea of Tranquillity. Of course, prices will be sky-high—and that may become the stock joke of lunar travel. Food will have to be dehydrated, then rehydrated. The people who are really "in" will have no choice but to rocket on to Mars. Fearfully exhausting, that jaunt. Two years one way. Our astronauts may come close to Mars in 1986. They may even land there. And die there.

By that time television will have advanced to such a point that we'll be with the astronauts virtually all the way. This could become one of television's longest-running cliff-hangers. Will our boys make it? We'll assume they land without duplicating that scene in a science-fiction film of a few years back. "Hey, whaddyuh know, MARS!" said the first spaceman to step into the Martian landscape.

It would be interesting to know if the 200 fantasists on Pan

Am's standby list have any clear idea of what they'd find on the moon. One jest has it that they will be greeted by creatures very like themselves—speaking Russian.

A cartoon of the early '60's showed our astronauts being welcomed by a bearded man in toga and sandals carrying a sign REPENT, THE MOON IS COMING TO AN END!

Pan Am is sensibly taking no deposits on moon flights. Experts at the Houston Space Center have indicated that round-trip fares ought to start at $20,000. That would seem to place certain limits on the sort of people who will be flying to the moon. They will be the jet-set types who've been everywhere, too often. But there'll be a few scholars, rumpled and bearded, traveling on foundation grants. There always are.

And all the way to the moon these passengers will be soothed, scolded, irked and admonished by one of those traveling spinsters. You know them. They come aboard in their sturdy shoes, toting a string bag full of books, an afghan and a stout umbrella. They decided to go to the moon this year because camping out in Tibet and digging for Roman ruins in Sardinia have got to be a bore. In their luggage you'll usually find a first-aid kit and a flask of good brandy.

I've always admired spinster travelers. Most of them are spiritual descendants of those splendid Victorian ladies who took their own caravans across the desert in the last century. Rugged they were, but they carried their own little Persian rugs, a few bottles of decent claret to go with the barbecued lamb and a morocco journal in which they wrote every single night. They were not, we learn from these little red books, icy or indifferent to the sheikhs of Araby they met en route. There was quite a sisterhood of Lady Chatterleys, and they loved to travel.

Neither the adventuresome spinster nor the jet-set traveler is going to like the moon very much. It's hideous to the eye and treacherous underfoot. Moon visitors will be scorched by day, frozen by night. They will hear no sounds, owing to absence of atmosphere—not even when the sun's heat cracks great rifts in the rocks. Meteorites will be falling continuously. Should a mete-

orite rip one's space suit, the blood will start to boil—literally—
and the other half of that round-trip ticket will go tragically to
waste.

As the astronauts can testify, the moon presents a nightmare
landscape, all shattered rock, desolate valleys and gritty dust.
Still, 200 persons are standing by, waiting for blastoff.

If you tilted the map of the United States very sharply, Frank
Lloyd Wright once wrote, Los Angeles is the spot where everything would spill out.

Wright no doubt was referring to the urban sprawl, the con-
gested freeways and the rococo architecture, built not to stand
but to stun. Los Angeles has much in common with the faded
film stars who live here with their memories. By night, they still
can put on grand airs and a bit of glitter. By day, you see not
only what time's fell hand hath defaced; you see that the glamor
was five parts illusion.

The "looseness" of Los Angeles strikes many Eastern visitors as
largely moral. It's a city of sudden ecstasies and fevered change.
All pendulums swing wildly. The very young who like to look
grubby and hairy seem much grubbier and hairier out here.
Strange cults spring up in the hills, sometimes attracting the lost
and the confused whose real need is for roots, for belonging.

It has been said that Los Angeles acquires 1,000 new residents
a day. In a city whose population already seems socially adrift,
this figure could have disastrous consequences. The state may
offer more swimming pools, more colleges, broader welfare policies and a gentler climate, but it's a state with more problems,
too. Problems involving taxes, housing, transportation, clean

water and air—in short, how to make life endurable in a state whose population goes up 50 percent every ten years.

Disturbing as it is to old-fashioned Easterners, in Los Angeles we are doubtless seeing the wave of the future. The society page tells of a hostess who became so harried about seating 500 dinner guests that she turned the whole thing over to a computer. After digesting brief biographies of each guest, the electronic brain assigned everybody a number.

Only one guest complained. He said he'd asked his hostess to ask the computer for a beautiful blonde with no gift for conversation. He got the beautiful blonde, all right, but said she talked nonstop all evening.

Besides praising the climate, Eastern émigrés seem to admire the high incidence of eccentricity. At a television party last Sunday, everybody was delighted with the little old lady who designs irreverent greeting cards.

Her Easter card was rejected by Hallmark, it was explained. "And it was so touching—a dead bunny on a cross."

With all its universities and museums, its far-out Bohemians and little theater groups, there's something ineradicably folksy and homespun in California. The Los Angeles City Council (which meets every day) has been known to table all business while a member rises to say, "I would like to present my sister Mildred who's visiting our fair city from Oklahoma and my niece Olga and my nephew. . . ." Nobody finds this church-supper sort of jollity out of place. In a metropolis so vast that one dials long distance for some intracity calls, the conventions of small-town America are a positive comfort.

Small-town America would be shocked by much that goes on in this city of golden sunshine. I don't refer to old-fashioned sin, but to a mood that's morally mindless. Nihilistic, in fact. The underground papers, hawked by small boys and mini-skirted girls with lemur eyes, recall the worst days of Rome and Babylon.

In the classified columns one reads of a "lonely clean man of forty-eight who wishes to share an apartment with sympathetic female." And we marvel at the desperation of the "widower over fifty" who desires only a "passably attractive female" in her forties. A girl named Annie Fanny advertises her willingness to pose in the nude, and a forthright orgy ad states: "limited to fifteen couples."

Where but in the California press would you read the announcement of a reward for a lost pet leopard, a request for "groovy pads" in which to photograph nude girls and a plea for a "refined, genial girl" to answer the telephone—all in the same column?

Two other small ads—shocking to Eastern eyes—offer "free marriage by ordained minister" at any time and free treatment for venereal disease.

Always a land of faddists, California now seems to be the holy see of astrologers. Astrology schools—though not astrologers—are now listed in the Yellow Pages. When you are introduced to a stranger in these parts, be prepared for the question, "When were you born?" It's the sign that counts.

Evangelists still flourish, too. My favorite is Miss Velma who makes a spectacular entrance on a white charger, a motorcycle or a flying trapeze, following which she intones, "Let us pray!" Always timely, Miss Velma now is coming to the faithful by a moon rocket. "High above the congregation . . . she will preach her entire sermon standing on the moon!" ran one of her ads. Her flock sees nothing bizarre in all this. In California, God is assumed to be a bit unconventional Himself.

They say that every man's death diminishes us all. But the death of a man who is wise and brave and good leaves us not merely diminished but wounded in our hearts. With some deaths, there passes a goodness from the earth, and we shall feel its loss a long, long time.

It was through a mist of tears that I read the news of Ralph McGill's death. This distinguished editor, gentle scholar and tough fighter for black rights died in Atlanta on the threshold of his seventy-first birthday.

I never met Ralph McGill, but he was my friend. I read his books and editorials. I watched him on television. On a few occasions we exchanged letters and clippings. His goodness often had an edge to it. He could be tough with hypocrites and crooks, merciless with oppressors. But the goodness had a depth and a warmth, too.

On the day my husband died, this busy, important man I'd never met found time to telephone me from Atlanta. He said how sorry he was and how much he had admired my husband. This was not the quick, embarrassed call from a stranger, the call that begins and ends with a hollow "Anything I can do?" The voice was warm, concerned, touched with the Southern courtliness that was implicit in all that he wrote.

The passing of Ralph McGill stills another humanitarian voice in the press. For this alone we have cause to mourn. But McGill the man was an ornament to our time for another reason. He was an old-line liberal. He spoke for the lost, the poor, the beaten, the despised, and he spoke from a Southern position of privilege.

When students of the twenty-first century ponder this troubled period of black transition, it is to be hoped that they will read McGill's book *The South and the Southerner*. It is one of the finest autobiographies of our time. For once the old saying is true: Whoso touches this book touches a man. To touch this book is also to be submerged in a region, a culture, a folklore. It's a painful book— and a glorious one.

It has been said too often that the tragic flaw in every Southerner is his blind allegiance to the past. McGill, born and bred in Tennessee, concurred.

"It is the fate of the Southerner to be involved in his region, always to feel himself held by it," he wrote. "He may never have believed the myths. The cruel injustices may have offended him and aroused him to open opposition. . . . But, nonetheless, he is part of what he has met and been. And the past, in tales of his grandparents, his great aunts and uncles, has been in his ears from birth."

Ralph McGill hated segregation because "it is a withdrawal from humanity." He sensed that decent Southerners often suffered from guilt, and he wrote of it in a simple, blunt way.

So many times, says the autobiography, a black, after an encounter with the white boss, would say to his family, "He knows it's wrong. He knows it's hard to be a nigger. But he can't do anything about it."

But what the black never knew, McGill told us, was how often the white man turned away from the tenant farmer or the store helper with a heavy heart—"Or how often that man went to the back pantry and poured himself a stiff drink and took it, saying in a half-whisper, 'Damn the first man to bring slaves here!' "

Two types of white Southerners drew the McGill wrath with special fury. One was the small-town rich man. The man who controlled credit at the local store or bank, used paroled black prisoners as farm hands and loathed Franklin Roosevelt because the New Deal took farm mortgages and loans out of his hands. He never forgave the Democratic Party for this insolence.

The second type was the able Southern politician who went to Congress and conformed to the mores of the old-time plantation types in the Southern bloc. This melancholy deterioration of good men has "further sickened the region's politics," McGill believed.

For his tireless work in the civil rights cause Ralph McGill and his family were shot at, suffered garbage thrown on their lawn and were persecuted by obscene phone calls. But his principles never faltered. He was a good man all the days of his life.

It's probably good for our souls to have a heavy snowfall once a year. The first sight of it on a frosty morning stabs the eye with beauty. The tasseled branches, the spangled drifts, the ermine muff on the windowsill all blind us for a moment. It's a new morning of Creation and, praise God, we're alive, we're here!

There's something chastening in all this icy grandeur, too. As we are dazzled, we are humbled. Like the Lord speaking to Job, a snowstorm puts us in our place.

In New York, a city grown sluttish with time, a special benison falls with the snow. It's the soft blanket of pity that hides scars, softens slag and puts a halo (snood?) on the Statue of Liberty. The meanest streets seem hushed and pure. Stalled cars look strange but snug under tarpaulins of ermine.

The trees in the park—"bare, ruin'd choirs where late the sweet birds sang"—seem dressed for a picture-taking. The fat little tree on the corner, all filigree beads and fluff, tosses her frosted branches as if to say, "I always was one for crystal, you know."

Snow in New York . . . and all the rubbish cans, all the rusted bedsprings and burnt-out overstuffed chairs, abandoned curbside for the sanitation haulers, now await their fate under great *poufs* of eiderdown. The softness is all. Let the Snow Queen be seated.

At the heart of all that is beautiful lurks a mystery. No doubt it's the *mystery* of the snow that awes us. Even the taste of it is strange on the tongue.

"Hast thou entered into the treasures of the snow?" the Lord asked Job.

We have. For we have watched things ugly and broken grow gentle and lovely in the thickening mist.

Beauty aside, this week's storm was a killer. Its scenic effects held little rapture for the 6,000 travelers marooned at Kennedy Airport. And it's doubtful that the families sleeping in frozen cars on the Jersey Turnpike passed the long night singing "Winter Wonderland."

Still, the snow did bring a sudden thaw to the hearts of winter-locked pedestrians. A jolly air of camaraderie livened the streets. Stranger hailed stranger, buses cheerfully stopped where there was no bus stop. Bearded lads in Ancient Mariner toggery—usually so self-absorbed, over there on the other side of the generation gap—gallantly helped old ladies over crossings and carried children piggyback.

Dogs wore their winter overcoats. Many of them—even great shaggy beasts—were carried to the curb by masters fearful of the rough salt's effect on the pads of little paws.

Taxis, driving slowly through rutted streets, permitted passengers to share rides home. Pigeon fanciers scattered corn on the snow. It was a *good* snowstorm. It reminded us of our common humanity.

The untrodden parts of the city kept their beauty longest. Central Park still has a few fairy glades, chaste bowers sealed in ice. Rooftops, naturally, escape that trampled-upon look. There's angel snow on church steeples and lonesome snow on the steps of town houses closed for the winter.

It is too bad that on the day after a beautiful snowfall the city engineer cannot flip an electric switch that will spread a quick thaw from Bronx to Battery. All the snow and fairy frost would be washed down the sewers before turning to gray slush and filthy puddles. For the next week the city would look freshly laundered and we'd all step a little livelier.

If snow stayed pure and sparkling, fewer people would feel impelled to take tropical vacations. A winter week spent in the sun always revitalizes one. But those of us who grew up with frostbite and the crunch of snow underfoot could never settle permanently in a warm climate. There would always come days, under the boring sun, when we'd remember the look of falling snow . . . and ache for a white dawn outside the window.

It Wasn't a Very Good Year

I remember a lovely story by Katherine Mansfield that perfectly described man's need for snow if snow has been the stuff of his winters. An Englishman doomed to live forever in warm places because of his wife's health hears her read a letter telling of snow back home. "Snow. Snow in London. Millie with the early morning cup of tea. 'There's been a terrible fall of snow in the night, Sir.' . . . 'Oh, has there, Millie?' . . . The curtains ring apart, letting in the pale, reluctant light. He catches a glimpse of the solid houses opposite, framed in white, of their window boxes full of great sprays of white coral. . . . Snow— heavy snow over everything. The lawn is covered with a wavy pattern of cat's paws; there is a thick, thick icing on the garden table; the withered pods on the laburnum trees are white tassels; only here and there in the ivy is a dark leaf showing. . . ."

When his wife, so frail, with "dark violets pinned to her thin bosom," asks him to fetch a shawl, a cape, the man does so, still in his dream. He remembers the morning paper, drying over a chair, the small boys with shovels clearing the walks for a shilling. But that night when his wife asks, "Do you mind awfully being out here?" he laughs at the very idea and tucks her tenderly under the mosquito netting. And he somehow goes on living out there among the palms and bright flowers . . . dreaming of snow.

Twenty years ago, when I was younger, swifter and innocent as an egg, I often nipped out to the corner mailbox at midnight. It never occurred to me that I was living dangerously.

In the late war years, when sleep would not come, my restless dog and I sometimes strolled the avenue long past midnight. And how we would have laughed had anyone suggested that a girl out alone at such an hour might be mugged, robbed or dragged kicking and screaming into Central Park.

That sort of thing, we knew, did not happen to nice girls who lived in the East Sixties and behaved themselves. Besides, on every late stroll one always met other nice people out posting their letters or airing their dogs or breathing the tender beauty of a starry night.

In retrospect, all that was long ago and in another country. I still live in the East Sixties, but after nightfall I wouldn't leave a burning building without an escort. Over the past weekend there were three holdups within a block of my house. (I say three; there may have been many more, not reported.) I must also add that at least half a dozen times in recent years I have heard in the dingy hours just before dawn a sudden scream in the street below. The cry is invariably followed by the sound of running feet. Then—silence. And the awful sound of my own heart.

We live in an age when it's essential to understand the social pathology of crime. It shames us all—and indicts our social order—that blacks bulk so large in the criminal statistics. The terror that stalks our streets, the shadows that move on little cat feet—sometimes carrying knives—are part of the price we are paying for years of neglect and injustice. We have created the culture in which young men decay early, turning to drugs, to crime, to any form of retribution.

What we must also face is that the crimes against peaceable citizens will no doubt increase sharply during the next few years. There is abundant evidence pointing that way.

The report of the U.S. Riot Commission, solidly researched and sober in its conclusions, is not precisely sanguine about the future. In the next decade, we are advised, the number of young blacks aged fourteen to twenty-four will increase sharply. This group is responsible for a disproportionately high number of crimes. For example, 75 percent of all larceny, 80 percent of auto thefts and 60 percent of reported rape cases are committed by young men under twenty-five.

This Kerner Report also states that the number of police available to combat crime is rising much more slowly than the crime to be combated. Large cities are particularly vulnerable. They are more likely to have a large ghetto population. The arrest rate among blacks is four times higher than that for whites.

I am haunted by the warnings expressed in that splendid, frightening book *Black Rage*. The black authors, both psychiatrists (Drs. W. H. Grier and Price Cobbs), warn that black aggression can only increase. "As a sapling bent low stores energy," they write, "blacks bent double by oppression have stored energy which will be released in the form of rage—black rage, apocalyptic and final."

How to quell the rage and direct this fierce black energy into a constructive channel is the major problem of this century. It will require the most enormous, expensive, *planned* social revolution in all history. A glorious revolution whose fruits we might be enjoying today were we not spending $10,000,000 every single day in Vietnam.

When out of grace with fortune, millions of Americans know where to find what the television commercials call instant relief. They visit a seer or a swami or a witch with a wild eye. She (or sometimes he) will read their stars, their palms, their tea leaves or the bumps on their heads. And hey presto! They not only feel better faster, but they become insufferably smug about their inside pipeline to the future.

"The stock market is going to rise very suddenly next September," they announce with authority. Dare to disagree and you're swept under the rug with a glance that says, "Poor clod. The things you'll never know!"

We are living, God knows, in troubled times. In consequence, astrologers, fortune-tellers and assorted witches are enjoying a bonanza. If you're a skeptic who regards the whole occult business as rubbish, it's futile to press your arguments. Rubbish the occult may not be—though I tend to think it is—but it's definitely a going business.

In this day of scientific marvels and free public education, Americans spend $200,000,000 a year on astrological literature and horoscopes. We all know people, otherwise sane and wholesome, who consult their "charts" every morning to see if it's a good day for taking a trip, making love or cleaning the closets.

Since fortune-tellers and mediums operate outside the law, there is no accurate means of determining their annual take from the troubled and the lost. Hypnotists (nonmedical), clairvoyants, mediums and bogus psychologists with mail-order degrees all take millions in fees ranging from two dollars to hundreds, all from gullible, troubled Americans. As the Bible noted so long ago, "The simple believeth every word."

A columnist recently expressed surprise that the Hollywood marriage of Jill St. John and Jack Jones had broken up. After all, hadn't her astrologist advised the marriage?

On television you may now see a celebrated English clairvoyant, Maurice Woodruff, perform his magic. Also from England comes a self-styled witch named Sybil Leek who casts horoscopes and TV spells. It seems that there's something eerie in the wind today. The world, say the seers, has entered a dark period. Could be. Anyway, from the witches' covens on the English moors to the gypsy teakettle in your neighborhood, the occult is now a fad. Suddenly it's more chic to be spooky than kooky.

As a token of our emotional health, this preoccupation with the supernatural is probably unhealthy. And as a means of coping with the tensions of the time, it's stupid and futile. Does it really make sense to say that the marijuana craze among the young is owing to the influence of the planet Neptune? And does anybody remember that serious "civil strife" was predicted for last Election Day because Mars was in conjunction with Jupiter?

It has always seemed to me that the most hilarious prose appearing anywhere today is in the astrology columns. "Get important data to higher-ups," one seer is fond of writing. Or, more imperatively, "Stand your ground with bigwigs!"

As a parlor game, astrology can be fun. As a key to personality or a guide to the future, it is nonsense—dangerous nonsense. It is a fantasy, embroidered with logarithms and a distorted astronomy. Horoscopes vary with each astrologist. And so absurd is the basic chart of the planets that one astrophysicist says the charts would be valid only for the year 3000 B.C. or A.D. 2300. That's how much the position of the planets varies.

People who set their life's course by what they fantasize to be the "influence of the stars" tend to be naïve and sometimes paranoid, psychiatrists say. The less educated accept astrology with firmer faith, which is hardly surprising.

Of all the spooky folk now at large reading the Tarot cards and throwing the I Ching, I am most fond of English witches. They meet in the New Forest when the moon is full to discuss what's new in magic and spells.

I'd love to meet the witch who was interviewed recently in one of the London papers. She keeps her broom in a corner of the drawing room and her cauldron atop the TV set. When she is seized by a desire, she told the reporter, she sets off a "magic current" that fetches it on the double. Recently the current brought her twenty alligator handbags.

"I don't know how the magic worked," said this night rider, "but I've got the bags."

The impassioned little "in-group" that somehow gets to read all important new books in galley proof is no longer divided over whether *Portnoy's Complaint* is the dirtiest novel of the twentieth century. Rapturously, they agree, it is, it is! The questions now troubling the air are: Can author Philip Roth fairly be called anti-Semitic, anti-female or—as some critics have suggested— anti-human decency?

In my view, Roth is all three. But he is also a legitimate, savagely funny, immensely gifted writer. Those virtues, considering his subject, are regrettable. A book about masturbation and adolescent sex fantasies ought to be written by a half-literate dirty old man. The pity is that Roth's effect on the American novel is likely to be as reverberative—and as unwholesome—as his effect on the morals and speech of young men. Yes, and young women.

The reactions of average readers to *Portnoy* become curiouser and curiouser. I received a letter from a lady who described herself as "a Jewish mother of four." She loathed the book. She stated her reasons cogently, concluding, "It's not even a *good* dirty book, right?" Right.

Another letter said, "I am an eighty-three-year-old shut-in and I enjoy reading. Do you know where I can get a free copy of *Portnoy's Complaint?*"

Still other letters complained that the library was not circulating the book, that teen-age girls were being "corrupted" by it and that Roth was "obviously some kind of maniac and should be put away."

Anyone who writes for the public prints is accustomed to bizarre letters, including screeds from full-blown lunatics. But I have been more interested in the responses of ordinary, average readers.

Portnoy, I have observed, ranks high with women who drop four-letter words into their casual conversation. And with the lemur-eyed girls in pants suits and fedoras. And with the sad, ill-favored types who go to bars alone at night.

Not surprisingly, the women I know who have found *Portnoy* loathsome and shocking are women who enjoy their own femininity. Older women, particularly women who are sophisticated in terms of life and literature, dismiss the book as a rather nasty aberration by a clever writer.

It Wasn't a Very Good Year

With people who rarely read a novel, *Portnoy's Complaint* is this year's *In Cold Blood*. With no standards of comparison, they waffle on about the book's "realism," its "authentic humor" and, above all, its "absolute honesty." It's that last phrase that has me longing to hurl a shoe at their heads.

I may have led a sheltered life, but I doubt that any young man, unless mentally deranged, could be as obsessive, as cruel, as foul-mouthed as Portnoy. Critic Marya Mannes rightly calls him "the most disagreeable bastard" she ever encountered.

With the book shooting upward on the best-seller lists, a reader who found it loathsome is obliged these days to defend her position. I fully agree that nature should, in a first-rate novel, be splendid and lustful. But in a good novel there are also moments of bloom and beauty. There are tender words mixed with the ugly. Portnoy knows only the ugly words. He repeats them to the point of nausea. And that, I keep hearing, makes *Portnoy's Complaint* a work of art.

The purpose of art, Tolstoy once wrote, is "the transmission to others of the highest and best feelings to which men have risen." Prostituted art, degenerate art fails of that mission. That was Tolstoy's complaint. It perfectly describes my feeling about this book. And I don't fancy paying three dollars to watch Portnoy complain in living color on the panoramic screen.

They may not know it, but those long-haired youngsters in slouch hats and flapping trousers strolling hand in hand through Greenwich Village have something in common with the giant panda. In both species it takes a medical examination to tell the male from the female.

I thought of these hairy young people in their scarecrow suits when my eye fell upon a letter to the editor on the women's page of a London newspaper. "Why," the letter asked, "do the young women one passes in the streets today look so wretchedly unhappy?"

Since every wretched girl is probably wretched in her own special way, we shouldn't attempt a full answer. It's also possible that many girls look more wretched than they are because they wear their hair like Rima the Bird Girl and copy their makeup from the Roman orgy scene in *Satyricon.*

In point of fact, though, I'd say that women are less serene and less womanly today because of the current life-styles affected by men. We can only be bewildered and anxious about the demasculinization of the male which has been going on before our wounded eyes for the past five years and shows no signs of abating.

Deep in their souls, where all women tend to be sweet-scented and sexy, the longing is for a rock to lean on, not a ringleted teddy bear to cuddle. Women will tolerate a man who occasionally borrows a nail file or a comb. But they're inwardly repelled by a man who uses their hair spray or wears their gold chains and medallions.

A proper gentleman of advanced years once suggested to me that young girls weren't attractive anymore because their young men preferred "unwashed nymphos on the pill." That struck even a Louisa Alcott type like me as extreme. But could it be that our young men are running about like hairy apes because no dainty lass ever stomps her foot and says, "Either get washed or get lost"?

It's my notion that new sexual mores, with communal sleeping arrangements and all that flower-child reverence for the Free Body, have led to further alienation of the female. By instinct women are hearth-hugging creatures. They need structure in their lives. The right to change one's lover every semester is not a cause worth marching for. Nor is a loose, casual relationship rewarding in the long run.

In adopting this free and easy style of sexual conduct, young women are not doing their bit for liberation. On the contrary, they are shouting down something basic and primitive that was better than they know.

In a book called *Woman, the Enigma* I came upon this fascinating statement concerning the crude drawings uncovered in the great caves of southwest France:

> Because Stone Age man portrayed woman's sexual characteristics, it does not follow that the sex life of the time was coarse or licentious. One of the oldest known representations of love was discovered in a grotto, scratched on a bone. It shows a man with yearning eyes and hands uplifted in supplication, gazing at the naked body of a woman.

The man's expression may have been stupid, he being not too long out of the trees. But it was also rapt, we are told, with anxiety and desire.

A famous sociologist has suggested that the generation now in its twenties may be "our last married generation." I'm not sure he's right, but it's a melancholy thought all the same. My heart is with that San Francisco woman who's petitioning for tax relief for the single girl. Her reasoning is that the number of eligible men has so diminished—due in part to rising homosexuality—that girls must spend more of their income on cosmetics and pretty clothes. It speaks volumes for our sexual climate, I suppose, that I read this dispatch and wondered, "Pretty clothes for whom? For *him*?"

Were it the custom of the government to bestow Distinguished Service Medals on gallant housewives, there are 150 New England ladies who should be summoned to Washington forthwith to be decorated.

These are the good wives of Westboro, Massachusetts—a comfortable suburb of Boston—who put their families on a strict welfare diet for the last week of Lent. By the standards now prevailing, this meant that a family of four could spend no more than $24.76 per week on food. The children in this experiment whined a lot—but they survived. And now they know what it feels like to be poor.

That, in brief, was the real purpose of this austerity project. Its success was immensely gratifying to a social worker named Paul Chapman. It is his notion that the "insensitivity of the middle class" perpetuates poverty. Doubtless we should all try the welfare diet for a week.

Being a good cook, I dare say I could manage a week of welfare food, provided herbs were not forbidden. Almost any cut of honest meat will make a savory stew provided you've got celery and onions and pinches of oregano, rosemary and thyme. One gift I'd like to present to all women who are trying to feed a family on $24.76 is a small herb cupboard and some simple recipes for beef, chicken and fish stew. (The last named comes to many fine tables as bouillabaisse.)

But before I go on this austere diet I'd like to strike a bargain with certain gentlemen in Washington. I'll gladly follow the welfare diet—and even omit the herbs—if Senators James Eastland, Allen Ellender, Strom Thurmond and all the others who have voted against the food-stamp plan (and similar acts of mercy) will also go on it. I might even stand these paunchy gents to the grits.

It's hard to forget, as we read that in some areas of the South three out of four children suffer from worms, that the Southern bloc stood firm against relieving this hideous suffering with any sort of legislation.

When a commission of six physicians testified that starvation was worse in the rural South than in many backward areas of Africa, the Southern Senators pursed their lips and said nothing. Oh, yes, Senator Ellender said he had a terrible case of worms as a child. And there were other murmurs about lazy, shiftless niggers with no git-up-and-git.

Still, one can't fairly call this pious, Pecksniffian attitude uniquely Southern. A similar harshness emerged recently in the New York Legislature when family allowances were cut back in the name of a balanced budget.

Besides an overhauling of the entire welfare system, which is inefficient and demoralizing, a vigorous program of nutrition should be launched. It's a pity that the great, rich companies processing and packaging foodstuffs do so little to advance the cause of sensible eating. In the long run it would be to their advantage, even if sales of artificially flavored cookies took a sharp drop.

The Department of Agriculture has announced a five-year program to assist low-income families in preparing more nutritious meals. Worthy pamphlets on wheat germ and dissertations on "the egg" will doubtless arrive in the surplus-food bags. And no doubt they'll be used to fire the stove.

What we need is a program similar to that set up by the first English nutritionist of note, Dr. T. R. Allinson, who went about the London slums setting up soup kitchens and teaching women to prepare nourishing meals for a few coppers. He wrote the first cookbook for poor people—*Wholesome Cookery*, one penny. His credo was "Good food is the best medicine." He distributed his "Balanced Diet" on street corners and in trains. He got poor people off their standard diet of tea siftings, adulterated white bread (containing chalk and bone dust) and gin. He showed them how to make cheap but decent bread from whole wheat. In short, he taught them how to eat decently on starvation allowances. He should be living at this hour to instruct our welfare mothers whose children deserve more than grits and beans.

The terrifying realities of life in New York were brought home to me last week when I walked into my kitchen and found the window cleaner crouched in the corner, injecting himself with a needle.

Two weeks ago I missed, by minutes, a fatal shooting on Madison Avenue a few steps from my house. The victim, who ran a haberdashery boutique, fled into the street when confronted by a holdup man. For losing his cool, he was shot in the back.

Generally speaking, mine is a sheltered life. Like the blind girl in the play, I'm always "home before dark." I live behind locks and bolts in a well-protected building. I've never known anyone who takes drugs, carries a gun or consorts with criminals. But I know scarcely anyone who has not been the victim of a burglar, a holdup man, a mugger or a car thief.

We are living dangerously every day—and taking it for granted! It rarely occurs to us, tucked away in our snug quarters in the nicest neighborhoods, that we are as vulnerable as night wayfarers in eighteenth-century London. Statistical odds are that some day, or some terrible night, somebody in everybody's circle will be caught up in a crime of violence.

The crime rate is most conspicuously high in New York and Washington, but our twenty-six largest cities also report sharp increases in crimes of violence. "We are closing ourselves into fortresses," the President's commission on violence reported last year. This at a time when, to quote the report, "We should be building the great, open, humane city-societies of which we are capable."

A letter from a reader describes the terrors and the techniques of survival in Greenwich Village. "I can show you the jackrollers waiting in doorways in Bleecker Street," he writes. "And the muggers who wait behind the fire doors on stair landings. By law, these fire doors must be kept closed to contain smoke and blaze. Tenants, fearing what might be behind the doors, regularly prop them open. When you climb the stairs at midnight, reach your floor and find the fire door closed, you RUN! . . . I have trained my German shepherd to proceed me up the stairs."

When you suspect a mugger lurking behind the door, this letter continues, "You race down the stairs, find a pay phone and call the police emergency number. The odds are 6 to 1 that no one will respond. So you get a stick or an iron bar and you and the dog go back up the stairs."

The statistical link between drug addiction and crime is well established. A New York legislative committee investigating crime has stated that heroin addicts in one slum district with a population of 802,000 spend a minimum of $115,000,000 annually on maintenance of their habit, equivalent to 40 percent of the welfare funds poured into the same area by federal, state and city agencies.

Curing drug addiction and reducing crime are part of one enormous problem: the rehabilitation of our poor, the clearing of our slums, the sweeping renovation of our schools, prisons and welfare agencies. All such reforms will cost billions, largely in federal allocations. Our leaders who control the purse and the power continue to seek—as a man on a sinking ship looks about for his gloves or his glasses—small, stopgap measures. Or they look to more police.

It is difficult, as law-abiding citizens have repeated brushes with criminals, to bear in mind that oppression is not the answer. At the close of the eighteenth century some 200 crimes were punishable by death in England. The law had grown capriciously, and crime increased as the urban population exploded. For some, crime was the only means of survival. And the death penalty was no deterrent.

Now we hear agitation to restore the death penalty, to deny the constitutional guarantees to offenders. Were we to fall into this trap we would, in the words of Mayor John Lindsay, be forced to choose "between the random terror of the criminal and the official terror of the state."

For my part, I am less frightened of a drug addict in the kitchen than of the specter of John Mitchell's Justice Department abolishing the Bill of Rights in the name of law and order.

A young English writer who rejoices in the name Mary Arden —or who *should,* that being the blessed name of Shakespeare's mother—has written a play with an indecent (unquotable) title and a wound-salting theme—namely, the oppression of women by men who resent their clever minds, noble hearts and adorable natures.

Miss Arden sounds grimly earnest and probably wears sensible shoes and tweed pants. "The central theme of my play and my life is the oppression of women," she told a London interviewer. "I'm stuck with it like Eldridge Cleaver is stuck with being a Negro."

Women have become a slave caste, "appendages of men without identities of their own," says Miss Arden. She despises the contented cows who accept this role. From across the water she gives the back of her hand to all you American wives, Spock-oriented, honey-giving women."

As a lifetime member of the slave caste, I suspect Miss Arden protests too much. To quote the wise son of that other Mary Arden, "A woman sometimes scorns what best contents her." Including, I should say, strained spinach in a porringer and a small mouth to receive it, smeared bright green.

Women who complain of feeling oppressed are often their own oppressors. But there's not one of us who's too noble to use this

Poor-precious-me argument in the battle of the sexes. ("If I hadn't given up my voice studies to marry you and have all these kids. . . .")

Miss Arden's talk of oppression sounds tiresomely familiar in most respects. One thinks of the suffragettes and Ibsen's "new woman" and *The Feminine Mystique*. But these reservations aside, I think Miss Arden is voicing a valid grievance against the men of our time. She speaks feelingly of the "hidden violence" lurking all around us. Violence is always frightening to women. And I gather she understands—from her frequent use of the word "pain"—the frustrations and indignities women suffer under the new hang-loose ethics.

I have just been looking at a candid photo of a cocktail party in the current *New York* magazine. All the women look bored, sloppy and unhappy. They have this in common with the women I pass in the street: The younger they are, the more wretched they seem. And the looser they hang.

You can't blame this female despondency on the bizarre fashions, the lemur eyes or the dripping seaweed hair. It's the tension, the despair. Too many nice American girls are beginning to fit Nina Epton's description of the average Englishwoman. To wit: "She looks unstroked, uncaressed and emotionally undernourished. She is also terribly unsure of herself." Unsure because she wants to retain her femininity and at the same time liberate herself from all the old symbols and clichés.

It's curious, I know, that women should look "uncaressed" in an age of rampant sexuality. With immediate satisfaction the goal and every smart girl on the pill, frustration is passé. We're wallowing in "fulfillment," a new malaise that comes of a surfeit of honey. ("Whereof a little more than a little is by much too much"—Mary Arden's boy Will again.)

Women who listen to their primal instincts may be affronted by the current emotional climate. We do not blossom in a sex-charged atmosphere that depersonalizes and demeans us. If we sometimes look sad it's because all around us there's so much easy sex, so little dignified, committed love.

When women lose their sense of security and well-being in the society of men, something is wrong. The fashion among the young today is the casual encounter, the one-night stand, the perverted experiment. Women, because of their innate needs, can only be the losers under such arrangements. If Miss Arden wishes to feel oppressed, let her feel oppressed by that, not by the dominance of the male in politics, in business or in bed. There are areas in which women should assert themselves; there are others in which they should—gladly, totally—yield to men.

There come weeks when much of the news is no news at all. The least newsy story last week was the one about quick-lunch restaurants adulterating their hamburgers with a variety of foreign bodies. Imagine! Well, our beautiful new commissioner of consumer affairs was outraged by this discovery. She was right, too. But when you live in a world as adulterated, denatured, defatted, freeze-dried and artificially flavored as ours, it comes as a relief to read that Chock Full O'Nuts is putting nothing more alarming into the hamburgers than flour and soybean paste.

This, after all, is the age of fraudulent food, most of it labeled "fortified." Or enriched, improved or simply NEW! When I read that the food-price index has risen again, my mind leaps to the probable cause. They've added another additive.

One hates to sound churlish about these thoughtful touches over which some unfrocked chemist with a stew pot has doubtless been laboring for years. Though the soup may taste like something left in the dog's dish, you may be sure it's bursting with niacin, riboflavin, oil of wheat germ and monosodium glutamate, the last of which we are now told causes headaches.

It Wasn't a Very Good Year

If Commissioner Bess Myerson plans to poke around restaurant kitchens, she may find herself suffering from more than a monosodium glutamate headache. I know two posh East Side restaurants, all gleaming damask and sham paneling, where the chef puts oatmeal in the wild rice. This gray, gluey mess is presented in a silver dish at wild-rice prices. I was told by a waiter that I was the only customer who'd ever isolated the secret ingredient and complained.

An unexpected note in the tale of the padded hamburgers was the restaurant owner's defense. Hamburgers, he said, taste better when buttressed with some form of starch.

Adding a rich variety of stuffing to hamburgers is an old American custom. At home it's a clean, economical practice. In restaurants it's apt to be dirty and dishonest. Miss Myerson may have to devise a recipe for plain, pure, unfortified hamburger and post it over every chef's range. Thereafter it will be honored when city inspectors come to call.

When I was growing up, all anxious mothers used to issue stern warnings about public lavatories, candy from strangers and hamburgers away from home. Dutifully, I obeyed every injunction.

Years later I was lunching one day in the garden of a handsome New York town house with a lady who enjoyed, at that time, a glittering reputation as a great cook and knowing gourmet. She even whipped up a few meals on television. Lunch that day included grilled hamburgers which had a savor, a texture I'd never encountered before. "What's the secret ingredient?" I asked politely.

"Let me see now," mused the great cook and gourmet. "Today I think I put mashed bananas in them."

"You're not sure?" I asked. No, she wasn't. It seems she made up batches of them, like mud pies, and then popped them into the deep freeze. Some were fortified, if that's the word, with corn-flakes, some with dry bread crumbs. "Once I mixed a batch with a cup of fresh orange pulp and raisins," she recalled, blissful at the mere memory.

The great cook's husband arrived as I was leaving. "Would you like some lunch, darling?" she caroled from the garden. "I've eaten," came the quick reply.

I heard a few years later that they were divorced. She, one would imagine, got custody of the deep freeze.

Are we the last married generation? Back in the Jazz Age, when no nice girl smoked *anything* and all brides were presumed chaste unless noticeably with child, a kindly, concerned judge in Denver decided something had to be done about America's rising divorce rate. His prescription was trial marriage. Not free love, another shocking notion in the '20's, but a marriage that could be dissolved by mutual consent if there were no children. In consequence of his views, Judge Ben Lindsey was denounced from the pulpit and castigated in the press. He was called a Bohemian, a heathen, a defiler of the American home—and a great deal worse. Ultimately, he was dropped from the bench.

In the forty years since Judge Lindsey's advanced theories were set forth, the divorce rate has tripled, and trial marriage in some circles is positively old-fashioned. Living together without the benediction of marriage is the new vogue on university campuses and among young people who dwell in those giddy habitations restricted to "singles." The affair is without commitment or any assumption of permanence. A psychiatrist at the University of California in Berkeley sees such liaisons as the wave of the future. "Stable, open, nonmarital relationships are pushing the border of what society is going to face in ten years," said he.

The downfall of the puritan ethic that began in the early 1950's was probably speeded by the pill and the loop. There were many who felt that the denial of guilt and shame about sex was all to the good. But the puritan notion that sex can be both dangerous and sinful, particularly among the irresponsible young, had a certain merit. Every society to hold itself together and go on functioning must have taboos. When contraception was chancy, when a fallen woman rarely rose up again, the taboo on sex outside marriage made sense.

Today, when a respected sociologist can write that marriage now "seems more a swinging affair based on mutual involvement than execution of a solemn vow," what can we expect of courtship? Casual friends become lovers for a night or a week, drift apart, are hard put to remember each other's names a year later.

Vance Packard reports (in *The Sexual Wilderness*) that individuals who have had many sexual encounters before marriage are substantially less likely to live happily ever after when they finally enter matrimony. He also reports that girls who have had sexual experience before marriage are more prone to infidelity than those who haven't.

The fallacy here seems to be in the importance attached to the role of sex in marriage. Couples who find the conjugal bed sheer heaven may find life in the rest of the house a hell. Inevitably, since sexual love must involve the whole personality, the conjugal bed takes on the storms and resentments that have swept too long through kitchen and den.

It's unfortunate that the officiating clergyman cannot amplify his ceremony to give the couple a foretaste of marriage. If he could turn to the bride and say, "Do you, Mary Lou, promise to be thrifty, punctual, and neat? Will you be crisp and smiling at breakfast? And will you promise to humor his bad moods and be very sweet to his mother?"

Saying "I do" to twenty such questions might put a bride into a thoroughly rum mood that would last through the honeymoon. But the practical aspects, the grinding reality of this most demanding of all human relationships, would be set forth plainly. The bride could not complain that nobody had warned her.

With contraception so easy and divorce so commonplace, it is obvious that we may have to live with this new marriage ethic.

Dr. Margaret Mead has acknowledged the permanence of the new morality and the prevalence of sexual adventuring by suggesting that marriage take new forms. She recommends a loose, easily dissolved marriage for couples who do not wish to have children—an unstructured marriage, if you will. But for a man and wife who have begotten children and created a home, divorce would be made a great deal more difficult.

In view of the changing morality, it seems sensible to stop clucking over student cohabitation and pregnant brides and shift our concern to marriage as an institution.

In a civilized society that cares for its young, marriage is a bedrock necessity. And the notion of a loving, faithful marriage should be refurbished—with song, story, and untarnished homilies from Granny's day, if necessary.

The prevailing theory that fidelity simply doesn't work in 1969 is one of the many idiocies we should erase from the credo of the young. It works a great deal better than infidelity. And it always will.

However commonplace trial marriage may become, it still is makeshift. And its defects are always more hurtful to women. One of the nicest elements in marriage is its public aspect. One's love for another human being is *sanctioned*. The traditionalists who see marriage as a sacrament, a civil rite and a total commitment of mind and heart see life clearly and see it whole. Being married is "being alive in the flesh." And it is being serene and whole in spirit. Sexual appetites may fade, adversity may strike, but love—and particularly married love—bears it out to the edge of doom.

Because it's a human arrangement, always involving two groping, ordinary mortals, their progeny and kinfolk, marriage will always be an imperfect institution. Are we the last married generation? Well, if we are, prepare for anarchy, chaos and a breakdown in all the civilized amenities.

In her fascinating book *The English Marriage*, Drusilla Beyfus quotes Lord Longford (wed many years to a writer of distinction, Elizabeth Longford) as saying: "I never think about our marriage at all. It's rather like asking myself how do I manage to breathe or how do I get off to sleep. . . . Once you are in love and you have a wife who has many interests in common with you, it seems to me the relationship wouldn't need further stimulation."

This suggests that we all may be too preoccupied with the technique of marriage at the expense of the spirit. One famous psychiatrist has said flatly that great love is not necessary for a good marriage. What is? "A wide area of common interest and an individual capacity for contentment." Neither of these traits can be properly tested, one would say, in a trial spin.

The Reverend Billy Graham, savior of sinners and unofficial chaplain to the White House, bobbed up on NBC's *Laugh-In* the other Monday.

And on Friday night in Madison Square Garden the Reverend Billy launched a ten-day pray-in. A true servant of the Lord, it seems, fulfills himself in many ways.

Having seen *Laugh-In*, I must confess I'd rather hear Dr. Graham jesting about sin than crying, "Woe unto sinners!" If that prejudice puts me a little short of the glory of the Lord, so be it.

A superb showman, ruggedly handsome and busting out all over with righteousness, the Reverend Billy handles jokes with professional skill. You like him. And you're delighted to see a man of the cloth—especially one who shares the burdens and, who knows?, the secrets of state—having such a jolly good time.

Clearly, Dr. Graham is a fine, impressive man. But when that great Graham carillon booms over New York, one always hears, like Hamlet, sweet bells jangling out of tune.

It isn't simply the Graham theology that repels—though it certainly repels me—it's his hell-fire and damnation preaching and his acceptance of Satan as a "personal devil" that belongs back in the Bible-thumping days when snake oil was sold along with the religious tracts. But the really distressing aspect is the way he mixes politics and social commentary with sin and salvation.

For example: We shall not solve our race problems, in Dr. Billy's view, "until Christ comes back as a benevolent monarch." Even a fundamentalist preacher might find that kind of sophistry offensive.

It is this sort of reasoning, one suspects, that has lost the Billy Graham Crusade the endorsement of the National Council of Churches and similar organizations.

In theory a man of peace and mercy, the Reverend Graham has been notably hawkish on Vietnam. His exhortation to the boys to fight on and on until "demon-inspired Communism" is wiped out distorts the true issues for many Americans. And it reminds me that not once during the dark years when Senator Joseph McCarthy was desecrating every tradition of freedom and justice in Washington did Billy Graham speak out against him. On the contrary, in 1953 he thanked God for "men who, in the face of public denouncement and ridicule, go loyally on in their work of exposing the Pinks, the Lavenders and the Reds. . . ."

There is a burning edge of hostility in Billy Graham's Christianity. He takes immense pride in his humility. His emphasis on purity and cleanliness verges on the fanatical. But like all of us, he's the product of his early years. And his is a virtual textbook case: the helpless child who was scrubbed and scourged, beaten and berated by insensitive parents and who now, in manhood, is compelled to scrub and scourge the world. One's heart goes out to the memory of a bright, handsome little boy being beaten in the vestry of the church one Sunday with papa's broad leather belt. His sin? "Fidgeting during the sermon." (The story is in his biography.)

When Prohibition was repealed, the Reverend Billy has told us, his pious father went out and bought a supply of beer. He forced it down the throats of his children until each one vomited. The Reverend Graham, not surprisingly, doesn't like liquor to this day. It's possible he doesn't like his father much, either.

Raised in a household obsessed with obedience and cleanliness, the Reverend Billy still carries a heavy burden of sin. He bites his nails to the quick, he has splitting headaches and he and his staff play practical jokes—the cruel kind, such as filling a man's new hat with shaving cream.

When Queen Victoria was asked to attend a service by the leading evangelist of her time, Reverend Dwight Moody, she replied that while she was sure he was "good and sincere," it was "not the sort of religious performance" she liked. The Nixons, one imagines, would consider the old queen rather rude.

Never mind about that Soviet first strike reducing New York to uninhabitable rubble. Like many another American city, it's going to be uninhabitable long before the Russians or the Chinese or even the Weathermen get around to blowing it up. And it will be uninhabitable for the simple reason that nothing, in terms of simple, functional living, works anymore.

Traffic is hopeless, elevators stall, air conditioners break down, letters are lost in the mail. But *that's* not the worst of it. No, the telephone system is the worst of it.

There sits AT&T—bloated, monstrous, cunning as a weasel with its $8 *billion* gross per year—demanding a rate increase. And there go the phones of New York ringing wrong numbers that have been dialed correctly six consecutive times. There goes the call intended for Grandma's birthday girl in Peoria alerting one of the eighteen phones in a Brooklyn bookie's hideaway. And there goes a scream in the night from a woman whose labor pains have begun and who finds, for the third time in a week, that her phone has gone dead.

On numerous days this year I have fumed away an hour trying to reach NBC, CBS, the butcher, the grocer or—oh, ultimate frustration!—the telephone repair service. Were it possible to dial *M* for murder—well, there are days when you just might.

Because of overburdened circuits, there are peak hours—usually midafternoon—when a telephone with an instant dial tone is as rare as a dog with perfect pitch. For several years now I have had two telephones, each with a different exchange. When BUtterfield lapsed into a coma, I could always arouse a thin whine on TRafalgar. Recently both lines went dead. I felt like a lorn creature abandoned on an ice floe.

When the phone you're calling is out of order and your message is urgent, the only efficient recourse might seem to call Western Union. If you're in New York, Los Angeles and certain other cities, don't try. You won't get an answer.

Frankly, I cannot imagine who could be tying up Western Union's phone service these days. The people I know are swearing off telegrams the way chronic coughers are swearing off cigarettes. It's more than a boycott. It's a protest steaming with moral outrage.

Probably nobody has been more discomfited by the breakdown of telephone and telegraph than newspaper correspondents. The ladies of the nation's fashion press in town this week for the autumn showings are discovering that the copy they dutifully filed "RUSH" at 11 P.M. is being received back home too late for the next day's editions.

Early on a recent morning I devoted two desperate hours to dialing Western Union. I'd wanted to send a message of sympathy to a dear friend whose husband had suddenly died. For two hours there was no response. Finally, I called the telegraph office in my neighborhood. "We don't take telegrams," a snappish voice (female) advised me. "Call 577-1234." That, of course, was the number I'd spent the past two hours dialing.

Offhand, the only solution I can think of to this communications breakdown is the revival of the "running footman." In the eighteenth century these splendid chaps ran night and day all over the British Isles. E. S. Turner, the social historian, quotes a contemporary description of a footman who "seemed all air, like Mercury." He could have beaten Western Union with weights in his boots.

"He never minded roads but took the short cut," runs the account, "and by the help of his pole seemed to fly over hedge, ditch and small river. His use was to carry a message, letter or dispatch. His qualifications were fidelity, strength and agility."

In Victorian London, pedestrians were accustomed to stepping aside for a tall, gaunt man who ran like the wind, carrying a dispatch box. Everyone knew him as Miss Nightingale's messenger, always jogging to the Foreign Office or to 10 Downing Street, presumably with another long treatise on sanitation.

Lucky Miss Nightingale! Her natural efficiency had scope and breathing space. She reorganized the British nursing service and cleaned up the British army, greatly aided in her labors by the fact that she never had to wait for a dial tone or a Western Union messenger.

What great thinker said that women were put on earth to gentle the raging beast in men? His name eludes me. But give him five minutes with the female liberation movement and he'd take back every word.

These strident, humorless ladies, with their ratty hair and eyebrows that meet in the middle, are fast becoming the scourge of the '6o's. Wearing trousers or shapeless tunics, chanting slogans and scattering leaflets, the liberators are theoretically pledged to improve the social and economic status of women. That's fine with me. But I fail to see how rúde manners and a rejection of all feminine graces are going to help their cause.

What puzzles me about this liberation movement is its real aim. Precisely what do these girls wish to be liberated from? In our society, equal educational opportunity is available to both sexes. A woman can enter virtually any profession. Offhand, the only jobs I can think of in which she might find her comrades a wee bit hostile are forest ranger, ship's captain and sandhog. Wearing standard liberation garb, however, a girl might just pass as any of these.

It has struck some longtime observers that women have never been so liberated. They wear pants, ride motorcycles, drive taxi-cabs, run for public office. They can even embrace the tradi-tional vices of men. Women play the horses, gamble in Las Vegas and, thanks to the pill, are as sexually fulfilled as any motorcy-cling, leather-jacketed wencher. What, then, do these young vira-goes want?

To a casual observer, it would seem that the liberation front wants, first of all, to look as drab, as revolting and unwomanly as possible. "We reject . . . the soft, sexy, slender, stylishly clothed body," says one of their tracts. To that end, the girls scorn cos-metics, girdles, pretty hairdos and all feminine fripperies.

"We will not be raped!" proclaims a liberation newsletter. ("You bet!" agree the men who've met the liberators.) "We will not be leered at, smirked at or whistled at by men enjoying their private fantasies of rape. . . ."

Women, it must be admitted, have their private fantasies, too. And one of the silliest is that they are continuously seduced in the private fantasies of men who have met them once.

It's regrettable that this campaign to raise the status of women had to originate with women who seem to be projecting their deep, inner neuroses—and undisguised hatred for men—into the arena of social justice. One must applaud their view that women should receive equal pay for equal work, that abortions should be made legal, that sex-linked monopolies—*i.e.*, professions that bar women—should be broken up. But are not women's greatest victories won by being womanly?

There's a harsh, totalitarian spirit in the hard-core liberators that can only be destructive. Members are urged to throw away their bras and girdles. Fashion magazines are taboo. So is perfume. The worldlier comrades would like to see ladies and gents using the same restroom, thus depriving man of his last sanctuary.

Officially, the movement appears to believe that karate lessons and coarse manners will scare men into promising them anything. Fools! Can't someone get through the lines with the message that it's the cool, feminine women—"soft, sexy, slender and stylishly clothed"—who win their battles with men? And they don't need karate lessons or unisex washrooms.

No sense shirking hard truths. Here's one we've got to face. Young men today are becoming too girlish, too foppish, too feminized for their good or the good of society.

Now this is not to say that our boys are turning homosexual in unprecedented numbers. Social scientists say they're not, though with those perfumed periwigs and clanking medallions, it's a moot point. Even among the "straight" lads, however, the fondness for long hair, brocade vests, pink silk trousers and reeky, hothouse perfumes has spilled over into Ronald Firbank country.

The reluctance of men to be men is altering our social landscape and upsetting the emotional climate. It's a fashion that must ultimately do grave damage to both sexes. I am glad for the first time in years that I am not a lass of eighteen and longing for a lover of twenty-two.

This dainty look in men, this preoccupation with hair and jewelry and fancy footgear, has stripped the rugged sex of all that made it fascinating. Gone is that dear, rough male mystery. One could cry, if one happened to be over thirty and sentimental, which I certainly am.

For a long time now, women have regarded men as strange and wonderful because they wore scratchy tweeds and kept their hair cropped close like a terrier's. We loved their cashmere sweaters with the odd little pockets and the way they sloshed on that stinging aftershave lotion smelling of lemon peel. We also loved the way they loved us—running fingers through our silky long hair and murmuring, "My, you smell nice!"

How, I wonder, can a 1969 girl love a man who borrows her hair spray and says he must have a pair of red boots exactly like hers? When the opposite sex begins to lose its oppositeness, we're all in trouble. The immediate questions now are: What has turned our boys into primping peacocks? And how can we bring them back to their nice rough male ways?

There's a new book that offers some interesting theories on this epicene trend. It's *The Feminized Male: Classrooms, White Collars and the Decline of Manliness.* I'm not in agreement with all of Patricia Sexton's notions, particularly about the remedies, but her thesis commands respect.

In brief, Mrs. Sexton blames female schoolteachers and over-protective mothers for the proliferation of light-foot lads. Boys are more vulnerable, she writes, and they are accepting too readily the pressures of the mother figures they encounter. Suburban life, with its commuting fathers, she feels, deprives boys of male companionship in the formative years. The slum child is deprived in another way. Jobless fathers, being impotent economically, do not give a boy a strong male image to emulate.

Mrs. Sexton also has a harsh word for the women who devote their lives to "the pursuit of adornment." Catering to them is a mincing army of eunuchs, men whose "castration is less a physical than an occupational matter." These men, pace-setters in fashion, have influence far beyond their merit, and we are all, at times, their victims.

It Wasn't a Very Good Year

Mrs. Sexton believes that college rebels and young black militants have this in common: They are trying to assert their manhood. The hippies, so docile and detached, are also victims of the system. They have been feminized to the point where rebellion in a healthy, positive way is beyond them.

What to do? "Quite simply, what we must do is masculinize the schools and feminize the power structure," Mrs. Sexton states. "We must balance out the sexes so that they don't corrode any one spot where they concentrate."

In short, boys might go back to being boys if rugged males taught elementary school and women infiltrated the power elite. If sneaking into the corridors of power is the only way we're going to bring back short haircuts, clean shaves and man-tailored suits, I, for one, am ready. Just show me the corridor.

Every time some anthropologist digs into the African veld and comes up with a bashed-in skull notable for its great grinding teeth and total absence of forehead, somebody is sure to exclaim in awed tones, "My God, think how far man has come since then!"

Well, indeed he has. Far enough to send rockets to the moon, make a live, jumping frog out of a single frog cell and refine the ritual of war to a simple efficiency that puts us all ten minutes from doomsday.

In such a world it comes as a pleasant shock to read of a man who directs his genius to improving the ordinary goodness of our daily life. Such a man is Neil Lyall of London. And if he ever comes here I should like to break bread with him. The bread must perforce be of my own baking. Mr. Lyall is a man who cherishes the taste of an old-fashioned, crusty, honest loaf, still warm from the oven. (God be with you, sir, and have some honey!)

Mr. Lyall is a food chemist and nutritionist. To my mind, he is also a great humanitarian. After seven years of research he has patented a mysterious potion—I'm loath to say "additive"—that will restore the home-baked flavor to store-bought bread. The potion is a blend of five ingredients, including wheat germ and processed yeast. English bakers have pronounced the enriched loaves delicious. Sales, they add, have "zoomed."

The last point is significant, bread buying having declined in England about 40 percent since the last war. Weight-watching is blamed, of course. But the repulsive taste and texture of modern bleached, aerated bread is an equally strong reason.

It would be lovely if the Lyall additive could be added at once to America's staff of life. There should have been a law years ago banning the deathly white, spongy stuff that masquerades as bread in our supermarkets.

But nobody, I hear you say, is obligated to buy that pale, wretched bread. Are not the shelves filled with neat, sliced, sand-colored loaves enriched with wheat germ and vitamins? Why don't people buy what's good for them?

The answer is that people, especially the poor, do not know what's good for them. Scores of studies by the government and various universities have shown that we are an ignorant and hence ill-nourished nation. The poor buy the loaf that appears to offer the most for the money. The not-so-poor believe that soft, white bread is somehow cleaner and nicer. Bakers have not been slow to take advantage of this unwisdom.

When I visit a supermarket it always saddens me to see mothers with a brood of runny-eyed, whey-faced little children buying the fat, squashy bread Alistair Cooke once described as "looking like dehydrated snow and tasting like blown-up blotting paper."

"The bread of the needy is their life," says the Bible, "and he that defraudeth him thereof is a man of blood." Updated, that means that the baker who sells a poor loaf that fails to feed more than the immediate pangs of hunger is a crook and a poltroon.

He can redeem himself somewhat, however, if he makes use of Lyall's additive. For it will build bones and teeth, as well as restoring that fine, brick-oven flavor.

In the Middle Ages, a time of hunger and plague, a man who dropped a crust of bread picked it up at once and kissed it. Bakers who turned out wormy or adulterated loaves were punished in the pillory. The most detailed history of eating I have ever read—J. C. Drummond's *The Englishman's Food*—tells of "nine bakeresses" being seized in the year 1310 and imprisoned for their short-weight bread.

It is not difficult to bake bread. It's splendid exercise, too, kneading the dough. More important, the baking of bread fills your heart with peace and your house with the most beautiful of the basic aromas known to man.

We live, it seems, in a world of tacky things. Of toys that break in a day, of TV sets that give off lethal rays and milk containers that can't be opened at the top but invariably leak at the bottom.

Maybe it serves us right. Having raised built-in obsolescence to a holy creed, we are now immured in insolent craftsmanship. We are helped through the day's labors by gaily colored appliances, all powered by precision parts that burn out in the night. We are mechanized, Lord help us, from womb to tomb to eternity.

But when the washer won't wash and the air conditioner refuses to condition, well, madam, you need a repairman. And you'd be in better luck if you needed an armorer to fix the dent in your breastplate. A museum might well send you an armorer. But nobody, in this golden age of technology, is ever around to put the pop back into your pop-up toaster.

This appalling breakdown in merchandise and service has

been attributed to "the roaring demands of affluence and workers' attitudes." So says the *U.S. News & World Report*.

Another reason may be the craven way we accept shoddy goods and services. "Things are in the saddle and ride mankind," as Emerson observed. We are cowed, we are conditioned to amassing possessions. We are willing to pay through the nose for the privilege. Thus do shoddy goods grow shoddier.

Remember the saying "built to last"? You hear it today only if a man is speaking of his 1935 Rolls-Royce, his 1780 farmhouse with the original oak beams or the sturdy peasant cook he just got by mail order from the Balkans. (And she is built to last only until a well-fed guest slips into the kitchen and makes her a better offer.)

Maybe the wobble and list, the general tackiness of today's goods and chattels can be blamed on our loss of Yankee thrift. Upward strivers all, we are seduced by a name on a label, dazzled by a commercial in living color. We buy on the run. And we're pushovers for salesmen with a sweet line of blarney.

In truth, salesmen don't have to twist our arms. Usually we are in urgent need of his wares because the glittering prize we had delivered six months ago has already slipped a gasket or chewed up its own nuts and bolts.

Across the gulf of years we read about English gentlemen who waited a year for their boots to ripen on the last at Lobb's—and wore the boots fifty years. Lord Tennyson wore the same velvet cloak for thirty years, then left it on a train. It is now in a museum.

Yearning for those dear dead days, I read wistfully of Mrs. Lydig, an Edwardian belle who had 300 pairs of tiny perfect shoes. All were made on plaster molds from the finest silk and kid. Each shoe was so incredibly light it could be balanced on a scale with an ostrich feather. Mrs. Lydig also collected old violins—and (terrible thought!) had the fine, delicate wood split up for shoe trees!

Now one is hard put to find a sturdy pair of boots that will stay

118

dry in a puddle. Everywhere we look, as some wit has said, we see craft ebbing.

What to do? Well, we could, in our roaring affluence, complain more. How often do we send back the tepid, ill-cooked dinner? How often, in buying a dress, do we say, "It's pretty, but those crooked, sloppy seams won't do"?

And where, oh where, is the man who will send straight to hell the wine steward, caressing his chain of office and bowing low, whose dusty bottle decants a thin and bitter brew?

The thought rises: Do all these artisans and servingmen hate their work? Kahlil Gibran once wrote that work is "love made visible." He was right. "If you bake bread with indifference," he noted, "you bake a bitter bread that feeds but half man's hunger. And if you grudge the crushing of the grapes, your grudge distills a poison in the wine."

Think about it.

Perhaps no holiday ever matches the dream. Fourth of July can dawn damp and drizzly. Hurricanes have a way of blowing in during the Labor Day weekend. And then comes Christmas. Our lovely fantasy of eggnog parties and strolling carolers, snapping yule logs and the perfect gifts under the perfect, sparkling tree can turn out to be an orgy of blown fuses, howling children and tippling guests. And, oh, those slushy trudgings up Fifth Avenue with two shopping bags, an oncoming cold and not a cab in sight!

This year it's difficult even to get the *fantasy* of Christmas into focus. You come upon a little list headed "Toys for Teddy," and there, unbeckoned, is the sudden vision of Vietnamese babies clutching their young dead mothers in a shallow grave.

You open the Christmas cooky book and wonder if there will be time this weekend to make the almond stars and the pfeffernuss crispies and Mrs. Schmidt's *spritzkuchen*. Then a voice from the television screen, weary with an old anger, says, "There are fifteen million people in this country who do not get enough to eat. . . . And being hungry they just can't cry very loud."

It is Senator George McGovern. He is addressing a special assembly of nutritionists, agriculture experts and sullen blacks who stand armed with the justice of the quarrel as well as the insolence of their hunger.

They are all members of the White House Conference on Food, Nutrition and Health. They are now gathered on the TV screen in this week before Christmas to tell the nation that we are a land where wealth accumulates and men decay . . . and that nobody cares. Nobody.

The debate—bitter, intense and deeply moving—goes on for an hour. Nobody talks of Christmas cookies. But we hear of children dying of malnutrition, of worms, TB and rheumatic fever. In the presence of such anger, such harsh, naked truths about the way we live now, an abundant Christmas seems almost sinful.

Throughout the hour it is the blacks who cut through the rhetoric, who pierce the hypocrisy of the Department of Agriculture experts, men who speak in pious, we're-doing-our-best tones of commodities and food stamps and welfare. A small woman stands up to say there are maggots in the corn meal. "That's a distribution problem," she is told. The manner clearly implies, "It's not a feast, but what do you shiftless lot expect?"

The hero of the hour is the Reverend Jesse Jackson. His wrath is Biblical. And he has more hard, brutal facts about hunger in America than any of the shifty, throat-clearing farm experts. Unerringly, the minister puts his finger on the greatest shame of all. More than 60 percent of our budget goes for the war machine, less than 20 percent for human needs.

We know it's a corrupt government, he adds, "when fifteen Southern states have 89 percent of the farm subsidy and the greatest area of starvation is the area where the greatest amount of money is going. There are more than 200 farmers in Mississippi receiving more than $50,000 a year for not working."

A number of myths—dear to the well-fed committees that deny federal funds to the poor—were put to rout by the impassioned voices raised during this hour.

The poor won't buckle down to work? Maybe they're too hungry to work. "I worked eight hours a day in a home without having eaten in two days," said a woman who'd failed at her job. "How could I go from the attic to the basement, scrubbing six floors and sweeping dust out of the chimney, *as a hungry person?*"

Some welfare programs provide twenty-three cents a day per hungry person for food. Senator McGovern finds this shamefully meager. Then he tells of a study made of the eating habits of the poor. "We found that, dollar for dollar, poor people do a better job of stretching that food dollar than middle-income people do."

No one should go hungry in America. It is therefore good that hunger is now a political issue. The White House Conference may have ended in frustration, but it's a beginning. Some year, before we are all too old to quaff eggnog and stand on a ladder to hang the mistletoe, Christmas may come and find us a land without hungry children and welfare mothers and food stamp scandals. Someday Saint Nick may step from his sleigh and say, "Blessed are the poor, for they are poor no more!"

At Christmas time, one dreams a lot.

"All passions in excess are female."—Lord Byron.

You said it, milord. And if anybody doubts it, let him consider some of the outcroppings of female passion now in the news.

I'm not referring to the bachelor motherhood of Vanessa and Mia. That's private passion and no concern of ours. It is evidence of darker passions, of perverse conduct, that upsets me. Frailty seems, at the moment, an extinct trait in women.

It is shaming to read that three of the five bedraggled hippies charged with killing Sharon Tate (and six others) were girls. Girls in their twenties with long, flowing hair and hurt, sad faces. Lost girls in love with a mad guru.

That the principal victim was a girl near their own age, great with child, puts the minds of the killers in a category beyond normal comprehension.

Reading of the agonizing final moments of Miss Tate, stabbed sixteen times, brought back to mind another widely publicized case of what one can only call "monstrous depravity." That was the Moors Murders of a few years ago. On trial were a twenty-three-year-old typist, Myra Hindley, and a queer bloke named Ian Brady, to whom she, like Susan, Patricia and Linda, was "enslaved."

When the trial brought out the fact that one of the victims, a ten-year-old girl, had been sexually abused and tortured with Miss Hindley either participating or looking on, the prosecutor was almost speechless. Finally, he uttered one trembling line that must have hung in the courtroom air like the eldest primal curse: "A child, madam, *of your own sex?*" he gasped.

It seems likely that the revulsion rising from the arrest of these vicious and pitiless young people will put the hippie culture permanently beyond the pale. We may even see some of the bearded strays returning to the fold, bathed, shaved and chastened.

But even as ritualistic murder by a coed gang of hippies reminds us that men have no monopoly on evil, so do the more bizarre activities of the Women's Liberation Movement suggest that hippies are not the sole practitioners of self-immolation.

There's a disturbing lot of exhibitionism and hostility among the liberation lassies. Of course, their grievance is valid and honorable in some respects. Women *are* discriminated against—in business, in the professions, in politics and, most brazenly, under our tax laws. If they've married dumb louts or insecure little popinjays, they're discriminated against at home, too.

But when they go about proclaiming, "Marriage means rape and lifelong slavery," they're common scolds. They're losing the citizens who could help them most. I mean the men. Decent, *concerned* men who jump to correct any situation that causes a loud female fuss. They jump faster, though, when some sweet voice asks, "Darling, would you . . . ?"

But no man is going to feel pleased with his role as supporter of a movement that psychiatrists have described as "essentially castrating." It just won't do.

I'll join any cause that gets more women into universities and wins equal pay for equal work. But I run from girls who take karate lessons or who cut their hair with a straight razor. I also sniff distastefully at any women who abjure lipstick, cologne, deodorants and other niceties in the name of "liberation." If you can't manage to smell nice, very well, go live with the animals.

Call me old-fashioned, but I sense something ugly and shrewish in a holy war that has among its slogans "Bitch, Sister, Bitch!" And which demands, according to an article in *Life*, that members leave their husbands (if they're old-fashioned enough to have such encumbrances), give up sex and start life anew with a new name, neither father's nor husband's.

Such a program has as much appeal as Carry Nation putting her ax to the town saloon and throwing shawls over nude statues. I may be less than enlightened in revolutionary tactics, but I can't see much future in any crusade that imposes such disciplines on its crusaders. The question keeps nagging: What ails these unsexed Furies? What vital stitch has slipped in their psyches?

If men worked at being a little more masculine, do you suppose women might get off the barricades and back into the boudoir?

1970

New Decade, Old Sorrows

. . . Spiro Agnew flew around the world, a Greek bearing a gift: the Nixon Doctrine. . . . Attorney General Mitchell, after prolonged study of judicial records, persuaded President Nixon to name Judge G. Harrold Carswell to the Supreme Court. The Senate decided he was unfit, setting off another Nixon tantrum. . . . ("What did he expect of a judge who can't even spell 'Harold'?" ran the joke.) . . .

On television, with a dramatic flourish of his pen, President Nixon vetoes the most humane education-health-and-welfare bill ever drawn. Troops moved the mail during the nation's first postal strike. . . . White demonstrators overturned school buses in Lamar, South Carolina, earning a mild rebuke from Spiro Agnew. . . . Bombs damaged offices of three giant corporations in New York. . . . The President announced invasion of Cambodia. In the ensuing national protest, four students were shot to death by Ohio National Guardsmen at Kent State. . . .

1970 was a sad, stormy year. The cost of living went up and up. The Penn Central went bankrupt, and even the Diners' Club had a deficit. . . . Robert Finch quit the Cabinet, leaving HEW in disarray and the public disillusioned. . . . Peru had an earthquake and 50,000 died. . . . David Bruce took charge of Paris peace talks, raising more false hopes. . . . Women's Lib paraded up Fifth Avenue, looking tired and tacky. . . . Palestinian guerrillas seized four jet liners, bringing hijackings to a total of 250, of which 184 succeeded. . . . The midi-skirt was launched—and sank.

This was the year of the finest, bravest of all Presidential commission reports. The Commission on Campus Unrest urged Mr. Nixon to exert "moral leadership." . . . The White House ignored it, sent Spiro out to denounce it. . . . Terror bombings were the plague of the year. . . . Angela Davis was arrested. . . . The November elections brought out the worst in Nixon and Agnew and made a hero of Senator Ed Muskie. . . . *Sesame Street* introduced small children to the delights of literacy. . . . Face-lifts became the new fad among the rich.

As if he didn't have enough to trouble his sleep, the President is now expressing grave concern over the decline of rural America. It seems there are fewer and fewer farms to keep the folks down on anymore.

In this case, at least, Mr. Nixon's instincts are sound. The decay of our green and pleasant villages is, indeed, cause for alarm. Not so long ago a rich, full life was lived here, with the feed and grain store doing a lively business and the public library open five afternoons a week. Of course, the big express trains roared right through town without stopping, but babies went on being born, cellars swelled with provender and "every rood of ground maintained its man."

I think we may count any man blessed who keeps the quiet landscape of a bygone village somewhere in the folds of his mind. It's all worth remembering—the busy mill beside the stream, the sturdy plowman (older than Virgil, who also honored him) and the girls in their summer dresses. They all live on, simple and true, back there where memory holds the door.

But now the villages are deserted and the curfew has tolled the end of an era. The last U.S. census warned that the country was becoming one vast urban sprawl.

New Decade, Old Sorrows

Citizens of Sprawl see little greenery. Smog lines our lungs, tension coarsens our voices. We buy ear plugs to muffle the din we're in. It seems incredible that people who lived in those long-ago villages sometimes said, "You can't hear a thing today but the wind in the poplars."

The poplars are gone now. And the laurels are cut down. And there's no mill beside the stream, no bashful virgins casting side-long looks of love. All that happened long ago and in another country. A country vanished under concrete and neon and chemical waste and the burnt-out hopes of good men.

Still, it's possible now and then, if you drive slowly through America's "back country" to glimpse occasional ghosts of our tranquil past. Prairie folk can see all their yesterdays in great, sagging barns, scoured silver by time and weather. You can still make out the letters GENERAL STORE on faded frame buildings. Rats and lizards live in the charred ruins of a once-grand mansion. ("Sent all the way to France for the mantelpieces, they did.") There are creeping vines in the cemetery. The depot is dark, the single track covered with rust . . . and there's nobody to say how long the train's been gone.

The census figures tell the story in simple numbers. Now, in 1970, 73.5 percent of us (or 149,300,000 people) live in urban areas. We're a land of city slickers. We're forgetting the way the wind blows the grass and how a night in April smells. Our roots have been cut. Only now and then are we aware that they are bleeding.

Paradoxically, as the small town has vanished, the suburbs have grown. The big city exodus grows every year. But nobody ever goes back to Grover's Corners. The move is always to the green edges of Urban Sprawl. A man can make a little garden out there. And the faces in the public school are mostly white. Crime is low, naturally, because "that element" isn't allowed.

If you have ever seen the living rot of a ghetto, you know the inhumanity of the so-called inner city. It's the hell that proves how badly we've bungled our basics. We have allowed millions of poor children to grow up half civilized, half human, sometimes

129

half dead. In our ignorance—and in the cupidity of our legislators—we've assented to their destruction. Now, awakened, we wonder why we cannot transport "that element" to those spacious small towns where the greatest need is for living people.

But what would a black family from Bedford-Stuyvesant do in a sleepy village of 500 souls? They'd leave, of course, exactly as the white folks left before them. On to where the good times are.

Significantly, the South is becoming urbanized more rapidly than any other region. California, though its growth has lately been slowed by unemployment and earthquake jitters, is now our most urban state. The East Coast, from Boston to Miami, is seen from the air as a pall of smog. Houston and Chicago have long since passed from big city to megalopolis.

Where, then, may we still find tidy orchards and rambler roses and "carpenter Gothic" churches fronting a village green?

Well, we can try Vermont, which ranks as our most bucolic state, with 68 percent of the population living in towns of less than 2,500. West Virginia, where too many residents live in poverty "down in the holler," ranks close to Vermont.

As one who passed some crucial years in villages of upstate New York and Connecticut, the death of small-town America is the death of a younger, more innocent self.

"Remember the place you came from and how it was," advises that gifted man of the plains Richard Rhodes.

I remember, and I am sad for the generation that has never glided down leafy streets in the summer twilight. I am sorry for all who do not remember houses with cupolas and porte-cocheres and banisters to slide down.

Pressed into our airless apartments and ticky-tacky houses, it's nice to remember the cool, spicy-buttery pantries where the coffee was ground fresh each morning, where molasses cookies and peppermints were stored and where many "nice girls" got their first serious kiss.

And attics! Pity the child who never spent a rainy Saturday up there under the roof, trying on the old plumed hats, playing the wind-up phonograph and reading boxes of faded postcards, tokens of the days when everybody was "having wonderful time."

When all the small towns are gone, the loveliest part of America will be gone. The wilderness will claim its own. Grass will grow on Main Street, just as the town drunk always predicted it would. But the ghosts remain.

"Remember us!" That's the whisper Richard Rhodes hears from leaning gravestones and box hedges now gone wild. He tells, in his book *Inland Ground*, of hearing sighs "from trees planted before we were reluctantly born, from sod that thickened red and black and yellow dirt, before we dared flatten its waving grasses . . . from cabins now become cities beside a hill. . . ."

Never do I drive past an old house set like a great ship on a rolling lawn without hearing ghostly voices. And I always see complete in a single flash all that lies behind the great veranda, from the threadbare Chinese rug in the hall to the big red thermometer outside the kitchen window.

First, there's a fanlight over the door. Graceful, elegant, practical. Then there's the vestibule, with an umbrella stand made from an elephant's leg. And a hat rack with a mirror in the middle and a bench below, solid oak. There are initials carved in the bench by children now called Granddad and Old Aunt Belle.

Then came the center hall, called in my childhood the reception room. A grand phrase for a tiny room with never a chair to sit on. From the "reception"—I can see it now—rises the heavy oak staircase, the banister worn smooth by generations of hands and by the steady whoooosh! of small bottoms.

Under the stairs a dark closet, slanting down to nothing. It's musty with old galoshes and camphor and dog leashes and a moldering mackintosh, left behind by a visitor twenty years ago. ("Throw it out! Why, it's perfectly *good*, and suppose he came back someday?")

Up the oaken stairs, turn left at the landing. The landing is lit by a stained-glass window, green and amber, hideous. There's a cushioned window seat where lovers say good night and children spy on their elders. The glass is thick, the light eerie. Boston ferns die there.

The landing fills many functions. It is the stage for family drama. From this four-foot elevation famous last words are hurled. Terrible threats are made, authority challenged, house rules defied. ("Nobody in this house is ever going to see me again, *ever!*") Then the tears gush, as Difficult Daughter bolts left, up the dark, closed stairs and into the soft comfort of her own room.

There was a blessed privacy in those small-town houses. One could *retire* from the parlor with dignity. Main Street may have known sorrow and shame and defeat. But it knew them in flower-papered bedrooms with GOD IS LOVE on the wall.

Every small town was unique in its way. But in memory all have the same elms, the same gossip, the same innocent, starry stillness at half past ten.

"Rural America is dying," says *U.S. News & World Report*. Not yet! we reply. Not dead while we remember the jaunty little parades on the Fourth of July. And the little boys in their summer haircuts selling lemonade, five cents a glass. And band concerts in the park with Otto the Butcher—so foreign without his bloody apron and straw boater—in the front row, bald and beaming, keeping time with his heel.

But never mind, Otto. It's the subtleties one longs to bring back. The way raspberries tasted, warm from the bush. The rambler roses that looked all wrong in vases. And the roses with names like Dorothy Perkins and Queen Mother Mary. And, oh, yes, the rose petals we ceremoniously swept up—we were a romantic thirteen at the time—for strewing in the bath. ("Those rose petals have clogged the goddamned drains again," roars a voice from the past. It was then that the strewing had to stop.)

After a passage of years, everybody's small town becomes "Our Town." And we're all Emily Webb, the birthday girl, back for one blessed day to turn fourteen, to say good-bye to mama's sunflowers and the smell of freshly laundered summer dresses.

The trouble would seem to be that America's small towns went on living in the past long after the past had become unprofitable and quaint. Progress, like spring in the North, came slow and begrudging. In remote hamlets with one church and a gas pump, in neat villages with a bank and a movie house, life was always hard. As late as 1935 only 5 percent of American farms had electricity.

Today we're nostalgic for that world. But is it the abrasions or simply the terror of urban life that persuades small-town living was idyllic?

All the pretty villages, if we face the truth, had their squalid side, too. There was scandal, there was thievery, adultery, abortion. Winesburg, Ohio, Gopher Prairie, Peyton Place, all had their own truth. But the truth was everywhere.

There was strength and wisdom in small-town America, too. People were closer then. They shared grief, laid out their dead in front parlors, kept secrets into the third generation. And, yes, Virginia, they really did hold square dances in the village hall and gather around the piano Sunday evenings to sing "Rock of Ages." All that was long before my time, but it happened.

Winters were hard, even in the comparatively recent days of my small-town childhood. My right ear still hurts under the hair dryer because it was frostbitten long ago. The snow came early and thawed late. Most people were in bed each night by ten— "snug as the Sunday roast," as Dylan Thomas would put it.

What killed small towns? Big cities. Progress. The airplane. Automation. Social mobility. The upward striving wanderlust of the American people. Today's young people, with their communes and caravans, are but another manifestation of that wanderlust.

The irony of the death-by-progress theory is that nobody worshiped the newfangled more than small-towners. Belief in progress, in America the invincible, was a form of religion back in 1900. Everybody marveled to see what American ingenuity had wrought.

Listen to papa chiding mama in the charming scrapbook Richard Bissell calls *Julia Harrington.*

"Just think," says papa, "you've got a telephone in the house and you can call up your mother six miles away. . . . Inside plumbing! Hot water! Caruso in your parlor on the talking-machine!" What more could any woman ask?

Speaking for myself, I just can't imagine.

In matters of housewifery, I've always considered myself reasonably competent. No Craig's wife, sterilizing the cigarette boxes and shampooing the velvet coat hangers. Just a nice, homey girl who keeps the mantel dusted, the ice bucket filled and green plants flourishing in every room to sweeten the city-burdened air.

I was wont to feel complacent about my domestic virtues until I opened my Christmas stocking and discovered one of those tiresome little books of household hints. The more I read the more incompetent I felt and the more disheveled my house looked. Had the census taker rung my bell the day after Christmas and inquired, "Occupation?" the only truthful answer would have been, "Slattern, sir."

And, indeed, why not? Have I ever oiled the zippers on the family galoshes? Do I set aside a quiet hour each month for cleaning our playing cards with cotton dipped in camphor? And how do I expect my loved ones to look well turned-out if I do not take the trouble to sew on their buttons with dental floss?

Creative economy, according to Waldo Emerson, is the "fuel of magnificence." I'll grant it's creative, but is it really magnificent to wash your nylons in hot water and pop them into the deep freeze to preserve their fibers? Holly Cantus' *Household Hints* book says it is.

Mrs. Cantus—whom I see as a small, round dervish in a cottage apron—supplies no instructions for thawing those nylons.

She does go on at length, however, about the proper way to thaw frozen bread. You slice it—never mind how—and then you press each slice with a steam iron. Should your phone ring and an impertinent voice inquire, "What are you doing?" you'd better have an answer ready. Say you're taking out your impacted wisdom tooth. No? All right, then, say, "I'm ironing some bread for dinner," and see how far you get.

Dear Holly Cantus, what a rich, full life you've led in that kitchen! Shellacking the cookbook covers, nailing a rustic mailbox to the wall to hold unpaid bills, braiding rugs out of old tea towels, upholstering the bottoms of ashtrays and coasters with bits of felt, turning plastic bread cases into cozy glove and shoe cases. If a sparrow falls, you can bet Holly plucks his feathers for doll house dusters.

All these little chores doubtless make some women feel creative. When a husband asks, "What did you do today?" it's a proud housewife who can reply, "Well, darling, I cut up those two old felt hats of yours to make nonskid bottoms for the coasters."

CUT! "Which old felt hats?" asks the husband, rising from his chair in a Neanderthal crouch that doesn't mean "How adorable of you!" Books of household hints never tell you how husbands respond to so much good wifery.

In my creative years in the kitchen I have done everything but stuff a boar's head and bake a pigges' pettytoes pye. I'm game for any recipe, however bizarre. But I've never put olives to soak in a cask to make my own olive oil. I've never weather-stripped my rocking chairs or spent a jolly Saturday night removing the kitchen wallpaper with a pancake spatula.

Call me a slacker, but I can make puff pastry and fine French sauces and arrange flowers better than Madame Butterfly. That loveliest of tributes to womankind—"Her ways are ways of pleasantness and all her paths are peace"—may not rise in every throat as I pass, but people always seem easy and comfortable in my house.

Maybe I don't wax the clothesline every Monday with an old

candle stub, but a man I once loved sent me a great tub of garden flowers on a May morning (my birthday) with a card that bore Archibald MacLeish's lines, "Wherever she is there is sun-/And time and a sweet air . . . /There are always curtains and flowers/And candles and baked bread/And a cloth spread/And a clean house." He never had to give me emeralds. I had in my jewel box that little card . . . those words.

The years pass, and like all tamed, wild creatures, I grow ever more domesticated. But I've yet to turn old ankle socks into jolly, misshapen mittens and wear them to bed, the insides squishy with hand lotion.

I do not vacuum my old velvet hats, as Mrs. Cantus advises, but that's because I rarely can find an old velvet hat. My bread box will never be lined with worn-out tea towels. And my pantyhose will never go into the deep freeze. I do not save pennies by shining the family shoes with the inside of a banana peel.

As I read over the above lines I can only wonder how many housewives suffer nervous breakdowns each year in the name of tidier, thriftier household management?

My digs will never be photographed in color for *House Beautiful*. But the linen is crisp, the floors clean, the laughter frequent and guests have to be dislodged with iron crowbars. And there's a household hint hidden somewhere in that paragraph for Heloise, Mrs. Cantus and all the Mrs. Craigs in their vacuumed velvet hats.

My advice to brides—and to weary wives—is: Forget the *Household Hints*. Keep the bathroom immaculate and learn to cook lovely dinners. For the rest, run an orderly house and be cheerful. Make house room for a dog and a cat. Encourage your husband's hobby, even if it's taxidermy or building an ark in the basement. Never prize possessions above love and comfort. You may not be asked to contribute to a new edition of *Household Hints* . . . but there'll be none of Beauty's daughters with a magic like to thee!

When we worry about the population explosion we are mostly worried about the proliferation of poor people. Rich families with ten or twelve children are dismissed as stupid or hilariously over-sexed or both. ("My God, what else can they do in the evening? *Converse?*")

But poor people who have a baby every year are condemned as immoral, not to say careless. Rarely does a prospectus for the better world of tomorrow reach this desk without an agenda that includes a massive program of birth control—for the poor, natu-rally. And quickly, please!

It is the poor, we are reminded, who devour our tax dollars. It's the poor who pull down academic standards and push up the crime rate. It's the poor who mar the environment with their un-sanitary hovels, pollute the beaches on Sundays and keep nice old ladies from getting a seat on the bus.

Well, nobody ever said the world would not be a prettier, ti-dier place if every family were deliciously stuffed and on the pill. But it is not the poor we must blame for the wretched condition of our society. It's the fat-cat legislators who make it a point of honor to withhold from the poor any and every benefit that might "weaken" their character. That includes such character-rotting gifts as sacks of government surplus corn meal (often wormy) and school lunches.

To those who would damn the poor for the ugliness and sorrow of life in the twentieth century, here's a sobering piece of news from Dr. Jean Mayer, the Harvard nutritionist and ecologist. Dr. Mayer damns the rich. It is the prosperous, uncaring folk who are making the world a mess, he says firmly.

"Fear of world hunger keeps us from seeing a more serious

problem," Dr. Mayer told an interviewer. That is overpopulation, "the most crucial problem of our time, not by the poor but by the rich."

What's wrong with having lots of rich people? Well, it's Dr. Mayer's notion that they "wreck the environment."

Specifically: "Rich people occupy more space, consume more of each natural resource, disturb the ecology more, litter the landscape with bottles and paper and pollute more land, air and water with chemical, thermal and radioactive waste."

This view coincides with that of conservationists who frequently chide real-estate developers for their "greed, ignorance and malice." It's the middle and upper classes who buy the "second home" in the country. The governor of Vermont recently blasted these second-home builders for creating, in that rugged state, a "man-made jungle."

The developers sell half-acre plots, put down septic tanks rather than proper sewage pipes and destroy forests, streams and wildlife.

"It might be bad in China with 700 million poor people," says Professor Mayer, "but 700 million rich Chinese would wreck China in no time. It's the spread of wealth that threatens the environment just as it's the spread of fat that threatens the lives of so many Americans."

The rich have lots of problems, it seems, in coping with the environment. A learned study of time and motion in the kitchen came up last year with the news that a housewife's drudgery time—*i.e.*, kitchen labor—increases in direct proportion to the appliances she owns. If you're blessed with blenders, mixers, freezers, ice-crushers, you've got to use them, that's all. And then you've got to clean them. And then it's time to eat again. Thus do we ripen toward the grave, blending, mixing, freezing, crushing. . . .

New Decade, Old Sorrows

Late bulletins from the lying-in hospitals suggest that it's going to be chic this year to have babies out of wedlock.

Mothers of teen-age daughters no doubt wish this form of chic an early death. And it's safe to say that most of the 300,000 women who will be giving birth to illegitimate children this year will not be admiring their swelling figures in the glass and murmuring, "How chic I look!"

Vanessa Redgrave and Mia Farrow may carry off their unwed accouchements with style and dash. But a lumpy fifteen-year-old who's suddenly taken to wearing a 42-long overcoat to all her classes, including gym, somehow lacks that style and dash.

Never mind that Ingrid Bergman was once an unwed mother. And that a pretty singer named Sandy, without a ring on her finger, presented singer Tony Bennett with a son. The awful truth is that an unwed mother is a sorry figure, more to be pitied than censured, but hardly a new goddess for the teen-agers' pantheon.

A touching interview with an unwed mother identified simply as Bridget appeared in a London paper not long ago. "No one would want to get herself into this situation," said Bridget. "Supporting a bastard is only one of the penalties of sex outside marriage."

Above all, sensible Bridget deplored the glamorous aura cast over illegitimacy by film stars, models and soldiers' girlfriends. Her three-year-old, she said, is "puzzled" by other children's daddies. "Where's *my* daddy?" he rightly wonders.

Bridget might also have deplored the new fad for equating illegitimate babies with "liberation." Tending a baby, managing a job and an apartment and putting down the inquiries of busybodies is a nerve-racking job, and it's anything but liberating.

It was all very gay and terribly emancipating when Miss Redgrave laughed down a reporter's question about her Italian lover with "Why should I marry him?" Why, indeed, when he is so much younger, so much shorter and not at all keen on getting married? Give Miss R. the palm for gallantry.

We may admire the dignity with which these celebrated young women go through their pregnancies—Miss Farrow was reported "rapturous" at the prospect of twins—but one's thoughts eventually must turn to the child. To allow a human life to take form without two parents wholly committed to its welfare strikes some old-fashioned folks as wrong.

The illegitimate child, be he a royal bastard or a movie star's petted darling, always suffers an emotional handicap. If there are other children legitimately born, the sibling rivalry can leave deep scars.

It is worth noting here that early abortion is now approved by 40 percent of America. This is progress.

For Vanessa and Mia, a baby born on the wrong side of the blanket may carry no stigma. Fame is a cushion. But the current notion that illegitimacy is a brave step forward for women, that it's "mod" and "liberated," is nonsense. It shoves women back into the eighteenth century—and beyond—when the lord of the manor had his way with any servant girl he fancied and when "fallen women" never rose up again.

Even royal families, with "three bastards in every litter," were properly embarrassed by irregular births. Louis XIV, who had thirteen illegitimate children, had them all legitimatized—but tactfully withheld the names of the mothers. William IV of England had ten children by an actress named Mrs. Jordan. (When he attempted to cut off her paltry allowance, she sent him the bottom half of a playbill that said, "No money returned after the raising of the curtain.")

A recent psychological study of unwed mothers indicates that they are as a group "immature, irresponsible and hungry for affection." This is said to hold true regardless of education or social status. Film star or file clerk, unwed mothers are all lost, sad girls when the lights are out.

> There was a young woman who lived in a shoe
> Who had so much contraceptive advice she didn't
> know what to do.

First, she took the pill. She took it regularly and happily, after her baby was born, until the pope said it was a sin. Then she began crying every night, and her proper Catholic husband took to slipping away to his study at bedtime—"To go over some papers, darling." Darling smiled bravely. She told her mother that at least he wasn't slipping away to visit some floozie.

Secretly, the woman in the shoe tried the loop, the coil, the cap and the method her ever-pregnant sister-in-law bitterly referred to as "rhythm and blues." Sometimes she wondered if it was too late to enter a nunnery.

Now and then the young woman in the shoe clipped such items out of the newspaper as POLL FINDS 54% OF CATHOLICS OPPOSED POPE'S PILL BAN. She stuck this and similar pro-pill stories to her husband's shaving mirror. "No comment" was his comment.

When the young woman read that French Catholics had been advised by their bishops that taking the pill was no sin—and, *alors*, hardly worth bringing up in confession—she wondered at breakfast if apartments were still scarce in Paris. "Yes, and so are jobs," said her husband. "And, anyway, I thought you wanted to live on a houseboat. That's what you said last week."

The turning point came when the woman in the shoe read in a nice, cheery ladies' magazine that the pill was not only the safest, easiest method of birth control but also gave women an emotional release that put them right up there with history's greatest courtesans. And she'd never realized it! In the warmer recesses of her mind, the young woman began to equate ecstasy with estrogen.

A few days later the young woman emptied her great-grandmother's teapot of all her hoarded cash and bought a gossamer nightgown of chiffon and lace and renewed her prescription for the pill.

For a year everything was roses and raptures around that old shoe. Then one evening the young woman tuned in Huntley-Brinkley and lo! there were the learned gynecologists and hormone researchers calling the pill a grave risk to a woman's life. Cancer, blood clots, sterility were a few of the possible consequences cited.

Mice, she learned, developed cancer in the most feared and terrible places after being fed estrogen. "But I'm not a mouse!" the young woman told Dr. Roy Hertz, the hormone expert who was telling Congress and American womanhood (via TV) how dangerous the pill was.

"Throw those pills out," roared her husband when she told him how, at the risk of her life, she was saving their marriage. After much argument, *he* threw them out for her. And now the young woman sits in her shoe, not knowing what to do.

If 10,000,000 women go off the pill we may expect another baby boom. The doctors at HEW will not be pleased. They'd like to see the birth rate take a sizable drop. If it doesn't, we'll have 300,000,000 people by the year 2000. "This means we'll have to build the equivalent of one new city for 250,000 inhabitants every forty days," Dr. Roger Egborg told Planned Parenthood not long ago.

Birth control is a deeply personal matter, but it affects the whole human race. Some researchers, every bit as reputable as Dr. Hertz, say that the pill is safe, much safer than pregnancy for some women. As for those blood clots, the British medical bulletin *Lancet* reported in December that "pill users smoke, on average, 20 percent more cigarets than nonusers." In short, the thrombosis deaths now blamed on the pill may be due to smoking.

Someday a safe, cheap and easy birth control pill will be devised. Meantime, what about the woman in the shoe and millions just like her? And what about the unwanted children of the poor, the welfare poor, who cost taxpayers $1 billion a year? Truly, we need a better pill—and quick!

Next to reading other people's mail—chiefly that of dead poets to their once-warm ladies—I most enjoy reading my own.

I may not write the most fascinating column in the land, but I'll match my mailbag against anybody's, including the ladies who, with tact that transcends despair and squalor, advise the lovelorn.

A good letter does more than state a point of view. It shows the texture of a soul, lets you feel the touch of a hand. A letter can also contain, as the Princess Bibesco once wrote to her love, "greater possibilities of murder than any poison."

The letters sent to newspaper writers are nothing if not frank. They tell you what troubled America is really troubled about. (Money, taxes, the morals of the young.) They agonize over Vietnam, marijuana and Merry Agnew. They wonder if you are possibly related to a family named Van Hooren that lived in Philadelphia in 1935.

Some passing references here to the pleasures of the table evoked one of my favorite letters. This from a woman who inquired, most politely, if she might come to my house someday with her young daughter and watch me cook! This is like asking Tiny Tim if you can watch him put up his hair. Will the results justify the time spent?

I fancy myself a dandy cook, but Les Amis d'Escoffier might think otherwise. Besides, I usually combine cooking with clipping the papers, polishing the silver and pulling the cat out of the refrigerator.

Oh, yes, the cat. Here's a letter that says, in block letters, "May I please have your cat's picture?—Sheldon." Now, Sheldon, if you'll just print your full name and address, Pouf, the cat, will try to oblige.

Pet lovers are a special breed. Their feelings are comprehensible only to *other* pet lovers. I am grateful to the reader who sent me a long press account of Lord Snowden's BBC film on pets. Among its more tender moments, a lady carrying on a warm, intimate conversation with her parrot: "People think we're a bit peculiar, don't they, but who's to judge? . . . Ten years we've loved each other. . . . We must die on the same day, when the time comes. We'll just ask God, that would be lovely." Dotty? No. Sad, loving and lonely.

Certain Republicans, not a bit lonely, feel almost as tenderly toward Spiro Agnew. "If some calamity were to strike President Nixon," writes a lady in California, "I feel sure that Spiro Agnew would fill his shoes to perfection and become one of the great leaders of history."

Following some doubts here about the wisdom and brilliance of Mr. Agnew there came a sack of what can only be called "hate mail." I mentioned this one day. And my heart is still full remembering the letters that came in a rush thereafter, all saying, straight off or in closing, "This is a *love* letter."

When I first wrote about the deplorable condition of my "luxury slum," a fine old house with flaking walls and damp ceilings, readers described their digs and invited me to "move in with us" —a bit of old-time hospitality I hadn't expected.

"I live in a sleazy, midtown hotel crawling with vermin," says one letter, "but, funny thing, we never lack for heat or hot water."

Oddest of the oddities was the number of letters asking, despite my lament about living in the House of Usher, if there were any vacant apartments. Well, there was a small dim one available last week but it was snatched up instantly—at $600 a month. A more eloquent comment on the New York housing shortage I've not heard.

It shames me that I'm not able to rip off instant answers to these letters. I'm particularly apologetic to the retired merchant seaman in Brooklyn who tells me he wrote to Somerset Maugham for sixteen years and always got an answer. Mr. Maugham, of course, sat in the garden of his French villa and dictated. That's the luxury way. Mine is harder. I'm teaching the cat shorthand.

And it came to pass that there went out a decree from the salons of Paris that all the women of the world should lengthen their skirts. And all went to be lengthened, everyone into her own city, just as in Biblical times.

And then a great howl and lamentation went up from the men. Some wept, some threatened to carry hedge clippers in a side pocket. With the demise of the mini-skirt, they said, there would vanish a glory from this earth. Worse, it would be no fun watching girls get on buses anymore.

Even Housing Secretary George Romney had a few words to say about the new *longuette,* as Paris calls it. "Interest rates have been up dramatically," he said. "But when the hemlines come down, interest lessens." That shows you how hilarious—and confusing—a proper Republican can be when challenged by a major social issue.

Mayor John Lindsay took the news of the mini's passing with cool pragmatism. "It'll make the girls run slower," he told *Women's Wear Daily.*

The same paper quoted peppery Mrs. Alice Roosevelt Longworth, now in her eighties, as receiving the new fashion decree calmly. "Occasionally I become acceptable," she mused. It seems that the "wild" daughter of Teddy Roosevelt has always worn her skirts twelve inches from the floor.

In general, it's the women over thirty who should be overjoyed to see skirts drop below the knee. Only young girls built along the lines of racing whippets ever looked smart in skirts that bared both knee and thigh. After a certain age, precious few women put one in mind of a whippet. Still, the fashion press reports a vigorous resistance in some quarters to the more sedate length.

Women who lead active, station wagon, horse-and-hounds lives are against the *longuette.* So are the women whose budgets do not permit a complete new wardrobe every time Dior or Cardin cries "Down!"

Another resistance bloc is made up of those misguided ladies who believe that short skirts are girlish. They cherish the same wild theory about bows in the hair. These are the youth-crazed matrons who now threaten to shorten their little minis. To where, one can't imagine.

The wife of the French ambassador, Madame Charles Lucet, says the shift to longer skirts will be a slow one. But it has been decreed in Paris and therefore must come. But while hems are dropping there will be an anguished chorus asking *"Why?"*

It's a temptation to blame each new trend on the calculated whim of designers who must periodically stimulate an upsurge in the dress business. But a more persuasive theory comes from the great fashion historian James Laver. (He admits to having picked up the theory from a psychologist named Dr. Fluger, but Fluger's fancy is now known as Laver's law.) The law says that

146

the lust of the eye is fickle. And that fashion, being only human, must from time to time shift its "erogenous zones."

Thus, for a few years everybody is in a tizzy about knees. For three years we've had a parade of melon knees, watermelon thighs, chunky ankles, fatted calves. Social historians may look back upon the '60's as the time when it didn't matter if a girl had Queen Anne legs. She showed 'em anyway. In a high wind she even got whistled at.

But now the eye is sated. "What else you got?" the men, all unawares, are asking of the ladies. The long-haired lads in the Paris ateliers may not have carnal desires where women are concerned, but their antennae are highly sensitive. It's time for a change. In the '70's, bare bosoms will be in—or out, if you must be literal. Why do women sheepishly follow what Paris dictates? Well, not to do so means looking dowdy. Women, says Laver, dress according to the "seduction principle." They can't bear seeing another woman look more seductive than themselves. Thus, Paris wins every single time.

Remember the nihilism that so obsessed Dostoevski? Well, there's more than a whiff of it in our polluted air these days. When people talk seriously of nuclear bomb shelters, when ecologists such as Paul Ehrlich give this befouled planet another fifty years to get straight, we are slouching toward our own Siberia of the soul.

One of the wittiest books of the past year bears the title *Due to a Lack of Interest, Tomorrow Has Been Cancelled.* Author Irene Kampen took her title from a notice she saw on a college bulletin board. That's college humor in 1970.

Given the trembling uncertainty of the times, I admire more than ever the people who still say *"Yes!"* to life. The people who go on building houses, planting trees, breeding babies and buying a diamond ring or a silver tea set to pass on to grandchildren still unborn.

In any society the most valuable citizens are those who believe in themselves and in their country. The people who in the face of Vietnam and the drug craze and sinister Dr. Strangeloves roaming the corridors of power maintain a sunny optimism about the human condition.

In this wild faith may lie our only sanity. It is knowing that somewhere radiant girls are being fitted for wedding gowns, somewhere housewives are putting down preserves and drying lavender that provides us with a sense of continuity—more security than you can buy with hoarded gold, more than you can build into the snuggest bomb shelter this side of the catacombs.

Frustration and despair come easily as one reads of the billions that go to the Pentagon and the pennies that go to maintain the decencies of life. Nobody can feel secure when the President's crime commission predicts a nation of "garrisoned city states" if our crime-producing slums are not turned into clean neighborhoods. Particularly when clean neighborhoods appear to be the last concern of a geriatric Congress which this week voted to maintain its tyranny by perpetuating the seniority system. (And how could we have imagined for an instant the vote would go otherwise? Do evil old men ever repent of their ways?)

The Pentagon view of the Vietnam War is repellent—yes, and terrifying—to those of us who would like to go on having babies, planting trees and putting down fine brandy to age for a golden wedding. The President repeatedly states that his goal is peace. Total peace, but with no honor lost, no concessions granted. Thus qualified, total peace may be achieved only through total destruction.

Clark Clifford, John Kenneth Galbraith, Senator Eugene McCarthy and others have stated that a purely military solution to the Vietnam problem is impossible. But there are voices in the Pentagon still echoing General Curtis LeMay's desire to bomb North Vietnam "back to the Stone Age." What the hawk mind fails to consider is the very good chance that such bombing would put the rest of us back in the Stone Age, too.

But the arms race goes on as crime mounts, the poor sink deeper into their miseries and the jails overflow. If tomorrow is canceled, well, "Vengeance is mine, saith the Lord." Meantime, somewhere out there people are still planting trees, building houses, preparing for the new baby—and savoring, not despising, the day of small things. If there is victory, it is theirs, now and forever.

What puts me off the Women's Liberation Movement is its sweaty virility. They shout, they swagger, they talk tough. Their approach to sex would shame a groom of the stable. They despise daintiness, and if they go roaring on this way they're going to lose all of us our hard-won privileges, to say nothing of our good name.

I concede that the "Libbies" are armed with the justice of their quarrel, particularly in economic and political areas. But what does it profit a girl to be armed with justice if she has disarmed herself of the only weapon with clout she ever possessed—namely, her femininity?

In their recent assaults on the fortress of male superiority, the liberators have lent fresh credence to the one male taunt they resent above all. They've acted like "a bunch of stupid dames."

Not all of them, to be sure. There are sensible feminists who would like to see more women in executive jobs as well as in political office. And there are freakish groups with names like Sisters of Lilith and WITCH. As in any reform movement, the wild militants and eccentrics give the whole cause a bad name.

A psychiatrist has noted the self-destructive quality of some women liberators. "Their most conspicuous feature is self-hatred," Dr. Abram Karder of Columbia University said recently. In its masochism, the Women's Lib resembles the far-out radical left.

Heaven knows we have all sat too long, like Patience on a monument, allowing ourselves to be downgraded intellectually because we are female. Any woman who lives by her wits—as I certainly do—has a vested interest in seeing the world made snugger, safer and more rewarding for women.

But the Women's Liberation Movement is ignoring the surest method of persuading a man to open his heart and hand—that is, speak softly, reminding him that he is male, you are female and there are old debts that must be paid.

To list the inequities built into our social order for the purpose of keeping women down takes some time. And it would cast me, for a few paragraphs, into a role I hate: the complaining female.

There are grievous wrongs, yes. But the female militants should remember that nothing much is ever won by "wronging the wronger till he render right." It's smarter—and infinitely pleasanter—to implore, cajole and, if necessary, shame him till he render right.

It's wrong to pay women less than men for equal work. It's wrong to give women an education inferior to that of men. It's wrong to brainwash women into believing they'll lose all womanliness if they become doctors, lawyers, scientists, architects or bank presidents. It is wrong to bar women from the Cabinet, the high courts and the podium of symphony orchestras.

Women have come a long, exciting journey in the past century. One hates to see their progress undone by the viragoes who imagine they can rule the world by becoming harder and meaner than the men.

Women who deny their femininity are women at war with

150

themselves. They have lost their most valuable weapons in the ancient and endless war of the sexes, their grace, their humor, their warmth and sweetness. A rough, tough, nasty woman can never put a man in his place as devastatingly as a soft-voiced, soft-fleshed, gentle woman.

My favorite statement on this thorny subject comes from J. B. Priestley in an essay recalling the great powers of old-fashioned women:

> It is the frail silvery old ladies with fine manners and much knowledge of the world who can put me in my place. And like all men I ought to be put in my place every now and again or I become insufferable . . . as for the free and easy banter of mannish women, their pontifical airs, their pedantry, their shrill sarcasms, they are simply ineffectual, a mere play of shadows compared with this older method of attack and defense, the method of politely smiling irony.

A final word to the Liberation Lassies: Read Jane Austen. She understood how women get power and how they use it.

One of the most sophisticated ladies I know entertains a curious fantasy about her role as a woman. "I'm really an Arab wife," she likes to say. "I know when to be hushed and reverent. And I always walk five paces behind, carrying the luggage."

In truth, this lady is no more an Arab wife than Jackie Onassis. And the only luggage she has ever carried is a jewel case, nicely filled and insured. Any Arab sheikh who tried to throw her across the crupper of his black charger would get a nasty shock. She'd unhorse him and filch his dagger in the process.

She's an iron nymph, this lady, but there is something rather touching—yes, and funny—about her dream role as the meek and humble wife trudging dutifully behind her lord.

In the American culture wives are supposed to be helpmates and jolly good sports. But there are girls who fancy the role of wife as obedient servant. One thinks of Elinor Wylie imploring her lover to "Set me where I bear / A little more than I can bear." And Shakespeare's Viola, dreaming of a willow cabin at her lover's gate where she may halloo her lover's name to the hills.

Old-fashioned girls, these. Absolutely unfit for picket duty on the liberation front. But you'd be astonished by the number of old-fashioned girls, Arab wives in the sorriest sense, who have given themselves to the young revolutionaries of the Third World. Given their all—body, soul and allowance from home. That's the way the boys want it these days.

In the vanguard of the revolution, girls with spirit, girls with a sense of "identity" are not welcome. They can't adapt to the gypsy life, to picket duty, bank burnings and such. Also, the male demands, as women often do. When you're planning a revolution, doing your bit at the secret bomb plant and turning out leaflets on your hand press, the little ceremonies of love and courtship can be a terrible drag.

Thus we have a new breed of woman. Call her the bride of the revolution. She's drab, dutiful and uncomplaining. And she walks five paces behind, carrying the burden—be it a bomb, a valise or a baby. Hers not to question why, hers to shut up and get on with the revolution.

So markedly different are the women in the revolutionary movement that an American sociologist, Professor Joan Rockwell, now teaching in London, has written a provocative essay about them. It appeared in a recent issue of the Sunday London *Observer*. Since I don't get about much in revolutionary circles, I was fascinated by Dr. Rockwell's disclosures.

It goes without saying that the girls who attach themselves to brutish, loutish young men are girls whose masochistic needs are fairly intense. They're spiritual descendants of Mathilda, the consort of William the Conqueror. This rough Norman lass repulsed all royal advances until one day the king waited for her outside her village church and knocked her down as she emerged. Of course, she fell madly in love with him and became his queen.

All dissident groups, says Dr. Rockwell, including criminal gangs, drug-oriented musicians, prostitutes, hippies and "groupies," degrade the status of women. Living outside society, they feel obliged to spurn its values. One of the values easiest to discard is the custom of protecting and honoring women.

Dr. Rockwell blames this churlish attitude on the breakdown of the family. When family ties are broken, women lose status and dignity. The family disintegrates, and the individuals in it are free to form a direct emotional relationship with the movement.

But there's an interesting paradox in the life-style of these revolutionists. The men dominate the women, abuse them and frequently deny them the status of marriage. But they do permit the women to support them.

Though she admits to a lack of statistical proof, Professor Rockwell asserts that revolutionists tend to marry upward. "Hypergamy," sociologists call it. The men count on the desire of certain middle-class girls to become Arab wives. They also enjoy taking vengeance on the upper class which, down through the years, has tended to look upon lower-class girls as one great, teeming brothel.

The brides of the underground usually enter the movement with starry eyes and hopes for a Brave New World the day after tomorrow. In a short time, writes Dr. Rockwell, they fall below the level of "a decent working-class girl." The men, we are told, rarely appreciate their sterling qualities. "She looked a right old slag," one English lad said of a girl ravaged by an abortion and a long, unhappy love affair.

This abuse of women by the young revolutionaries explains, in Dr. Rockwell's view, the bitterness of the Women's Liberation

Movement. "Many of these women," she writes, "go from meetings at which they denounce men directly home to wait on their own men hand and foot."

In times of stress, bewilderment or bereavement, people do odd things.

We become quirky in a compulsive way. It would seem that a fierce focus on one consuming passion screens out other, possibly threatening passions. It also puts down loneliness and fear. In that sense, we might call it therapy. One becomes a nice, benign nut to avoid becoming a sobbing, hysterical nut.

There comes to mind sweet, loving Lady Elizabeth Raleigh toting Sir Walter's severed head all over England in a moroccan hatbox. The locked box never left her side, day or night. Seeing to the box, explaining the box, talking to the box saw her through the long years of widowhood.

Then there was Sir Isaac Newton, unstable, as a boy-genius should be, resting his higher brain cells by constructing a tiny, perfect model of a windmill operated by a *mouse*. Getting those wee blades to turn and keeping that mouse's nose to the grindstone may have delayed Newton's law by quite a few years. But it may well have delayed or abated some of the periodic fits of melancholia that used to plague Sir Isaac.

History also records mass escapism: the witchcraft craze of the seventeenth century, the dancing mania that swept Europe in the Middle Ages and the fads taken up to relieve the tedium of war and depression.

The "ecology kick" of the moment is dismissed by cynics as a passing fad. One hopes this is a misjudgment, since life and death are involved in the drive to clean up the environment. The mossbacks argue that pollution cannot be eliminated without draining the economy of billions, thereby lowering our standard of living. Of course, they shrug, this Earth Day nonsense is just another passing fad.

Because our food and water supply, our climate and the health of our lung tissue are all bound up with the "ecology kick," it would behoove us to become more involved, not less. But there is one aspect of the new ecology that is clearly a fad, and it may do more harm than good. That's the current uproar over "organic foods."

The true believers are a cult unto themselves. Some are downright cranks, insisting that organic foods will cure ulcers, arthritis and poor eyesight. They bore you into a coma telling what they ate last night and how superbly they digested it. Gourmets have been known to turn green and leave the room listening to an organic eater describe the locked-in goodness of soybean pudding or goldenrod tea. ("I don't keep tonic on hand anymore," said an organic hostess recently, "but do try this gin and papaya juice.")

The secret of organic food is supposed to be its pure, undefiled progress from seed pod to dinner plate. It is grown without DDT. It is packaged without hormones, artificial coloring, emulsifiers or vitamin enrichers. You don't need to read the fine print on the label because there isn't any.

Over the years I have sampled all the goodies in the health food shops and read all the leaflets and broadsides sent to me by the food nuts. My original criticism of this back-to-nature diet holds. It is dull, bland food. It spoils quickly. And it is absurdly overpriced.

The price appears to be no deterrent, however. Health foods are a $750,000,000 industry. A few years ago it was only little old ladies in tennis shoes and fussy bachelors still living with Old Mum who patronized health food shops. Though they popped in every day for a noggin of carrot juice and a sunflower-seed muffin with sassafras jelly, they looked no ruddier, no more durable than the folks who ate hamburgers at Joe's Tavern.

Moved by the common need to escape the ugliness and sorrow

of life in the '70's, I spend considerable time concocting lovely little dinners and in reading the source books that inspire these lovely little dinners. To date, nothing in the literature of organic cooking measures up to Escoffier or Craig Claiborne or Fanny Farmer. I'll admit, though, that I've not yet tasted cat-tail muffins, sage wine, burdock salad or persimmon beer. Some treats can wait.

Doing my face in the small, dark room I keep for that purpose, I fell to thinking—as women alone with mirrors will—of the faces one sees today on the young.

This sort of reverie is known as giving a windy night a rainy morrow. Let the young admire the young. And let's hope there's enough admiration to go around. For the youngsters I see in the streets today are neither as handsome nor as appealing as children of affluence, vitamins and sunshine ought to be.

Some, in fact, look like vagrants. Vagrants with a wasting disease. Young hobos who slept on a park bench last night and will try for an abandoned car tonight.

They are a sad lot, the restless, hairy youth of our time. They make you glad, glad, glad you're not that young anymore.

To be young today is to look, in the eye of beholders over thirty-five, like creatures from another planet. With grotesque eyeglasses—small and squinty or saucer-size and silly—and masses of hair everywhere, they have evolved a wholly new American face. It's a defiant face, droopy and dour. Its look suggests in the female a budding slattern, in the male a cultivated incivility.

One sees exceptions, of course. Glowing young faces quick with sympathy, guileless and vulnerable. Still, the new face is suf-

ficiently common to warrant generalizations. It is a mask the
young have put together to hold off the tensions of our times. It's
a look born of the wish to be as unlike the previous generation as
possible.

Certain kinds of faces, as we know from the portrait galleries,
belong to certain epochs in history. In our mind's eye we all carry
the clichés absorbed from masterpieces.

We tend to think of the Flemish face as ruddy, the Renaissance face as sallow, the early American face as lopsided and out
of focus. The female face of the '20's was distinguished by bad
makeup and frizzy hair. The New Face will probably be remembered as the Hippie Face. But it is not the only distinctive face of
our time.

At twenty paces one easily spots the Activist Face, the Drugged
Face (subspecies, Drugged Hippie Face) and the trying-to-be-
with-it Middle-Aged Face.

But some of us, even when ninety winters have besieged our
brows, are not going to feel at home with any of these New Faces.
To be sure, some of them are very dear. Some compel admiration
by the sheer intensity of the eyes or by the wild ingenuity with
razor and scissors. But in years to come I shall always feel a
twinge of sadness remembering how early in the '60's the serene,
healthy faces of the young gave way to whiskers, matted, ropy
hair and a look that grew too old too fast.

The all-American-boy look is now as outdated as little white
gloves on Sunday or the "last waltz" at the junior prom. Only
the astronauts—lean and bronzed, hair close-cropped, big,
healthy-toothed grins—are preserving that look for the picture
albums of the 1970's. Foreigners often say that the astronauts all
look exactly alike—and that they all appear to have married the
same girl.

A recent cartoon in *Punch* showed a man in a space suit holding out his arms and crying, "I'm back from the moon, Betty
Anne or Mary Lou!" as a smiling, wholesome blonde falls into
his padded embrace with a gladsome, "Oh, Tom or Dave or Ed,
is it *really* you?"

A somewhat myopic gentleman of my acquaintance swears that every time he goes to the movies he sees the same actress: "Lots of long, straight hair and gummed-up eyes. She gets into all the foreign films, too. Same girl, I swear."

Standards in beauty seem to have slipped more in the past decade than in the previous half century. The fashions of the '60's punished the beautiful and made the plain look pitiful.

Only a girl with superb legs ever should have been allowed out of the fitting room in a mini-skirt. And only a girl with classic features, divinely young and fair, should ever wear the long, straight hair that parts in the middle and just *hangs*.

The fat ones look like dish mops, the tall, skinny ones like knitting needles. And the shy ones use the hair as a shield, a veil, a screen against the harshness of the times.

The true Hippie Face—often sick, grimy and marred by running sores—is clinically, rather than aesthetically, interesting. One turns from it in sadness.

Of all the new faces, the funniest is the cherubic boy with a full set of mutton chops or a curled mustache out of an 1880 tintype. I am always positive that the whiskers are fake, a bit of fuzz bought at the joke shop, maybe a villain's prop left over from the school play. It's impossible at times to resist the query, "Dear boy, are you coming unglued there on the left side?"

"Europe isn't the same this summer," said my jet-set friend. "THEY are everywhere, you know."

They, of course, are the young. The hairy, the hippy, the unwashed, the unrepentant. "Swarming all over the Continent like rats. Some of them even turned up at Biarritz."

The barbarians, in short, are inside the gates. "They make it so hard for *nice* Americans," said my friend. "They travel in gangs, living off the countryside. And, of course, they're having a high old time on drugs."

That a good many of these young tourists are having a rather low time in some of Europe's worst jails seemed to be news to my friend. I told her about the beautiful American girl, a former "Playmate of the Month," who had served ten months in a Greek prison for carrying hashish. My friend was unmoved. "They should all be in jail," she opined. "Then the rest of us could visit Europe in peace."

And what a deep American longing is embodied in that last sentence. The balance of payments may go on tipping in Europe's favor. The unwashed, pot-smoking young may turn up at the queen's garden party and under the pope's balcony. They may yodel dirty words up and down the Alps and leave graffiti on the walls of the Alhambra. But "nice Americans" will continue to flock to Europe every single summer.

If anybody stays away from Europe it will be those rich, vulgar types who prefer Hawaii anyway. The superpatriots, the flag-wavers will stay home, too. Not to help the dollar problem, not to express disdain for the expatriate young, but because they hate all foreigners and weren't planning to go in the first place.

A few years ago, when Lyndon Johnson threatened to tax airline tickets and impose daily penalties on all Americans traveling abroad, one could fairly say that the government was being beastly.

For these stay-home laws, had they passed, would have fallen hardest on the people who most needed the trip. On graduate students headed for the British Museum, on professors on sabbatical and all those lonely widows and eager spinsters who each summer jog over bad roads in horrid buses, somehow managing to "do" six countries in ten days for $1,000.

One of the happier aspects of social progress is that the summer trip to Europe has become a central fact of life to increasing numbers of Americans. The memory of such summers lends an inner grace to the long winters back in Kansas or North Dakota.

Never mind what sorrow waits over the next hill. Never mind how drab the weekends in that one-room-and-kitchenette in East St. Louis. Who can reckon the value of a few golden yesterdays tucked away in memory? One is forever richer for having known the taste of the *vin du pays* at an old French inn or the slant of light through a cathedral window—thus is present sorrow lightened by past pleasure.

In the words of Dorothy Parker, "So long as I have yesterday / Go take your damned tomorrow."

While abroad, Americans may ostentatiously take pride in America's bigness, her glittering splendors, her dark lust for power. But we go abroad because of the unfed hungers in our souls. Something we never knew we lost is miraculously restored to us by the sight of old, weathered buildings, winding cobbled streets and sudden patches of tranquil green. The pure air, the honest bread, the little parks that appear out of nowhere like emeralds in the dust bin remind us, with an ache, how much we have lost on the bloody road to world power.

Granted, there are many wonders to behold on this side of the Atlantic. But some deeper springs are fed by pilgrim inns and Gothic spires and stones that have known great Caesar's tread.

Hippies may be selling hashish in the cathedral close . . . but the cathedral stands. The hippies are just passing through.

Dark thoughts come unbidden in the night. And the most piteous of these is the image of oneself as old and sick, out of funds and out of friends, shuffling down the long corridor to Death.

It's rooted in reality, this grim fantasy. And its grimness is hardly lightened by the knowledge that most pension funds provide a bare subsistence, that most nursing homes are prisons for incurables. Add to that most physicians too overworked—and too cynical—to give more than perfunctory care to the aged.

Most of us cheerfully grant Time the right to collect his due, to steal fire from the blood and passion from the heart. We accept the ancient truth that every bed, presently, is narrow. But what we cannot face is the chronic disease that renders one helpless, a helplessness worsened by poverty.

Dearer than life itself are those last shreds of dignity and control that separate the mobile man from the bedridden, the alert from the inert.

"I'd rather die than shuffle and slobber," said the twenty-year-old daughter of my neighbor after visiting an old aunt crippled by arthritis.

But this old auntie at least maintains her independence. She lives in her own apartment presided over by a nurse-companion. There's money in the bank and she can still sign checks. More than 2,000,000 of our aged folk make do on social security alone. One out of four lives below the poverty line. Hardly 10 percent of our nursing homes, my doctor tells me, are decently kept and adequately staffed.

I recall a television play in which a new inmate asked an old-timer at the nursing home, "What do you do here?" and got the answer, "We wait for the undertaker."

Any society is judged by the way it cares for its infants and its old folks. Still despised, after twenty-four centuries, are the Spartans who banished the weak and unfit to die of exposure and hunger on mountain ledges. How much nobler the Chinese and the Hebrews who, believing that "with the ancient is wisdom," have always surrounded their elderly with comfort and respect.

"When thou shalt be old, thou shalt stretch forth thy hands and another shall gird thee," says the Bible. Today the old stretch forth hands to empty air. The ears of the young are being blasted by rock music, the hands are busy with other matters, such as lighting up a joint of grass. Tumultuous social change has widened the gulf between young and old. They speak a different language, they march to different drummers.

Today 10 percent of our population is over sixty-five. And we are beginning to discover that one of our greatest blunders is the practice of compulsory retirement at sixty-five.

A man's health, mental and physical, takes a sharp downturn once he loses touch with the workaday world. He feels lost, unwanted, impotent. Enlightened physicians and social workers are beginning to agitate for a change in this mandatory retirement policy. Studies here and abroad indicate that older workers, while slower, are more efficient and reliable than young ones.

A splendid British physician, Dr. Donald Gould, has written a moving plea for the restoration of old people to useful work. He firmly believes that forced retirement hastens senility and death. With idleness, he points out, "there is actually a decrease, all too often to a dangerous level, in the secretion of hormones which are essential to health. Established diseases worsen. New diseases find a foothold. Quite literally, the rot sets in."

Our current attitude toward the aged is summed up by Dr. Gould as cruel, ignorant and callous. Dr. Howard Rusk, New York's leading authority on medical rehabilitation, is fond of saying that "Age is psychological, not chronological."

To keep old people busy and happy is not simply an act of benevolence by the young. It is insurance against joining the scrap heap.

What this country needs—and quickly—is a *Sesame Street* for adults.

That is to say, an emergency crash program to reclaim the 20,000,000 or so Americans who live in the dark country of illiteracy. We need a national crusade against this crippling ignorance before it permanently alters our character and forever stains our pride.

The Census Bureau has stated that 1 out of every 10 Americans over twenty-five is illiterate. A Harvard study of far greater depth suggests that the Census Bureau is taking the optimistic view.

The awful truth is that over half the adults in this country are "functionally illiterate." That means reading at the fourth-grade level or below it. Since hardly anything worth reading, save street signs and billboards, is written at that level, we're a pack of dullards, getting duller.

Ours is a complex society. And these are revolutionary times. We must have an adult equivalent of *Sesame Street* before we are one foot deeper into the mire of pig-ignorance and one step closer to the native fascism whose advance guard of Brown Shirts has already given us fair warning.

And I do mean the hardhats and the red-neck policemen of Mississippi and the National Rifle Association and that horrid little town in New Jersey that ordered every motorist to stick a flag decal on his car.

We had an earlier warning from Thomas Jefferson in a letter he wrote in 1816. "If a nation expects to be ignorant and free, in a state of civilization," he told his friend Colonel Yancy, "it expects what never was and never will be."

The mission of *Sesame Street* is to develop a society of free men by teaching small children, particularly poor children, to read and write. It accomplishes this mission by making the alphabet into an enchanting, tuneful game.

To be sure, the gentle ploys of *Sesame Street* would hardly rivet the attention of a twenty-year-old black youth who was streetwise and cynical at six.

Nor is a television program likely to pierce the pall of ignorance that lies over Appalachia and the subhuman barracks of the migrant farm workers. But if we're clever enough in wartime to teach thousands of draftees to read and thousands of inexperienced civilians to make the intricate machines of war, we can surely find a way to unlock the printed page for adult illiterates. It isn't enough to stamp out pollution and VD; illiteracy is every bit as menacing. And its potential for destruction is almost as total and terrible.

Walter Cronkite, among other observers, has noted sadly that too many people receive all their information from television. We are experiencing, he has said, "a genuine crisis in communications."

"Most American cities now have but a single newspaper," Cronkite wrote recently. "And these monopoly survivors, in many cases, are not doing the thorough job of coverage that they should. . . . Since a democracy cannot flourish if its people are not adequately informed on the issues, the problem becomes one of the nation's survival."

It isn't simply the gap between the totally illiterate and the literate that is disturbing. There is perhaps more potential danger in the gap between those of the Silent Majority who rarely read and the studious citizen who reads hundreds of periodicals and books each year. Knowledge comes, wisdom lingers. We may here translate wisdom as compassion, tolerance, insight and hope for tomorrow.

When Joseph Goulden went out on the road for *Harper's* interviewing some of the self-styled Silent Majority who had written to President Nixon, he repeatedly asked if they'd ever read a book about Vietnam.

"*Are* there any books on Vietnam?" replied a Detroit man.

A nineteen-year-old girl in Florida was so delighted to hear that there actually were books about Vietnam that she got a pad and pencil and begged reporter Goulden to suggest some titles.

Perhaps the basic tenet of the Silent (and ill-read) Majority is summed up in the remark of a man in Sandusky, Ohio. "I don't believe we have enough information to know whether policies are right or not. *Leave it to the leader.*"

It took no flight of vultures to announce that Rome was in decay, Gibbon tells us. The signs were everywhere and among them "a savage contempt for letters." Finally, the shameful day came when many Romans no longer could read the inscriptions on the monuments to their noble past.

Our monuments will never match the grandeur of Rome's. But we've already outstripped that fallen empire in illiteracy.

Next to telling her age, the most horrible mistake a woman can make is believing the lyrical promises of the cosmetic ads.

Studying the poetry, the golden fantasies of these ads is a hobby of mine. What puzzles me is why there are millions of forty-year-old women in this country who look forty years old. So stupid of them when they can be forever young and fair simply by treating their sallow, dried-up skin to the rich emollients that remove wrinkles and banish all bags and sags in ten days or your money back.

If you are a woman you do not simply buy a jar of Biogenic Miracle Night Cream.* You buy a jar of hope. Naturally, your life will be transformed the minute your skin has shed those dry, lifeless cells—that is, the minute it begins to absorb the amazing scientific blend of hormones, enzymes, proteins and—think beautiful, now!—extract of placenta.

And while your deep-down girlish skin is coming up through the trenches of time, don't you want to add sparkle to your eyes? I mean, who wants plain old eyes like that crone Mona Lisa? And what's the point of wondering in the dark of night, "*Do* blondes have more fun?" Be a blonde and see.

---

* The Biogenic Miracle Night Cream referred to in this piece is nonexistent. I made up the name. Six months later letters were still arriving with the question, "Where do I buy the Biogenic Miracle Night Cream you wrote about recently? My druggist says he has never stocked it." As I was saying, a woman buys a jar of *hope,* call it what you will.

Never Go Anywhere Without a Pencil

On television, cosmetic ads take on an added dimension of witchery. Drab mouse hair turns into a soft silky cloud blowing in the breeze. And there, Myrtle, is a younger, lovelier YOU, skittering across a moon-drenched terrace in a Dior gown. As the violins sob you are clasped in the arms of a spavined male model with weedy sideburns who naturally wears *his* hair long and loose in the breeze, too.

For some women those moonlit terrace scenes—even with Jake the Unbarbered waiting in the potted palms—make that $40 jar of Magic Youth Dew an exciting investment. Some women would slosh themselves with snake oil and stale beer if guaranteed that Count Dracula would take a nip out of their neck.

Americans spend $7 billion a year on what are loosely called "grooming aids." Having just this week cleaned nearly 100 bottles and jars out of two medicine chests, a linen cupboard and a vanity table, I clearly have spent my share. And if I do say so, I've always smelled delicious. But I have concluded that nothing helps your skin as miraculously as soap, water and a good diet— and that without artful advertising most cosmetic houses would have to diversify into axle grease and finger paints for kiddies.

As I hurled bottles and jars into rubbish cartons, my mind kept composing an urgent letter. "Dear Ralph Nader: Would you please apply this rare frog sperm lotion to your face five nights in a row and let me know if your beard is softer? Is your chin line firmer? Do people remark on how young your eyelids are looking?"

Darkening my already jaded thoughts on cosmetics was a story I heard about a pretty young woman who was so terrified of "offending" (that offensive TV word) that she prepared herself for the hostile, sniffy world by slathering on gobs of deodorant.

She walked in beauty, this lass, perspiration at the daintiest permissible minimum. She wafted the perfumes of Araby all over the subway—until they took her to the hospital for plastic surgery on her armpits. Sadly, she is not the first deodorized lady to suffer this cruel fate.

In a highly readable—and very shocking—little book, *Cos-*

166

metics—Trick or Treat? Toni Stabile writes about a woman who became "sore and disabled" after using a deodorant fortified with antibiotics. True, she didn't catch pneumonia under her arms—but she did develop what her doctor called a "chronic suppurative involvement of the sweat glands." She, too, had surgical repairs. And she sued the manufacturer who finally changed the magic formula of his germproof deodorant.

There have been cases, documented in Miss Stabile's book, of blindness caused by eyelash dye (not mascara) and baldness caused by hair dyes and home permanents. Giving oneself any sort of beauty treatment at home appears to be a high-risk procedure. But home is where most women try to make the fantasy of a Younger Lovelier Me come true.

Representative Leonor K. Sullivan of Missouri has been trying for at least ten years to get a tough cosmetics law through Congress. But the "lipstick lobby" is as potent and as sly as the oil and gas lobby. The bills are defeated—if, indeed, they get out of committee—and women continue to use lipsticks that take the skin off the lips and eye pencils containing coal tar that create welts and splotches.

Truly, women were better off in Elizabethan times when a book called *Delights for Ladies* suggested that any woman could achieve a perfect complexion if she would simply "wash her face in the wane of the moon with distilled water of elder leaves."

Well, it probably worked as well as the biogenic miracle youth dew with protein and placenta. Sounds prettier, too.

Fear, the cloak under which we city folk huddle, is giving way to the tatters called terror.

A neighbor, young and fleet of foot, reports that whenever she walks her dog after 11 P.M. it is she and not the dog who comes home panting, with racing pulse, dry throat and, in the doggy-talk she affects, "very trembly paws."

A shopping center in Minnesota now keeps policemen on the rooftops with binoculars, spotlights, walkie-talkies and guns. They are part of a "car-clouting squad" whose mission it is to spot the parking lot prowlers who will steal anything from a truck to a sack of groceries.

As crime rises, so does the anxiety of every householder, shop-keeper, air traveler, motorist and nighttime pedestrian.

"I have this awful recurring dream of a knife being drawn across my throat," a woman remarked at dinner the other night. Why? "Because one night I actually felt the knife. Two young boys pushed me to the wall, next to my own front door, snatched my purse and ran."

The crime statistics, like the defense budget, are becoming too enormous to comprehend. Thefts—all kinds—totaled more than $3.5 billion last year. Larceny, burglary and car theft accounted for 3,800,000 of the 4,500,000 reported crimes. But remember this: *Most crimes are never reported*. Of those reported, our police and courts have chalked up one conviction for every 50 crimes. That old warning to the young, "Crime doesn't pay," has ceased to be true. For most criminals it pays, simply because they rarely get caught.

Another reason for our mounting anxiety is the surly reluctance of insurance companies to protect our persons and property. Burglary and vandalism are just too commonplace. The nicest people are the worst risks. Private home rates are up 16 percent in New York, 25 percent in Illinois. Many people do not report small thefts because they fear their insurance will be canceled.

Even the traditional clauses insuring us against arson, riot and civil commotion are being revoked. Schools and colleges are finding that some companies simply will not write policies for them. The $1,000-deductible policy for "damages" has shot up to $100,000 and more.

As we hasten through darkened streets, put extra locks on the doors, it is a shock to realize that no matter what we do in this affluent technological society, we are still vulnerable, naked to our enemies.

Along with muggers and lunatic bombers, these enemies include a generally underpaid and ill-trained police, weakened by corruption and deep racial prejudice. We must also recognize among our enemies the legislators, state and federal, who refuse to pass the laws that would reform our inhuman prisons and reform our archaic court system.

These enemies actually are strengthening the vicious grip in which the criminal world now holds us all. When it is dangerous to post a letter late at night or to drive through city streets with car doors unlocked, we are not living in a free and open society.

We've another set of enemies whose attitude has steadily worsened this sorry situation. These are the people whose fear has numbed their better instincts. The people who have found in the criminal a new target for pent-up hatreds. Such people, however valid their fears, are irrational in their solutions. They see crime reduction only in terms of more police, more guns in every home and harsher sentences for the young men cast into our miserable, crowded jails.

The final report of the President's commission on crime predicts that unless crime is reduced, all our cities will become medieval fortresses, especially by night. It speaks of the "defensive city," bustling with workers and shoppers by day, totally sealed off by police sentries and armed guards after dark.

This is an ugly and shaming situation. It ought not to exist in a civilized nation. Shaming, too, is the fact that young Americans, eighteen to twenty-four, commit most of the violent crimes (four times as many as those over twenty-five). Not surprisingly, our poorest people, the urban blacks, loom largest in all sorts of crime.

The crime commission's report, prepared under the aegis of Dr. Milton Eisenhower, points out that young offenders are hardened in their criminal ways by our jails. The bad go to worse. The system must begin to rehabilitate, or we shall discover that the bulk of our tax dollar is going to maintain our garrisoned cities and their dungeon jails.

Some wise thoughts on this agonizing problem are set forth by Ramsey Clark in his book *Crime in America*. He finds it alarming that we spend only $5 billion a year on our police, courts and correction system. The Eisenhower report sets $20 billion as the necessary figure, a figure Mr. Clark seems to find more realistic.

If our correction system continues to fail, writes our former— and some say our very best—Attorney General, "then all the efforts of police, prosecutors and judges can only speed the cycle of crime. Longer sentences tend to harden people who spend years waiting to be released; they do not deter others on the outside."

Mr. Clark deplores the citizens who "blinded by prejudice . . . will not see that through decades of civil wrongs we have bred and nurtured crime."

Here, in this sentence, you have the essence of this firm, quiet man some would like to see give Nixon a run in '72. "We must not be ashamed to speak of humaneness, to be gentle, to seek rehabilitation—these are essential to the spirit of man. Without them he will be hard, cruel and violent." Amen.

My grandmother used to tell us a story *her* grandmother told about a giddy ancestress of ours who lived in fear and dread of Indians. Let a twig snap or a shadow cross the garden path and this Colonial dame would scream "Indians!"—and hide the baby.

Her fear, it must be said, was not entirely unfounded. Women did live dangerously in those early New England settlements.

More than one wilderness bride was ravaged and scalped by a painted savage with white man's liquor on his breath. (That the savage may have been squaring an old score for the white settlers' crimes against his womenfolk was not a consideration then.)

Anyway, this quaking goodwife was alone one night "with a babe in the cradle and another one on the way," when she heard ominous sounds outside the window. ("What kind of sounds, Granny?" "Oh, bushes breaking and a man's deep, rumbling voice.")

And what did our long-ago grandmother do? Well, she snatched up a musket and, for the first time in her life, aimed and FIRED! (Here we all gasped.) Abruptly, the sounds ceased. The baby slept. The lady musketeer slept. In the morning she discovered she had killed her one and only cow.

This long-dead grandmother comes to mind today because it strikes me that she had all the requisites for active membership in the National Guard. She panicked easily. She shot straight only by accident. And she slaughtered an innocent creature. Today's Guard would make her an officer.

At the cost of a great many innocent lives, we are beginning to learn that the National Guard in time of riot and civil commotion is a national menace.

The President's Commission on Campus Unrest report on the shooting of four students and wounding of nine others at Kent State distributes the blame with perfect justice. It condemns the irresponsible acts of certain students. It deplores the rock-throwing and the burning of the ROTC building. But the commission, in a ninety-two-page document, calls the shooting "unnecessary, unwarranted and inexcusable."

William Scranton's commission also concluded that the Guard should not have been armed with M-1 rifles. These are high-velocity weapons with a range of two miles. At the time of the shooting, students were engaged in a peaceful lunch-hour rally on a grassy knoll. There was no sniper fire. The mood of the crowd suggested "the circus was in town."

All that stood between the students and brutal death was "the flick of a Guardsman's thumb." And, of course, some fool flicked. Specifically, twenty-eight fools fired sixty-one shots at boys and girls showing high spirits on a fine spring day.

Such behavior is not at all inconsistent with past performances of the National Guard. The Commission on Civil Disorders noted that the Guard's behavior during riots in Newark and Detroit "raised doubts about their capability for this kind of mission."

Raised doubts, indeed! Renata Adler sets down the appalling record of the Guard in *The New Yorker*, and every bloody-minded citizen of the land should read it.

The Justice and Defense departments have reviewed the Guard's deportment in various riots, Miss Adler writes, and have found it "surreal." An odd word in this context, but Miss Adler clearly means something beyond the irrational.

In the Detroit riots, the Guard fired 13,326 rounds of ammunition, compared with 201 rounds fired by the regular Army. Some units got lost and panicked.

"Guardsmen were in the habit of arriving by tank or truck, weapons loaded, and shooting out street lamps at night," Miss Adler writes, "then deluding themselves that the sound of their own shots in the dark was 'sniper fire.' "

Since their aim was bad, she continues, "the rounds of ammunition required to dispatch a single street lamp often injured people in apartments blocks away or in cars on other streets. The first person killed by Guardsmen in Newark, for example, was a small boy in a family car."

The final report on the Watts riot listed 34 dead, "several of them killed by mistake." By the Guard, that is, called in to restore order.

A Harvard boy said of his National Guard training, "It's a farce . . . a stupid movie. . . . The equipment is all bad. They're all badly trained."

Stupid and dangerous, a national disgrace, the law-and-order force that escalates the violence. Guardsmen called to quell a riot in a Southern high school bayoneted each other. Two guardsmen who got lost in Detroit remained at one intersection from Monday to Friday. At four one morning a regular Army unit had to rescue a Guard troop crouched behind a high school, claiming to be trapped by sniper fire.

Generally speaking, the Scranton Commission report is too easy on the Guard. In the name of public safety, the National Guard should be abolished.

Sometimes when I read about the marvelous technology of the future, I'm almost glad I won't be around to test its dazzling efficiency. I have enough trouble with the dazzling efficiency I've got now, especially my TV set that picks up phone calls from city officials' limousines and the electric can opener that will yet take my hand off at the wrist.

Looking ahead to the next century, it would be nice having a robot maid who vacuums the rugs, scours the sink, pops the roast into the oven at half past five and then tucks herself (excuse me, *itself*) into the closet for the night.

Trouble is, you'd have to "program" these robots. Feed the proper instructions into them via your handy kitchen computer. If my past housekeeping record is any criterion, I'd push the wrong computer dials, and my marvelous mechanical maid would spend a full day vacuuming the sink, scouring the roast and practicing the tango on the dirty carpets. After a while something would blow up, probably the house.

Furthermore, this outbreak of domestic mayhem would undoubtedly occur while madam was off conferring with the bank manager, apologizing for the aberrations of the desk computer that went berserk and paid every creditor three times. ("The computer is not careless, madam; it is the human being *instructing* the computer who is careless.")

Housekeeping by computer will not, I predict, simplify the daily life of old-fashioned, ten-thumbed housewives like me. Given two switches, one marked MANUAL and the other AUTOMATIC PILOT, I'd push MANUAL every time. Life will lose a certain savor, I suspect, when all you need to run a gracious home is a sound knowledge of electronic engineering.

I don't look forward to living in a world where everybody shops by TV, pays bills by computer and has books piped into the house (page by page) from a microfilm center. Nor am I eagerly anticipating a world where babies will be carried nine months in the womb of "surrogate mothers" to free affluent ladies from the nuisance of pregnancy. (The babies, in tomorrow's brave new world, will be formed from the loving couple's own sperm and ovum. The proxy carrier will simply surrender the infant on birth.)

Another thing: That robot housemaid is sure to be the ugliest contraption this side of a bulldozer. It's no wonder she—I can't help thinking of it as *she*—is referred to by engineers as a "robot slave." Only a slave would consent to looking so drab.

Here is a description of your future maid by Professor M. W. Thring of the University of Sheffield, England. "It will not look like a human being," he writes, steadfastly neutral about the gender, "but rather like a box with one large eye at the top, two arms, three hands and a pair of long narrow pads on each side to support and move itself with."

Three hands, please notice. Never mind if she's a pantry drinker, a slattern at the sink and a Lucrezia Borgia at the stove. What every woman needs to fulfill the requirements of gracious living, as set forth in the magazine ads, is three hands. Or a three-handed maid who puts herself away in the closet and never entertains gentleman callers after the beds are turned down.

If you feel disinclined to leave the snug efficiency of your own

174

hutch in the twenty-first century, nobody will blame you. Country life, as we know it, will have disappeared.

Professor Arnold Toynbee, whose specialty is charting the rise and fall of civilizations, says every nation will be one huge, teeming city in the twenty-first century. To escape the traffic, the noise and the pollution you will have to travel to the Sahara, the Himalayas or to a polar ice cap.

Professor Toynbee calls this sprawling global city Ecumenopolis, not to be confused with Megalopolis or even Indianapolis.

He foresees the time when the East Coast will be one enormous urban sprawl from Boston to Washington. In Middle America we shall simply have a colossal Chicago, a totterin' rather than a toddlin' town. It will extend on through Texas. The West Coast will be called Los Angeles.

All industry will be urbanized, including food production. Huge farms will exist under glass—and under water. That we are already heading that way is suggested by a new butter churn I've read about. It makes four tons of butter in one hour.

Nobody has devised a replacement for the cow, but the technologists are working on it. They've got a machine in England that makes synthetic milk, first chewing clovers and nettles and, one imagines, mooing a lot. Some samples of ersatz milk have been produced, but to date the product has one flaw. It's bright green.

To have witnessed the slow decay of New York City over the past decade is to have seen beauty vanquished by greed, and a free, open spirit replaced by fear and cunning.

Living through the declining years of a great city is like watching a lovely woman waste away with a hideous disease. You never look upon the ravages without wincing for the grace and style and gaiety that are gone.

New York is hardly unique in this terminal illness, call it urban blight or what you will. The God of wrath who destroyed the cities of the plain (including those toddlin' towns, Sodom and Gomorrah) appears to be repeating Himself all across America.

Inevitably, some cities are coping with urban blight more successfully simply because their populations are smaller and their services to the public cheaper.

When word went out last week that New York expected a $300,000,000 deficit and was therefore launching an immediate austerity program, the hard-working, hard-pressed citizen made his customary response: "If the mayor would take some of those no-good cheats off welfare. . . ."

As the nonwelfare public sees it, cutting off welfare payments would mean that people who now lie abed till noon, drinking gin or shooting heroin, would suddenly be hopping on the subway at 8 A.M., shoes shined and the help-wanted ads tucked under the arm.

The sad truth is that most welfare clients have no skills to offer in the job market. And as our welfare program is now constituted, they're too busy filling out forms and trying to feed five or six small mouths on a $1-a-day food budget ever to learn any useful skills.

A survey of welfare mothers a few years back disclosed that seven out of ten would rather work than receive public assistance. And two of the remaining three said they'd gladly work if their children could be looked after during their absence.

The worst evil of the welfare system is that it's self-perpetuating. Until the system is reformed, with a comprehensive federal program ranging from Head Start to mandatory job training, our cities will continue to rot. Crime will soar, slumlords will go on fattening their purses with welfare rents and we may envy Sodom and Gomorrah, which at least had a clean, quick end— damped down with salt.

New Decade, Old Sorrows

How pleasant it is, in this city of menacing streets, foul air and subhuman subways, to think of the New York that used to be. Henry James secretly loved it, though he lived abroad. He was awed by our great harbor which flashed upon his jaded eye as a glittering canvas filled with "bleached sails, stretched awnings, scoured decks and new ropes." He also looked fondly upon our "divine little city hall." He saw this edifice as elegant and gallant, "holding out for the good cause through the long years. . . ." (Mr. J., thou shouldst be living at this hour!)

It's just as well that James never met Jimmy Walker, to name only one tenant of our divine little City Hall.

If you would really weep for the tender grace of a day that is dead, you must dip into *Lights and Shadows of New York Life*. This fine, fat tome, originally published in 1872, has just been reissued in a facsimile edition (with lovely steel engravings of New York sights), and you can scarcely believe your eyes.

Here is what author James D. McCabe says about Central Park:

"All classes are proud of the park, and all observe the strictest decorum there. No crime or act of lawlessness has ever been committed within the limits of Central Park since it was thrown open to the public."

And here is McCabe on the police force 100 years ago:

"The strictest discipline is maintained in the force, and offenses are rigidly reported and punished. The men are regularly drilled in military exercises. . . . They are armed with batons or clubs . . . and revolvers. The latter they are forbidden to use except in grave emergencies."

Sanitation note: "Snow seldom lies in the streets for more than a few hours."

How innocent, how sweetly moral our forebears were in old New York! "There are not many first-class houses of ill-fame in the city—probably not over 50 in all—but they are located in the best neighborhoods, and it is said Fifth Avenue itself is not free from the taint of their presence."

Author McCabe was a high-minded man in all respects. "The

177

Sunday papers," he wrote, "are generally high priced and nasty. They are entirely sensational in character and devoted to a class of news and literature which can hardly be termed healthy."

One of the ads from the nasty Sunday papers reads: "Sure cure for ladies in trouble. No injurious medicines or instruments used. Consultation and advice free."

Well, in that respect at least, we have moved toward sanity. But, oh, to have lived here when a guidebook could say 'New York is remarkably clean . . . the great center of all that is good and beautiful in life." Backward, oh backward, Time in your flight!

The air bites keen, the light in the west is purple at half past four and once again the year-end holidays are upon us.

And it is at holiday time that the paradoxes of the American system strike us most vividly. This year, while millions of Americans owed their Thanksgiving dinner to food stamps, welfare doles or some local charity, shop windows across the land were bursting with all-cheering plenty from a flowing horn. Resort business was brisk this year, and every airport turned away hundreds of standby passengers.

Thanksgiving is, perhaps, the most unifying of all our holidays. It is so touchingly American, so familial, so nonsectarian. Unlike Christmas, Thanksgiving simply arrives. We do not greet it in a state of exhaustion, nerve ends frayed from weeks of shopping, cookie baking and all the rest.

Most Americans keep Thanksgiving with dignity. The mood is gentle, the wassail minimal. A Thanksgiving hangover is apt to be the result of gorging, not guzzling. This dignity endures, one would like to think, because Thanksgiving calls back the best tra-

ditions of our American heritage. For one blessed day we are all
Pilgrims again, chastened by experience, grateful that the Lord
has brought us through another year.

The Lord, let's admit, had a rougher time of it this year. Since
our last holiday season the world has not ripened noticeably toward goodness and wisdom. I asked a friend who travels exten-
sively up and down this vast land how the country has changed
in the past year, and he replied simply, "There's more hate."

There's also more unemployment, more pollution, more crime,
more drug addiction, more pornography, more bankruptcies,
more suicides, more breakdowns of public service, more fear and
despair, more cynicism and more screams in the night. But this
groping, blundering creature, Man, still summons up the spirit to
celebrate the holidays in style.

This autumn we lived through one of the most vicious political
campaigns in history. We saw unemployment rise to a new high.
We're bombing North Vietnam again, and peace never seemed
more remote. But on Thanksgiving Day the nation, as usual,
made a joyful noise unto the Lord and gave thanks for being
alive. Come Christmas, there will be lights and songs and presents and kisses under the mistletoe. Such are our human needs.
And in these needs lie our hope and our salvation.

The heart breaks a little brooding over the mixed harvest of
blessings this year has brought us. We're closer to a cure for cancer, but we're more remote than ever from our young. We've unlocked the secret of the gene, but we haven't learned the secret of
living together in peace and love. In high places, wealth accumulates. And across this land of plenty, men decay and children
starve.

But the troubled America of today stubbornly clings to its
comforting rituals. Considering the violence in the streets, the decline of decency in the arts and the duplicity in Washington, it is
good to remember that somewhere out there, west of Manhattan's topless towers, the harvest is home, the preserves are down
and the storm windows up. Somewhere cats are purring on the
hearth, children are being very good because Christmas is com-

ing and loving hearts are assuring each other, "Next year will be better."

And if it isn't, the heart of man somehow will find ways to reconcile, if only for a day, the contradictions that make up America today.

When the young hurl rocks, burn banks or drift into a life of dope and dereliction, the common excuse is "the System."

It's the System, we are told, that erodes youthful goodness and punishes nonconformity. The System betrays those who trust and punishes those who feel. It's rotten, all the way. Therefore, a triple obscenity on the System.

But what of those who somehow accommodate to the System—the young who never riot, never freak out on speed or LSD? Does their very act of accommodation somehow corrupt them, too? Is the System so bad that every kid with red blood should be out there on the barricades with a placard and a grenade?

Behaviorists suggest that youngsters who stay in college, out of trouble, off drugs and in reasonable rapport with their elders have had a head start in life. They've come from homes where both love and discipline abound. They grew up respecting their parents and, in consequence, transferred this respect to the surrogate parents charged with educating them. Lucky, beloved children, these, who usually grow up to be valuable members of the community.

But what of the others—the juvenile offenders, the young anarchists with their homemade bombs, the addicts who must steal, the avengers who must lay violent hands on something or somebody? Can we blame the System because it failed to give them loving, enlightened parents?

We can't, of course. But we can blame the System for not putting out a kindlier hand to children in desperate need of help. For the cost of one month in Vietnam we could build and staff 1,000 children's shelters. We could set up farms and camps and communities for young addicts. We could begin, in short, to tend our own.

Even if we continue our madness in Vietnam, our priorities should be put in some humane order at home. Schools, hospitals, day-care centers do more for America than four-lane highways and the supersonic transport. It often seems that the two grand passions of our government are greed and war. If you view the System as driven by those twin forces, then the young are armed with the justice of their quarrel.

Whatever you may think of Charles Manson—and words like "depraved" and "monstrous" will always cling to his name—you cannot fail to be touched by his address to the court in Los Angeles last week. He spoke for all the beaten and twisted young who never made it in the good, straight society.

"Most of the people at the ranch that you call the family were just people that you did not want," he said, "people that were alongside the road. I took them up on my garbage dump and I told them this: that in love there is no wrong."

No doubt Manson was shrewdly aware of the melodrama he was creating in the courtroom, but his words were a bitter indictment of the System.

"I have always been in your cell," Manson said. "When you were out riding your bicycle, I was sitting in your cell looking out the window and looking at pictures in magazines and wishing I could go to high school and go to a prom."

For the cost of one month in Vietnam, we could begin—and handsomely—to reform our prisons and our criminal courts. We could spot the Charlie Mansons before they struck the garbage dump. We could correct, salvage and restore the casualties of the System. If we fail to respond to the aching human needs in this area, we shall one day be living in armed stockades with day-and-night sentries.

The young who despise the System are further disenchanted when they look around and see our leaders, men looked up to with grave respect, fighting to preserve the evils inherent in the System.

There's something pitiless and mean in the determination of J. Edgar Hoover to give no man a second—or, in some cases, a first—chance. Clothed in righteousness, as always, the FBI director has started a court action to maintain the agency's authority to circulate arrest records of persons *not convicted* following arrest.

"Distrust all in whom the compulsion to punish is strong," wrote Nietzsche. Instinctively, the young do. And they see the compulsion everywhere.

From time to time my mail turns up a letter from a righteous citizen aflame with patriotism who advises, "I have submitted your name to the FBI for investigation." Rarely—I might even say never—does the righteous citizen sign his name.

Here today is a postcard that says, "If you aren't careful someday your name will be on the Attorney General's list, and I hope it is."

Someday? I'm on every list but the Ten Best Dressed, and that, I suspect, is because the judges haven't seen me in my new terry cloth robe. I grow dizzy thinking of all the lists our vigilant government has compiled starring people like me. People who must be watched because we oppose: the Vietnam War, the apotheosis of J. Edgar Hoover, the arrogance of the Pentagon and the buffooneries of Spiro Agnew.

We're a dangerous lot, because we should like to see civil liberty for all, an end to poverty and a vow of silence from Martha Mitchell. This makes us enemies of the state. The American Legion will never salute us. The DAR will never award us a plaque. But somewhere in Washington there's a computer stuffing our names into its memory bank with the notation, "Suspected radical. Bears watching."

None of this surprises me. While there's a liberal element, I'm in it. While there's tyranny and injustice, I'm agin it. While there's a neo-Fascist right wing, I'll spit in its eye. And when the tumbrels begin to roll Suspected Radicals to the gas chamber, I'll be in the procession. So, sending my name to the FBI is like recommending me to Macy's for a charge account. I have been a customer for twenty years.

That I can write the above with an easy mind demonstrates a certain stubborn faith in our American freedoms. That I am prompted to do so by a persistent kind of crank mail suggests that we have, as a nation, moved away from the decent, open society our forefathers envisaged.

A great deal has been written of late about the growing threats to our privacy. The right to be let alone is becoming obsolete. Big Brother is watching—and he is now computerized! The average citizen, regrettably, seems to miss the dark threat in that simple fact.

Big Brother wears many guises. He's in the FBI, the Justice Department, the CIA, the local bank, police and credit bureau. Every time you fill out a form that asks for your Social Security number you are providing the magic key that will permit various government agencies to exchange confidential information about you.

And every time you apply for a job, especially in government or defense industry, your private life in its most intimate details goes into a file, a computer, a data bank. It's a fearful, mistrustful society that sanctions such snooping.

Perhaps the most revolting aspect of this Big Brother business is the role played by the U.S. Army. For several years now, the Army has had spies, costumed to blend with the crowd, attending all political protests, antiwar rallies and civil rights meetings. A former Army captain, Christopher Pyle, said last March that

Army spies are given orders to infiltrate all protests and marches, gathering "intelligence" however they can.

The intelligence thus gathered, said Captain Pyle, is distributed by the Army on a weekly, sometimes daily, basis to every major troop command from Alaska to Panama. Do you detect a note of sheer lunacy in this? You're right!

Just how inept and foolish these Army spies are was made clear when TV's *First Tuesday* gave us the candid confessions of five former secret Army agents. One told how the Army picked up the check for the liquor he bought for protestors who made a small, vulgar display at President Nixon's inauguration. Another related his difficulties in trying to keep track of the mules at Martin Luther King's funeral.

"It was a very strong requirement of the Army," said this secret agent, "to know the exact number of mules and the exact number of horses at all times."

The Vietnam Moratorium, the Poor People's March to Washington—and their pathetic bivouacs at Resurrection City—all were spied on by Army agents. An Assistant Secretary of Defense, Daniel Z. Henkin, conceded that Army agents were guilty of certain "excesses" but said steps were being taken to correct them.

Senator Sam Ervin has conducted hearings on the whole squalid business of government snoops, questionnaires and data banks. Nothing came of them. Unless some strict laws are passed to protect our privacy, he warned, "We stand to lose the spiritual and intellectual liberty of the individual . . . which our founding fathers so meticulously enshrined in the Constitution."

Since I rarely go to the movies, it's difficult for me to tell the players apart. In some of the long shots I can't even tell the sexes

184

apart. My friends have expressed similar bafflement. This, I suspect, is one of the reasons naked love scenes are now mandatory. They give the nonregulars in the audience a clue as to who's him and who's her.

To find delight in today's films you must be a member of the counterculture—that is, you must use four-letter words with dirty abandon and fall down in rapture when anybody says "Woodstock." It also helps if you can turn on, see God and repair a motorcycle in the midst of traffic. I fail all these tests. And if you're showing *Trash* or *M*A*S*H* at your next dinner party, don't count on me.

For those of us who remember the dear dead days when all nice girls tried to look like June Allyson, going to the movies today is going slumming. You are obliged to watch the undressed behavior of people you'd never invite to your house fully clothed.

Call me reactionary, but I cannot stomach this new cinema full of sweaty Elliott Goulds and naked nymphs with blemished backs. Dull, depraved, stupid and sick, that's the New Wave in films. And it helps explain, I think, the astonishing success of a book devoted to the olden, golden days of the cinema. It's called *Hollywood and the Great Fan Magazines.* Now in its third printing, this delicious anthology has been chosen by five book clubs, including, with perfect logic, the Nostalgia Book Club.

The book is a glorious memento of the days when most people lived such drab, pinched lives that the local Bijou, smelling of incense, old galoshes and gum wrappers, was a veritable palace of art. It provided the only beauty and romance some mortals ever knew.

We were, intellectually and otherwise, an undeveloped country in the days when movie stars were royalty. Most people lived all their lives within a radius of 200 miles. Only the lucky few went to college.

As late as 1938, the unemployment rate stood at 19 percent. People went to the movies to escape the pain of real life. And poor as they were, they could always find fifteen or twenty-five cents for the magazines that told of the heartbreaks and triumphs of screen stars.

It helped to know, for example, what kind of man Clara Bow really wanted. Strangely, she wanted a man who would "mother" her. "A man who would stroke my hair and talk softly and let me tell him things." Poor Clara's problem was that she lost her own mum while still a tot.

And have you any idea, you in the granny glasses and brass-toed boots, what motherhood meant to a girl like Helen Twelvetrees? "An emotional revolution!" that's what. "Forgetting herself and gaining spiritual values!"

The exclamatory style was *de rigueur* in fan magazines. Audiences wanted lavish descriptions of clothes, houses, parties and how stars suffered for their art. The beautiful people of filmland may have had *Everything*, but they also had a peck of trouble. They sacrificed so much, as *Silver Screen* put it, "on the Terrible Altar of Ambition."

Thus we read that when Fredric March went to the hospital with a stomachache the doctors' official verdict was "nerves shot." The brutal Hollywood star system put Renee Adoree in a sanitarium. It also "sent Mabel Normand away and she never came back."

It's significant, I suppose, that the subjects movie fans found most fascinating are the subjects that have titillated us forever and always will—marriage, separation and pregnancy.

In 1931 a simple, boxed announcement appeared in *Screen Book*. It said: "I regret more than I can say that my marriage with Hal Rossen didn't work out.—Jean Harlow."

Fan writers strove mightily for the philosophical angle. Olivia de Havilland admitted to an ill-advised love affair with an older man, a romance that "came into conflict with all the ideals bred in my bone." But, she added bravely, a broken heart makes a better actress.

Janet Gaynor, "wearing whiffs of lavender mules," also confessed to a regrettable love affair. "I know now there is no Seventh Heaven," said she. And when the interviewer spoke of Janet's "touching childhood," the star replied, "Every childhood is touching because it is untouched." Think that one over.

On page 130 Ginger Rogers asks, "Did I Get What I Wanted Out of Life?" Answer: No. Ginger always wanted to go to college.

Among the items I cherish in this marvelous book is Shirley Temple's last letter to Santa Claus. (She was twelve at the time.) She asked Santa for "a doll, dungarees and a pair of six-shooters to wear when I ride the pony Mr. Schenck gave me."

"No-More-Divorce Lana!" describes Miss Turner's anguish over her divorce from Artie Shaw (roughly eight husbands ago). Deanna Durbin longs to have fudge parties like other girls. A story describing the "real Christmas" Barbara Stanwyck arranged for her son contains this touching note: "Very carefully, the butler stole outside to ring the sleigh bells." There's more, much more . . . and anybody who pops by my house can expect the choicier read aloud to him—with feeling.

1971

More of the Same

. . . It was the year our ping pong players went to China and a Chinese restaurant in New York changed its name to the Ping Pong Kitchen.

It was the year of the Pentagon Papers, the Berrigan Brothers and Nixonomics. . . . Lieutenant William Calley was found guilty of murdering at least twenty-two civilians at My Lai.

The Attica Prison riots disclosed subhuman conditions, left forty-one dead in the prison yards and Governor Nelson Rockefeller politically dead with millions of outraged voters.

In 1971, we continued to pray for peace while the Pentagon ordered stepped-up raids on North Vietnam, with seven-and-a-half-ton bombs the new thrill for the generals. . . . Tricia Nixon, the last of the sugar plum princesses, married Nader Raider Edward Cox in the White House Garden. . . . Three more astronauts flew to the moon, but Tricia's wedding got a higher TV rating. . . . Women's Lib decreed that the proper written address for all females was "Ms," pronounced "Miz." . . . Some of us demurred.

It was not a vintage year for J. Edgar Hoover, Charles Manson or the New York cops. . . . The voting age was lowered to eighteen. . . . The President took a helicopter from San Clemente to Burbank to tell us, via TV, that he would visit Red China in '72, by odd coincidence an election year. . . . Jimmy Hoffa was pardoned by the President and, after due thought, announced that he would support the Republican ticket in '72. . . . The cleanest word in the mouths of the young was "ecology."

The drug problem reached the crisis stage with Vietnam soldiers among the tragically hooked. . . . To enliven the economy, the President froze wages and prices for ninety days. . . . Nothing helped. . . . Mayor John V. Lindsay turned Democrat, saying he had no Presidential ambitions. By unanimous vote, the House reinstated the school lunch program abolished by President Nixon.

A May Day peace protest saw disabled veterans giving back their medals and decorations. . . . The day was poorly managed and resulted in 12,000 arrests, virtually all of them illegal. . . .

In 1971, everything we deplored in 1970 got steadily worse: inflation, unemployment, violence in Northern Ireland, skyjackings, street crime, strikes, duplicity in Washington. . . . A survey disclosed that nobody trusted the government anymore. Nobody doubted the survey.

My next husband will probably be a brute and a scoundrel. I say that because my last husband was much too good for me. I also say it because I happen to be widowed, not divorced, and carry no memory of bitter parting words over who failed, who lied or who should have custody of the cat.

I also say it because it has lately struck me that men are being subtly damaged in their self-esteem—and, therefore, in their ability to love—by the more ferocious partisans of women's liberation. Good guys are encouraged to become cads. And this is a bitter irony.

A basic tenet of Women's Lib is that the female has been degraded by the man who deflowered her—and by every male encountered thereafter, in the boudoir and out. The truly liberated woman, runs the theory, finds fulfillment in sex only to the degree that she asserts herself, demanding gratifications nice girls never dreamed of until the Red Stockings and all those now in the vanguard of the movement insisted they were her "natural rights."

If the liberation ladies have their way, it's the men who will be assuming the passive roles, casting sidelong glances of love at dinner as they murmur, "I made this soufflé just for you, dear. Isn't it nice?"

Give the girls on the barricades another five years and there may be a parade up Fifth Avenue by the Men's Liberation Front. It continues to astonish me that each time I write about Women's Lib, deploring the obsession with karate and "equal orgasms," I get letters from outraged men. Men who say they are *for* the liberation movement all the way and why don't I get back into my crinoline and go bake a tipsy cake. Sometimes—not always—the letters add, "I'm not one of the Gay Liberation boys, mind you." (Well, I *did* wonder about that.)

If men are to become working advocates in the liberation of women, they must be prepared to give up certain male privileges. Duties formerly regarded as strictly feminine will have to be shared. And come to think of it, why shouldn't men be den fathers to the Cub Scouts? Why shouldn't they help with the Christmas pageant and share the heady excitement of discovering a new low-phosphate detergent?

If women are to become surgeons and judges and ministers of God, why shouldn't men have the right to be baby nurses, manicurists and Avon ladies? Fair is fair.

Of course, this turnabout could lead us into strange pathways. The liberated man may one day feel free to accept jeweled cuff links and a mink-lined opera cape from his rich lady love. He may even withhold his favors and complain of after-dinner headaches.

Wives can retaliate by having sly affairs with cute Mr. Brown from the typing pool or the new receptionist whose sideburns are all golden ringlets.

All these notions are on the jokey side, of course. We are witnessing a sexual revolution, marked by dramatic—not to say traumatic—breaks with the past. We are groping our way toward a new domestic order in which woman will be more of a person and less of a sex object. (Though what's so terrible about being a sex object I really can't imagine.)

Let's not deny that women's frustrations, their anger at having to accept kitchen drudgery and baby tending as a full-time career, have damaged a great many marriages. It's not the shrill, castrating females of Women's Lib who will restore balance and tranquillity to the American marriage, however. They may even do positive harm by introducing new tensions into the man-woman relationship and by transmitting to the male, through the contagion of ideas, some of the neuroses now thought to be exclusively female.

No. The consequence of Women's Lib that I find alarming is a new hostility in the female sex. I also notice that some of the girls are so overanxious to be oversexed that you wonder how men can stand them. "Bitches in heat" hardly says it.

Ever since Women's Lib moved away from the sensible aim of equal pay for equal work and full human status in law and began "liberating" us from pretty clothes and perfume, men have been restive. They feel we are forgetting the male animal we used to love—and I daresay we are.

Men, let us freely admit, can be adorable. They're marvelous at getting out the ice and opening bottles and cleaning the fireplace. They help you out of your long slinky boots and give you wanton lace nighties for Christmas and know just what to say to surly cab drivers. They walk the dog when it's raining and they perform endless tender, clumsy little services for you when you're ill. Also, if you've chosen right, they're bigger, stronger, smarter and richer than you are. What woman in her right mind would change all that?

So many of women's troubles vis-à-vis men are her own doing. One of the best books I have read on the woman problem, *Love and Liberation* by Lisa Hobbs, makes the point that women are far more prone to "victimize" themselves in marriage than are men.

"Men can scarcely be blamed for wondering whether such dedication to one's own demise as a human being is not a rather cunning psychological game," writes Miss Hobbs.

Miss Hobbs also states that woman has for too long denied her own intelligence and "repressed her authenticity" because of the dominant male ego. Maybe so. I'm a strong champion of better education, richer careers and the full flowering of intelligence in women. But when we come to the word "authentic," I know what's female. I do not care to have it defined for me by a bra-burning virago with a black belt in karate.

There's no doubt whatever that the cuisine at my house could be greatly improved by removing the television set from its pedestal beside the stove.

The evening news once more is curdling my sauces and burning the biscuits. An artist should work in an atmosphere of truth, hope and serenity. I can't even mince a mushroom without catching the President or some member of his official family in another whopper. As a citizen and a gourmet, I'm finding this a hard winter.

By 7:15 every night I'm either shaking my wire whisk at Spiro Agnew or wiping the gravy off Senator Fulbright—at whom I really didn't mean to shake my whisk at all.

But the one who got gravy in the face the other night deserved it. That was Defense Secretary Melvin Laird. Emerging from a Senate hearing room, Mr. Laird was asked by reporters to comment on the intensive new military operations going on in Laos. The Secretary, looking, as always, like a well-tailored owl, faced the cameras and paused briefly to make it clear that he had heard the question and would now consider the answer.

Then, slowly and deliberately, he told reporters that he had some interesting facts to impart on new draft quotas. He imparted them in tedious detail, casting a cold eye on the circle of reporters swarming around him with nervous pencils. "Just stand back, boys!" his manner seemed to say. The arrogance of power, the insolence of office—there it was. And it was there that Mr. Secretary got the gravy in the eye.

Had his reply been an affable "Well, something is going on but I'm not at liberty to comment," I might have restrained my shootin' hand. But the Secretary has grown smug in the service of death and destruction. His replies are self-serving, always a little slippery.

When reporters again asked about Laos, offering the incidental information that the foreign press, including *Izvestia*, had reported the massive buildup of forces in the jungle area near Laos, Mr. Laird replied in a patient-father-to-demented-child tone: "*Izvestia* does not tell the truth."

The whole world may have known about this new allied operation—in which no U.S. soldier is supposed to cross the Laotian border—but the Secretary of Defense declined to comment. Not a word of information to the millions of taxpayers whose cities are rotting and whose jobs are vanishing because too many of our tax dollars are going into the war machine.

That brief, surly exchange with reporters widened the credibility gap a bit more than the Pentagon brass had expected. And it hardened at least one viewer's conviction that this administration may go down in history as the Era of Mendacity. Not only are we lied to, the lies are delivered with eggy-faced ineptitude. When official liars lack the wit to lie well, that great slumbering beast, the People, is prodded awake.

Colonel James Donovan sums it up in his fine, angry book *Militarism, USA*. To wit: "The deceptions, the fabrications, the deliberate distortions have revealed to the perceptive that during much of the Vietnamese war the decision-makers didn't know what they were talking about."

And never mind, for the moment, that some of the distortion is assumed to be in the interests of national security. The point is we don't believe what our government says anymore.

As George Orwell noted bitterly, history is a series of swindles. Where the people are not vigilant, he added, power gravitates to the wrong hands.

It is interesting, in a purely clinical sense, to observe how the White House strives to put a ruddy new glow on the Nixon image. His recent appeal to youth was a beautifully crafted speech. There was a certain grandeur of vision in his State of the Union message. And at a religious breakfast this week the President reminded us that excellence and virtue are still the best attributes of a good society. That's Norman Vincent Nixon thinking positively.

Had we not lived through so many disenchanting episodes with Mr. Nixon we might accept the historic notion that the office dignifies the man. But some things—the Carswell nomination, the duplicity on health and education bills—just won't wash.

That the new image aspires to studious calm may be adduced from the White House campaign to establish Mr. Nixon as an intellectual. Such effort presupposes a simple, nonbookish electorate, easily impressed. To give out a list, as Press Secretary Ron Ziegler did, of the books President Nixon would be reading in the Virgin Islands is movie press agent stuff.

And the books! Now, please, be impressed! When not discussing philosophy on the beach with Bebe Rebozo, Mr. Nixon will be reading Lord David Cecil's *Melbourne*, Robert Blake's *Disraeli* and that old spellbinder *The Crime of Sylvestre Bonnard*.

John Kennedy would have been reading the James Bond stories, having read *Melbourne* and praised it warmly, which may or may not have propelled the book into the Nixon luggage. Now, what I'd *really* like to know is what books is Bebe Rebozo reading?

Postscript: When the President returned from the Virgin Islands, an enterprising reporter spread the news that our man of letters in the White House had read none of the books in his luggage. He did, however, see *Patton* seven times in 1971.

With the world growing dirtier, noisier, bloodier and meaner, it behooves all of us to become cleaner, quieter, kinder and more militant in our battle for a decent life.

If ever our society needed activists, people who give a damn, it is now. The times demand an expression of outrage. Not muttered curses, not an occasional letter to the editor, but *outrage,* expressed in a socially constructive manner.

While we grumble and mutter, certain beauties are passing from the earth. While we gasp in horror at the day's news, certain basic agreements that uphold civilization are being violated. While we cry "How terrible!" the terribleness grows.

The trouble with too many of us is that our outrage is pent inside us, dark and fearful. An anger close to tears clots the throat when we read how Lieutenant William Calley spent an hour shooting unarmed villagers as they ate their breakfast and hear how he dismissed it at his trial as just another day in the life of a soldier—"no big deal, sir."

A different sort of outrage comes when we read that this same officer is hailed as a hero in the taverns and shops around Fort Benning. As so often in the past few years, the thought rises, "Dear God, what kind of people are we?"

Our outrage at this point can't touch Lieutenant Calley. But it can and should reach the White House and the Congress as the war worsens in Southeast Asia. One feels, at times, like that frightened child sent to jail by a cold, stupid judge who wrote on the cell wall, "Won't somebody *lissen?*"

To catalog all the outrages one feels in a normal week would take hours. That fact alone speaks volumes. If you read a great many periodicals—and I must—certain stories haunt the mind for days.

I read the other day of the children in certain depressed areas of the South who are so hungry they eat clay. In some counties all the children below a certain family income level have worms. All of them. Retardation is common, and it's usually a direct consequence of infant hunger. The people are without hope and without energy. Millions of dollars in antipoverty funds have found their way into the pockets of local politicians and the rich who control the economy.

When these facts were brought to the attention of Arthur Burns, the President's economic adviser, he was unmoved. He wondered why the poor didn't plant gardens. (This and other tales of horror you may read in Nick Kotz' little book of outrage, *Let Them Eat Promises.*)

Faced with a page of newsprint, my eye is unfailingly caught by one word: widow. That's me. There are 10,000,000 widows over sixty-five—no, that's not me, thank heaven—but it depresses me to read in the *Christian Science Monitor* that 3,000,000 of these widows live below the poverty line.

One of these, an elderly woman in Boston's Back Bay, "enters a restaurant, orders a cup of hot water and then pours catsup into it. That's lunch." It's also poverty and a brutal commentary on a country that can somehow find $80 billion a year for the Pentagon.

Another widow, sixty-eight years old and living on $45 a month, told a reporter for the *National Observer*, "When you keep busy you don't mind being hungry so much. I don't hardly notice when mealtime goes by if I am playing the piano or reading my Bible."

It takes less emotional energy to be outraged by the steady befouling of this good earth. I am taken aback to read that Lake Erie has aged 15,000 years since 1920! At this rate it may soon be a bog. This horrible news would stir considerably more outrage in me if I lived in Buffalo. Then I would be obliged to smell the sulphuric fumes, see the miasma rise from the scummy water, hear children complain that they've no place to swim.

What to do about life's daily outrages? Well, we can sign petitions, write letters, join Common Cause, march, picket, write checks and be willing to serve as mister or madam chairman—we can give a damn. It may not be instantly effective, but it's a beginning.

In the matter of pollution there are specific instructions. They arrive in every mail, and I respectfully file them away. Some of the admonitions I try to follow. They're worth passing along: no detergents, just good, clean soap; take the train or bus, don't drive; use as little electric power as possible (this will be bad news for power companies, and that's nice, too); use sand on your icy street, not salt; compost your garbage; don't use tinted tissues or toweling; reuse envelopes and answer letters on the reverse side of the sender's notepaper.

I'm not sure I'm managing to follow all those warnings, but here's one I shall find easy to obey. In *The User's Guide to the Protection of the Environment* it says: "Don't buy a jaguar coat." I promise. Never. After all, a jaguar is a *cat.*

"Somebody who brings serenity, calmness and strength into a room. That makes a great difference."

The words are President Nixon's, describing that rare creature, the perfect wife—in this case, his wife. The President paid her a fond and tasteful tribute in a special interview with the ladies of the press. It was a rare occasion in that Mr. Nixon was saying, as President, what he deeply feels as a man. This, of itself, was significant enough to be page-one news.

Inspiration for the interview was Mrs. Nixon's fifty-ninth

birthday, which fell on March 16. Certainly this homage from her husband will be among the First Lady's nicest gifts.

It might also be said that one of the nicest traits projected so far by Mr. Nixon is his devotion to his wife and family. Here is something solid and good, the kind of conventional decency Americans always expect of their leaders. We may not be a highly moral people, but we expect all men who hold public office to be awash in private virtue.

After two years, Mrs. Nixon's image is firmly stamped on the public mind. Nature was in earnest when she made Thelma Ryan Nixon. When a reporter once asked if she were afraid of hostile crowds, she replied, "I'm not afraid of anything." Who could doubt her? This is a First Lady who could have gone West in a covered wagon, her hair and dress in perfect order and no nagging complaints about rutted trails or lurking Indians.

Because she projects so much strength, her admirers often wish she'd invest some of it in social causes. But she is an activist only in the lighter social sense. She enjoys parties and always looks elegant and composed. Age has brought a marble-hard beauty to her face. The President says that his wife, like all First Ladies, loves her role and plays it with great efficiency.

Despite the pleasures and "perks" of her job, there must still be gray, if not black, moments. A correspondent who asked Mrs. Nixon what sort of movies she liked to see after dinner was told, "Something gay. I have enough troubles."

Of course Mrs. Nixon misses privacy. She longs to go window-shopping and walk on the beach with the wind in her hair, says the President.

Whenever I read these cries from Fame's captives, I remember the comment of Helen Thomas of UPI on the petulance Presidential families occasionally show the press. "Considering how hard they've worked to get there," she wrote, "their protestations about privacy are just a bit much."

Though Mrs. Nixon does virtually nothing in the way of espousing worthy causes, she is surrounded by the largest, costliest public relations staff ever assembled. Their job, apparently, is to make sure that she does nothing in a graceful, casual way. Promoting the image of the President's wife costs the taxpayers $150,000 a year. One reporter has said bluntly, "Pat's press is a computerized, Madison Avenue snow job. She comes out like a statue of the Holy Mother."

In spite of that public relations brain trust—or maybe because of it—Mrs. Nixon has remained remote and cool. The Madison Avenue touch has not humanized her. Probably her finest hour to date was her trip to Peru following last year's horrendous earthquake. Deeply distressed by the suffering she saw, she wept and the people loved her. It might be said that she's at her best in a disaster.

Certainly her first cross-country trip to encourage volunteer social work was not a glittering success. She had requested no greeters, no officials at the airport, and in consequence she had few.

On the First Lady's next trip, ten months later, advance men signed up throngs of cheering Republicans to cry "Welcome!" at the airport. They also enlisted the Girl Scouts. As Winzola McLendon, a veteran White House correspondent, tells it, Mrs. Nixon's tour "brought out every damned Brownie in the country." Because the little girls were always in the front row at the airport, a regular cry went up from the Secret Service, "Don't squash the Brownies!"

Unlike Ladybird Johnson, Pat Nixon has no gift of phrase. When she tries to be glib, she sounds phony. Speaking of Mrs. Eisenhower (while she was First Lady), Mrs. Nixon said, "Her sparkling personality immediately captivates all who see her."

And at the first White House reception after the inaugural, the new First Lady addressed a teatime throng of some 500 distinguished guests and said she hoped this would be the first of hundreds of similar parties. "Instead of having just the big shots," she said, "we're going to have more people like *you*."

Hundreds of parties the Nixons certainly have had. Guests pour in at the rate of 45,000 a year. The bill for food, drink and help is so enormous that the Republican National Committee has been paying part of it. The Nixons entertain ten times as many guests as the Eisenhowers did, and Washington regulars say the parties are ten times as much fun. The ladies on the White House press beat do not praise the President and his lady for their social grace, however. The press is usually barred from dinner. Now and then, as a grand gesture, the Madison Avenue PR staff has the afterdinner toasts recorded and played back.

It must be said, despite the chill that exists between her and some of the press ladies, that the First Lady plays her part with dignity and correctness. And if she brings serenity, calm and strength into the room with her, well, she's performing a great service—to her husband and hence to her country.

It's hardly news anywhere that the streets of New York are unsafe after dark. They've known it for years in Grand Forks and Medicine Hat. And now they know it in Milan, Italy, and in Bonn, West Germany. Worse, the European press has pointed out that among Manhattan muggers, the female is often deadlier than the male.

In recent weeks an Italian businessman and the former Defense Minister of West Germany have been attacked in Manhattan by streetwalkers. The Italian was stabbed to death by a trio of black prostitutes as he was strolling near the Hilton Hotel. Franz Josef Strauss was luckier. He was simply robbed, also by street solicitors, not far from his hotel.

It's not uncommon for a girl to act as decoy for two men who, instantly the victim has been stopped, step in for the kill. A man who has seen two such holdups says they are executed with the swiftness and precision of a ballet.

Naturally, one hates to think of women as participating in

such vicious crimes. But the social conditions that generate crime are beginning to mark both sexes. Last year an elderly woman who was waiting for a traffic light on East Sixty-eighth Street found herself assisted across the street by two teen-age girls. When they got her safely to the other side they stole her purse.

The prevalence of prostitutes, particularly on the West Side, has moved one city official to suggest legalized brothels to reduce this illicit traffic. A municipal doss house under the watchful eye of the police and the Board of Health might have its advantages. But one doubts that such establishments would reduce street crime. The average prostitute is not a knife wielder. She's more apt to be a pathetic, inadequate female who needs money for drugs.

More and more the terror of New York after dark evokes a comparison with the London of long ago. In the eighteenth century most streets were unlighted and the lantern carriers were not above leading a customer straight into a gang of "footpads," as muggers were then known. Horace Walpole wrote to a friend that "One is forced to travel, even at noon, as if one were going into battle."

In 1720 a duchess was robbed as she was being carried across Bond Street in her sedan chair. And ladies on their way to court armed themselves with blunderbusses "to shoot at rogues."

Private citizens don't shoot rogues in the street anymore. But if the crime rate continues to mount, they doubtless will. And innocent persons will be killed in the melee. Crime will not cease, the streets will simply become more perilous.

In 1753 novelist Henry Fielding (author of *Tom Jones*) was asked in his capacity as magistrate to draw up a plan for purging London of street crime. He reorganized and upgraded the constabulary and paid informers, or "thief-takers," to turn in criminals. He insisted that newspapers report every crime, with full descriptions of the suspects. Pawnbrokers and stable keepers were put on guard. The public cooperated enthusiastically, and the streets for several years thereafter were comparatively safe again.

Conditions worsened considerably during the Regency, becoming far more hazardous than those plaguing us today. Street gangs, such as the Mohocks and the Bold Bucks, committed barbarous acts against pedestrians for the simple "thrill" of it. A particular delight was encasing a stunned citizen in a barrel and rolling him into a ditch. A marvelous thrill.

New York's current troubles come back to mind as one reads that "foreign visitors" were particular targets. Small wonder that Continental visitors never walked abroad without a sword or a dagger.

In the annals of crime, physical violence by women is rare. The Newgate Calendar, a compendium of historic crimes, does list one Mary Young, alias Jenny Diver, hanged for street robbery. "Her depredations," we read, "were executed with the courage of a man and the softer deceptions of an artful female." And certainly no more depraved and violent a cross section of women has ever been gathered in one place than in the famous "dusthole" of Victorian London. These women were so degraded, social historians report, that "even abandoned men refused to accompany them home."

"A policeman never goes down this street alone at night," says a contemporary account, "one having died not long ago from injuries received there. But two Salvation Army lasses go unharmed and loved at all hours. . . ."

Thinking of New York's after-dark terrors, I am always reminded of Jane Jacobs' theory that "There must be eyes upon a street." Eyes belonging to the street's "natural proprietors"—that is, the shopkeepers, news dealers, cops walking a beat, old-time residents.

The sidewalk, Miss Jacobs writes in *The Death and Life of Great American Cities*, must be in fairly continuous use. The mood of the streets controls the behavior of the people who use them. By that standard, New York's mood must seem to visitors ugly and cruel.

So a Boy Scout leader in Idaho imagines his troop would find it educational to visit the Soviet Union. Well, now, you just know that Boy Scout is a dangerous radical. He's obviously got Commie leanings, and some true-blue American should turn him in before he corrupts all those brave, clean, reverent kids.

This being America, the home of the Red Menace, of course somebody did turn him in. The FBI makes it all so easy. The Boy Scout who wished to show his troop how Soviet citizens live— perhaps to remind them of how comfy things are in Idaho—is now listed in the FBI's suspicious file. Big Brother is everywhere.

The name of the Idaho Boy Scout turned up in the copies of stolen FBI documents now flooding newspaper offices. They were mailed anonymously, and the Attorney General has asked that nothing be revealed of their contents. He says that disclosure "could endanger the United States and give aid to foreign governments." He omits the most potent reason: Disclosure can only embarrass the hell out of the FBI, the Justice Department and the Nixon administration, which has continued the tradition of regarding J. Edgar Hoover as a holy relic whose removal might cause the Lord to smite the earth with plague and fire.

Some of us, after reading what sort of garbage goes into an "unevaluated" FBI file, would settle for the plague and fire. They're cleaner.

In compiling dossiers on possible enemies of the state, the FBI's methods appear to be simplistic, irresponsible and immoral. For example: A telephone operator fancies there's something suspicious about a certain professor of philosophy. Maybe he never praised her hyacinth hair and classic face. Maybe he never suspected she was sending box tops to Big Brother.

At any rate, the FBI attaches sufficient weight to the word of disgruntled telephone operators—and the general spookiness of philosophers—to persuade this switchboard spy to keep a record of the professor's long-distance calls.

This in America, the land of the free! The land where we began by eliminating dissent and are now eliminating—by intimidation—dissenters.

While one never can condone the stealing of documents from anybody's files, it is possible to say, without apology, that this particular theft may be a great public service. The documents are so absurd, so light-minded and so malevolent as to be terrifying.

We are closer to the classic police state—such as now exists in Greece—than we'd ever suspected. Any lunatic, any crank, any rancher in Idaho with a fourth-grade education can send the FBI a list of persons he "suspects." And the FBI, God help us, will carefully record all the names and have a local agent give the suspect the once-over.

"When we relax our standards to accommodate the faceless informer," Justice William O. Douglas has written, "we violate our basic constitutional guarantees and ape the tactics of those we despise."

According to these pilfered documents—whose authenticity the FBI admits—this mighty agency can demand bank statements, can tap telephones and has sufficient funds to plant an informer in every PTA, every rock band, every philosophical and literary society. Only the John Birchers and the American Legion can be reasonably sure they're not harboring one of Mr. Hoover's agents on the rolls.

As recently as 1965, it is well to remember, one-half of the membership in the American Communist Party was comprised of FBI agents. Their dues, plus artful PR, maintained the myth of the Red Menace.

One of the more repellent aspects of these FBI documents is the continual reference to informers. To keep abreast of Communist plots on campus the FBI is willing to pay students for reporting anything "suspicious," such as that philosophy professor lecturing on liberty and the right to dissent.

One newsletter from the Philadelphia office of the FBI suggests interviews with members of the New Left "to get the point across that there is an FBI agent behind every mailbox."

Funny, that's the point some of us have been trying to get across for some time now, but people have cried "Nonsense!" and reminded us of how bravely J. Edgar Hoover was battling "subversion." It would be helpful if the Supreme Court finally defined subversion.

The more one reads about the FBI the more muddled and out of touch Mr. Hoover seems to be. Hank Messick's book *Lansky*, the story of the crime syndicate leader, offers a fascinating footnote on the FBI chief's gullibility. It says:

> Hoover was unbelievably naive where gangsters were concerned. An FBI agent has related how "the Chief" would attend gangster-owned race tracks in Miami and find himself posing with notorious hoods. To protect himself, he created a special Hoodlum Squad based in Miami. Its duties were simply to identify various gangsters to Hoover when he came down each winter . . . to keep Hoover from hurting his image.

It is interesting to speculate. Would Mr. Hoover be humiliated to discover that he'd inadvertently had his photo snapped with a Boy Scout from Idaho who once contemplated a trip to Russia?

The great warm gush of sympathy for William Calley begins to make one sick. It is as shaming to this country as the massacre for which he was tried and found guilty.

Charitably, one must assume that this sudden apotheosis of Lieutenant Calley rises from ignorance of what transpired at My Lai and not from patriotic pride in acts of atrocity.

Lieutenant Calley, in the words of the one juror who has spoken up, was given "every benefit of every doubt." That jury, comprised of officers who have risen from the ranks, was loath to bring in the verdict "guilty." But the lieutenant's deeds, weighed on any moral scale, are as wanton and savage as the Tate murders. Some would say they are infinitely worse. But nobody is sending telegrams to Governor Ronald Reagan beseeching him to pardon the Manson family.

It should not be overlooked that the wildest indignation over the Calley verdict rages in the states of the old Confederacy, in the land of the night-riders and lynch parties, the bloody ground where racism and contempt for law have flowered most evilly. Citizens who ten years ago were erecting billboards that said IMPEACH EARL WARREN now are carrying placards that say PARDON LT. CALLEY.

The liberals and the peace militants who have joined in the mindless uproar over the Calley verdict would be wise to look about and see whose barricade they have mounted. Do they truly want to stand with George Wallace and Spiro Agnew?

To say that Lieutenant Calley was only one of several thousand soldiers who slaughtered unarmed civilians in no way lessens Lieutenant Calley's guilt. To stress that issue as if it were all is to overlook the moral point made by the court-martial.

While draft boards are resigning in protest and thousands of telegrams are pouring into the White House, it might be sensible to pause and ask again, "What specifically did Lieutenant Calley do in that unarmed village on March 16, 1968?"

The best account of the My Lai incident is found in Richard Hammer's book *One Morning in the War*. It is a sober, quietly understated recital of cold-blooded murder. So keen for accuracy is reporter Hammer that he insists on referring to the village by its proper name, Son My. He also states that there were two separate and distinct massacres that morning killing upward of 500 civilians. Lieutenant Calley originally was charged with 100 murders. At his court-martial the figure was pared down to 22.

Here is Hammer on the carnage: "Houses were blown apart and burned. Dead bodies were tossed into the pyres which had once been their homes. . . . Animals were slaughtered. Haeberle [a combat photographer] remembers one scene of a GI stabbing a cow over and over again with his bayonet while other soldiers stood around watching and laughing. Dead animals and dead bodies were thrown down wells to pollute the water supply. *And everywhere, it seemed, was Lt. Calley.*" (Italics mine.)

Then there's the testimony of the helicopter pilot who happened to fly over the village and noticed an irrigation ditch jammed with bodies. He also saw Lieutenant Calley about to shoot a small child. The pilot, Warrant Officer Hugh C. Thompson, landed and started toward the child as Calley began moving in.

"Calley made a motion with his rifle," Hammer writes. "Thompson, blazing with rage, turned abruptly and strode across to the helicopter. There he told one of his waist gunners to aim his machine gun 'at that officer' and if the officer attempted to intervene again, to shoot him. Thompson then went back, picked up the child and carried him back to the chopper and took off once again."

When the helicopter and the child had departed, Lieutenant Calley, Hammer relates, said to his radio operator, one Charles Sledge, "That guy isn't very happy with the way we're running this operation. But I don't care. He's not in charge."

Daniel Ellsberg,* a Vietnam analyst for the Rand Corporation and one-time assistant to our ambassador in Vietnam, has said that My Lai was beyond the bounds of permissible behavior and all the soldiers involved have recognized this fact.

"They knew it was wrong. That is why they have tried to hide the event, talked about it to no one, discussed it very little even

---

* Later to become famous as the man who delivered the Pentagon Papers.

among themselves," said Mr. Ellsberg (quoted in *War Crimes and the American Conscience*).

Television, to which we turn so eagerly when a dark passage in our history needs illumination, has not done itself proud this week. Instead of keeping the Calley case in perspective, it has fanned the flames of hysteria, stressing the sentimental outpouring in the lieutenant's behalf. Not until one of the jurors, a decent man virtually numb from his ordeal, came on did we hear a voice of reason.

If you can stomach the story of what sort of war our boys are fighting in Vietnam, read Dick Hammer's book. Read Jonathan Schell's *The Military Half*, in which he describes how casually we have destroyed peaceful villages, wiping out 70 percent of one province, Quang Ngai. Read *Casualties of War* by my old friend Dan Lang. Read Murray Polner's book *No Victory Parades*. Learn what this war is all about, and you'll join every peace march that passes.

Well, I missed the Easter Parade this year—and didn't feel a single pang.

I have seen the girls in their revolting Sunday pants suits. And the camera-courting lass with a live chick on her hat and the overdressed little girl with a bunny rabbit in mummy's hatbox. And the smart little models who wear the labels inside out. All this to honor Christ among the lilies.

I'm old enough to remember the days when we donned our Sally Victor bonnets and our little white gloves and went to the Plaza for Sunday tea—not brunch, that was for the TV mob—and felt deliciously feminine and chic.

I date the "uglification" of women's fashion from the invention of the unbelted shift. It was those gunnysack dresses that demeaned the female form and took away the joy of having a slim, graceful figure. High necks added to the general hideousness, and nothing was improved by the addition of paillettes and sparkling braid. Bits of rope would have done as well.

We have gone through some appalling fashion cycles since 1965. There was a long stretch when the only pretty dresses available in the shops were those designed for baby's christening. The stiff, geometric shape, the mini-skirt that showed maxi-thighs, the rip-offs from the Romany gypsies and Indian street beggars all contrived to make young women look grotesque. Not surprisingly, young men began to vie for grotesquerie, too—and being naturally messier, they won.

By not going to the Easter Parade I spared myself the sight of the girls I think of as the drowned Ophelias. Their hair drips dankly. Their dresses are skimpy, drab and usually askew at the neck. They are commonly sold in a choice of three fabrics: calico, challis and old dishrag. Adding a fanciful touch are necklaces of shells, pods, fertility symbols, bits of tackle and now and then a wilted garland of flowers. "Ophelia's weedy trophies," piteous and tacky.

With her skimpy dress and necklace of hand-painted peach pits, our Ophelia wears laced boots, a cartridge belt and, on chilly days, a cloche hat. The hat may be crocheted out of butcher's string or old nylon stockings. Anyway, it's worn pulled over the eyebrows, in the style that somehow evokes retarded children. Ali McGraw wore just such a cap the other evening on television. Despite her fresh young beauty, she looked terrible.

Now and then, out of a mad desire to accent her beguiling femininity, our Ophelia adds two coin-size spots of rouge to her cheeks and draws thick, spiky lashes above and below her eyes.

The new grotesquerie takes many forms. Hot pants have introduced a look as vulgar as the name. I was astonished—and maybe a little flattered—when a matronly saleswoman stepped into a booth where I was being fitted and said coyly, "Would modom care to try these on!"

"Heavens, no!"

"But modom has the figger," she said archly. She held the hot pants, which were embellished with long ribbon streamers, in front of her firmly corseted girth. The ribbons fell in pretty disarray. I murmured my disapproval, wondering had the pants been designed for some kind of Maypole dancing? My pants saleswoman looked confused.

"Would modom care to slip into them?"

Modom would not and allowed as how hot pants should be outlawed.

"They're very *in* with society," my new clothes counsel persisted. "Joan Kennedy was photographed in them for *Newsweek*." And who was I, her tone implied, to differ with such undisputed fashion leaders?

I have decided that there are two kinds of exhibitionists in the fashion world: those who dress with great style and those who dress like Joan Kennedy. Regrettably, it now seems to be the Joan Kennedys who set the styles for young girls.

Each time Mrs. Edward Kennedy visits the White House she manages to create a sensation. Once it was her glittery micro-mini-skirt. Another time it was a see-through chiffon blouse. Recently, at a luncheon for Senators' wives, breezy, "mod" Mrs. Kennedy wore gaucho pants, a bolero jacket of tie-dye leather over a tight sweater and suede boots. With her long blond wig, she looked like a faded film star on her way to a ranch cookout. And one must, in all charity, wonder: Does this swinging young matron have any idea what she is telling the world by wearing such costumes to the White House?

In her mode of dress, a woman is making a public statement. She is proclaiming her respect—or lack of it—for herself, her hosts, her husband and the milieu in which she lives. Naturally, she is also reflecting her time. But more obviously she is projecting her inner conflicts. One wishes, therefore, that pretty Mrs. Kennedy would discard those cheap novelties and hie herself off to the Paris couture—or to a good New York dressmaker. She can, one may assume, afford to dress well. Her mother-in-law, at eighty, looks elegant and womanly. In tasteful clothes, Mrs. Ted might one day inspire the poor Ophelias of America to get out of those weeds and rags.

What I like about the young people who are trying to clear the air, freshen the water and save the earth is their total lack of guile. Everything from their homemade handbills to the heavy tomes by their bearded young professors is blunt, tough and urgent. And fie on you, Uptight, Buttoned-down Bourgeois, if you can't grasp the desperate urgency of it all. ("Fie on," I should add, is my own quaint euphemism, and it's in no danger of being taken up by any of the earth-savers.)

The simple, direct approach can be stunning. A little book that came in the mail, *Earth Day—The Beginning*, is dedicated "To the Tree from which this book was made."

A chapter on the ravaging of the landscape by powerful interests is cogently titled "Sue the Bastards." Young activists come straight to the point.

A handy test for the urgency of any movement is how much mordant wit it generates. By that token, saving the earth is now our number-one priority. Trouble is, only the young—and the scientific community—seem to feel the urgency.

On Earth Day last year, Kurt Vonnegut quoted President Nixon's proud statement that America has never lost a war and he wasn't going to be the first American President to lose one. But: "He may be the first American President to lose a planet," said Vonnegut.

As one who remembers how the air used to smell on a fine spring morning and how sparkling Adirondack lakes used to be and how vegetables tasted fresh from the garden, I can only cheer the young ecologists.

Were I a brisk twenty-one again I expect I'd be gung-ho for ecology all the way. I'd be writing my Congressman, burning candles instead of electricity and recycling everything in my wastebasket. Alas, I have read all the instructions and now must live with the fear that I'll be named Mrs. Litterbug of 1971. My rubbish bin runneth over. I'll never be able to make my own nonbiodegradable soap. I can't imagine keeping house without plastic bags. If we care about our environment, if we are going to fulfill our duty as recyclers of our household waste, we'd better not buy detergents, aluminum cans or plastic anything.

To deprive the average American of plastic products isn't going to be easy. We use more than 100,000,000 pounds of plastic wrapping every year. When incinerated, plastics smell awful and produce something very nasty: hydrochloric acid aerosol. It eats away the insides of the incinerator. But does the average consumer care? No. Therefore incinerator makers had better adjust their product.

Paul Swatek's book *User's Guide to the Protection of the Environment* says the average person pollutes the good earth with five pounds of trash every day. By that standard I should be arrested.

My unopened mail, the press releases and such flotsam, weighs five pounds. The garbage accounts for another five. I subscribe to thirty magazines and five newspapers. Besides that, my cat sheds a lot. And everything seems to come in plastic bags.

The environmentalists are bursting with helpful hints. I get a new volume of them every day, and the suggestions exhaust me. I am to return all wire hangers to the cleaner. I am to use only cloth napkins, never paper. If I care about tidying up this blessed land I will carry a litter bag wherever I go and be willing to pick up other people's refuse. In 1967 it cost $28,000,000 to remove the litter from our primary highways. That's a big stash of trash. The price suggests that the concession for litter-picking, with or without plastic bags, is giving somebody a vested interest in an untidy America.

215

Enzymes and presoaks are high on the *verboten* list. This I consider social progress in the best sense. We are now to be spared the nightly TV messages from those lumpy homemakers with the nasal twangs who have found happiness in the laundry room. As good wives, they have presoaked everything but their heads.

An ecologist's manual, *Living on the Earth*, arrived the other day, and it's quite the oddest book I've read in years. For one thing, it's written in longhand by a nut-brown maid who calls herself Alicia Bay Laurel.

Dutifully, I read this book straight through, including the handwritten index. I'm now able to tell you how to make laundry soap, shoe polish and something you've always wanted, a toga.

I also have instructions, should life cast me away on an island, for making a bamboo flute, a burnous, a loom, an outdoor latrine, tire-tread sandals (to wear with the hand-woven burnous) and magic elixirs that drive away rats and lice.

Miss Laurel thinks of everything that will get us back to the good, simple life, even to home delivery of babies. Like Paul Ehrlich and Paul Swatek and all the others, she is terribly earnest. But to save the earth must we make our own soap and have our babies at home to the music of a bamboo flute?

One of the hazards of being seriously ill or seriously banged up in an accident is that your doctor might order a blood transfusion. And then . . . Lord help you. A catalog of the dangers lurking in hospital blood these days would provoke all but the comatose to pick up their beds and walk.

The very sick child I once heard about who said he wouldn't mind a transfusion if the blood came from his older (and much admired) brother was wise beyond his years. If one needed blood, it would be a great comfort to know that it had been drawn from a dear friend or relative whose type matched and whose body harbored no sinister microbes.

The commonest ailment lurking in donated blood, of course, is hepatitis. One study reports a serum hepatitis rate of 8.7 percent, or 75,000 cases a year. Of these, 10,000 are fatal.

A mild form of malaria has long been a transfusion risk. But now, according to reports, a highly virulent malaria has been occurring in a few samples of hospital blood. A parasite known as falciparum has been brought to sick folks at home by Vietnam veterans who are also drug addicts. For the price of a fix, they sell a pint of tainted blood. Commercial blood banks too often are remiss in examining donors. Desperate donors invariably lie and give fictitious addresses to avoid being traced.

It's almost axiomatic that bought blood is bad blood. In one Tokyo hospital where 98 percent of all deposited blood is paid for, hepatitis occurs in more than 65 percent of transfused patients. That makes our 8.7 percent rate reassuring. But in all of Great Britain the posttransfusion hepatitis rate is only 1 percent. There's a reason. Over there bought blood is illegal. All contributions are voluntary. And there's never a shortage of blood.

How a nation manages its blood banks may be taken as an index to its decency and altruism. By this standard, the British—who never charge a patient for blood—are easily among the nicest people in the world.

By contrast, we're a pack of poltroons, selfish, scared, irresponsible shirkers. We lack a sense of "community," says Professor Richard Titmuss. He's a distinguished scholar at the London School of Economics, and it's his notion that the "quality of life" in any country can be measured by the willingness of its citizenry to make regular gifts of blood to strangers voluntarily, without hope of reward or honor.

Anyone who reads Professor Titmuss' book *The Gift Relationship* is immediately going to add up his visits to the blood bank and classify himself accordingly. In a dire emergency I did donate blood to a friend many years ago, but that was my only high moment of altruism on the Titmuss scale. Every other time I volunteered I was turned down because, as a sporty young intern once put it, "You can't make the weight, honey."

Once, after I'd written a plea for blood donors in behalf of the Red Cross, a snarky letter arrived from a reader asking, "How many pints have you given lately?" Stung by this query, I asked one of the Red Cross chairmen if I might give *half* a pint, please. I explained that even though I was a ninety-eight-pound weakling I had a high hemoglobin and was in excellent health.

I presented myself at the appointed time, with a nip of brandy in my purse to guarantee quick recovery. This time I weighed in at ninety-six. Instant rejection. "But what about your friend here?" asked the lady in charge.

My friend was a pale young man not long home from the wars who was planning to take me from my bloodletting to a hearty dinner. As things turned out he needed the hearty dinner. Though he'd been wounded three times, suffered malaria and various other war ailments, his blood was eagerly accepted.

So, you see, Professor Titmuss, I have tried.

It gives one a terrible sense of inadequacy to read how splendidly the British manage their blood banks. Because of the National Health Service, plus a mounting accident rate, the demand for British blood has risen steadily. So in the past twenty years have the donations—269 percent! Even private patients receive free blood.

In America we have a derelict class known as "blood indigents." These are the skid row drunks, the addicts, the professional donors who find bloodletting easier than working. More than half the donors, one study shows, are chronically unemployed.

Blood donors in England are a cross section of the population, with the upper classes giving a bit more than others. Middle-aged people, particularly women alone, are frequent donors. Their motive is, quite simply, "altruism."

The Soviet Union offers a variety of inducements for blood. A day off, an excursion, special foods—blackmail in a worthy cause. South Africa segregates its blood. A similar fastidiousness prevails, by law, in those citadels of altruism Arkansas and South Carolina.

Blood donations cannot be left to the whim and hazard of the marketplace. Bad blood in the bank not only discloses a bad society, it kills innocent people. Scientific standards slip. Patients will lose faith in their doctors. Litigation involving blood transfusions has been increasing, we read, "with geometrical progression." Small wonder.

Someday, if current Russian experiments prove fruitful, we may be able to draw usable blood from cadavers. Meantime, our hospitals purchase more than half their blood for transfusions. The blood is good for only twenty-one days. Shortages are chronic and acute. Our method is fifteen times more costly than Britain's. We're always short. Donors have to be paid or dragooned. In sum, we are not only less dutiful than the British in these matters, we are a good bit less shrewd.

Some jests never go out of date. And the most enduring are those reminding us of imperfections in ourselves—and our institutions—that go on forever.

I'm thinking of this passage from Mark Twain: "Reader, suppose you were an idiot. And suppose you were a member of Congress. But I repeat myself!" A good jest in the 1880's; perhaps even better today.

No matter where you look in 1971 you are affronted by the gap between what ought to be done for the people and what is being done by the Congress. Our priorities have been out of order for generations. All our social ills, including crime, unemployment, urban blight and the Vietnam psychosis, can be traced to a Congress whose general tone suggests roll-top desks and frock coats in an age of computers and love beads.

To get decent social legislation through the modern Congress is a feat comparable to orbiting the moon in a Piper Cub. The Congressional mind is totally unlike the mind of Caesar, which "rejoiced in committing itself."

The ordinary citizen no longer believes in that time-honored protest, "I'll write a letter to my Congressman." He knows he'll receive a reply three months later written by a computer and signed by an "autopen." These devices save your Congressmen precious hours each week. Most have pens equipped to write, depending on the status of the correspondent, "Senator John Doe," plain "John Doe" or, for a few thousand intimates from back home, "Yours as ever, John."

Some letters to Congressmen are of a nature that makes any reply gratuitous.

A good friend of mine wrote to Senator James Buckley not long ago: "Sir: Your vote on the SST confirms my excellent judgment in not voting for you." No reply expected.

The recently retired Senator Stephen Young of Ohio will always be remembered for his zinging replies to constituents, such as, "I feel obliged to inform you that some raging lunatic has been writing me threatening letters under your name and address."

Insulted Congressmen can also take heart from the replies Representative John S. McGroarty of California used to send to irate constituents. "One of the countless drawbacks of being in Congress," he wrote, "is that I am compelled to receive impertinent letters from a jackass like you. . . . Will you please take two running jumps and go to hell."

Peppery McGroarty is no longer in Congress. The jackass backlash, we may assume.

Though 90 percent of a Congressman's mail is answered by a push-button form letter signed by a robot pen, all the mail is counted and categorized. Every lawmaker with a competent staff knows if his constituents favor quick withdrawal from Vietnam or an accelerated bombing campaign. They know if the school prayer issue outweighs the pollution issue in their districts. But, generally speaking, mail from back home doesn't carry as much weight with Congressmen as pressure from the special interests and arm-twisting by the President's men. One call from the White House means more than 25,000 letters from constituents.

In his fine book *Congress: The Sapless Branch*, former Senator Joseph S. Clark says that relying on mail as an accurate guide to public opinion would be "folly."

"On the whole," writes Senator Clark, "mail is more trouble than it is worth. . . . Public sentiment can be more accurately checked by reading the newspapers, corresponding with leadership groups and conducting or following polls of public opinion."

A recent news magazine had an arresting summary of the "Real Issues in Today's America" based on the comments Congressmen hear when they go back home. Not surprisingly the single greatest worry coast to coast is the state of the economy.

When the government fails in its prime function—"to do for people those things they cannot do for themselves"—there is an inevitable disenchantment among the voters. Their only recourse is to vote the rascals out and vote honest, devoted public servants in. In theory, this is fine. But in practice, the rascals cannily perpetuate themselves by maintaining the creaky machinery—corrupt election practices, the seniority system, and so on—that keeps the system from working and denies the average man full opportunity for the good life.

With all the fuss about Tricia Nixon's wedding cake—an uproar that may just compel me to test the recipe myself—I haven't had time to read the story in a new pocket magazine "Tricia—The Last of the Sugar Plum Princesses."

To be totally candid, I was somewhat put off by the fact that this gush over Trish is tucked between an article on abortion and another called "Group Sex—Is It Happening on Your Block?" If Miss Nixon is affronted by this juxtaposition, she has a right to be.

But brides traditionally are more concerned about the costuming and coiffing of the wedding party than about the cake and champagne. We can all rest assured that Tricia will be the prettiest bride ever to say her vows in the White House. But some of us are awfully worried about that cake.

In my culinary library there's a handsomely illustrated volume titled *The First Ladies' Cookbook*. The only recipe I have ever attempted is Thomas Jefferson's Madeira jelly. It was delicious. And making it gave me a feeling of utter abandon because I did not have to follow the original that begins, "Take four calves' feet and wash them well without taking off the hoofs. Or, take 1 oz. of deer horn. . . ." I took instead two envelopes of plain unflavored gelatin. (Deer horn does sound more dashing though!)

The closing chapter in the new edition of this book offers the favorite recipes of the Nixon family. Excellent they are, too. Beef Wellington, stuffed tomatoes, vanilla soufflé and walnut cookies. *But no lemon pound cake.*

The New York *Times* test kitchen followed the White House recipe exactly and got, for its precision, a pan of soupy mush and a filthy oven. Instead of rising, Tricia's cake dripped. "Are they going to cut it with a spoon?" somebody wondered.

But then on television we saw a chef taking a perfect cake out of the oven, a cake made according to Mrs. Nixon's directions. The reporter who nibbled it cried "Delicious!" I still don't believe it.

A pound cake, if you care deeply about these things, is a classic sweet loaf, solid, more gritty than velvety and highly "keepable." An eighteenth-century pound cake recipe calls for a pound of butter, a pound of sugar, a pound of flour and eighteen eggs, yolks and whites.

Queen Victoria, who left a collection of recipes in her own hand, demanded a pound of currants in her pound cake. She was a fussy but hearty eater, and her banquets were four-hour events. (One of my old cookery books also records instructions for making "Prince Consort's Favorite Tart." The queen was humorous only by accident.)

No doubt Tricia's bridal cake will be an item in all the social histories of the Nixon years. It has set off one of the few amiable controversies in this administration. And what is most agreeably astonishing is that everybody seems concerned that every detail be perfect for the wedding.

Being a nation without royalty, we tend to regard certain White House doings as royal affairs. Tricia's wedding will probably have a TV rating comparable to an astronaut's moon walk. Disavow her father's politics we may, but there is something infinitely touching and beautiful about a June bride in a historic setting. The marriages of the Nixon daughters may prove to be the only unanimously applauded events of this administration.

It should be noted also that liberals, the people who were horrified by Tricia's professed admiration for Lester Maddox and Spiro Agnew, find it a delicious irony that she is marrying a young man Martha Mitchell might easily describe as "radical liberal."

Edward Cox is a social activist who, according to the latest story, refuses to tell his betrothed how he votes! He once spent a summer as one of Nader's Raiders, investigating consumer frauds. He seems, on the whole, the ideal man to complete the political education of Richard Nixon's daughter.

As for that wedding cake, the recipe may be faulty (halfway between a Tipsy Cake and a Quaking Pudding, it strikes me), but the wedding is bound to be lovely. Considering the many disillusions the Nixon years have brought, it might be said that the First Family owes us a bit of pageantry, a heartwarming spectacle to banish for a little while thoughts about hard times, lost liberties and justice denied.

Wanted: For those of us who came of age in gentler times, an emotional shock absorber. More precisely, a muffler for outrage, a relaxant for unbecoming revulsion. In this world that's too much with us there's an alarming erosion of the qualities that steady us, beginning with innocence, decency, wholesomeness. All those old square-toed words one can scarcely say without embarrassment anymore.

Naturally, it's the little things that jar one most. For example: I went to the pet shop to buy fresh catnip for my cat. "I just can't keep it in stock," said the woman in charge. "The kids are smoking it now."

Smoking catnip, for God's sake! That lovely aromatic herb that grew wild in the land when I was a child. Hairy catnip, first cousin to peppermint, the leaf country folk brewed as a sedative tea. They sweetened it with honey and the cat lapped the dregs. Now it's a joint of pussycat pot, a (more or less) bangless bhang.

I told a friend about this new vogue, the "catnip high," and he told me about nutmeg and morning glory.

Now, I happen to be a nutmeg fiend. Little brown flecks of it turn up in the popovers, the chicken broth, in any dish made with bananas. But it seems the medical journals have been onto nutmeg's magic properties longer than I have.

In heavy doses, nutmeg produces a nasty sort of intoxication. Rapid heartbeat, numbness in the arms and legs, a flushed face and sometimes nausea. Freshly grated nutmeg packs a bigger kick than the tinned powder.

The secret ingredient in nutmeg is an oil called myristicin.

224

The secret ingredient in morning glory seeds is ololiuqui—a word I hope I never have to spell again—and is a close kin to LSD. When members of the drug culture began cultivating morning glories in window boxes, the seed packagers became alarmed. To forestall the banning of the seeds, packagers decided to coat them with an emetic. Now all you get from chewing morning glory seeds is very sick.

Trifling matters, this cheap thrill-seeking via nutmeg and flowers. But how sad that the craving for euphoria or nirvana by our young people has reached such extremes. The physician who signs himself "Doctor Hippocrates" ("Dr. Hip" to the underground press) reports that he was once asked by a "head" who'd tried everything if hydrangeas gave a stronger psychedelic effect than pot.

It was wise of the "head" to put the question to a doctor. The reply was, "The component of hydrangeas causing the high is probably cyanide. You might get so high you'd never come back." It's strange to realize that there must be thousands of "heads" trying everything from carpet dust to toothpaste in search of a new "high."

How prevalent is the drug culture? In the world a young friend of mine describes as "black shoe, buttoned-down bourgeoisie," one simply doesn't know. But I cannot forget the barefoot girl, beautiful and emaciated, who sidled into a little Third Avenue boutique one day. The proprietor watched her with a fierce eye. "On drugs," she whispered to me. It was the whisper of one who knows. I looked at the girl, so frail and unkempt, so lost. "How sad!"

What else does one say? Are there any words?

It has been borne in upon me repeatedly that we who live outside the youth culture and the drug culture are insulated from the most agonizing problem of our age. A little book, *Heads, You Lose*, by an eighteen-year-old named Pamela Hall has seared some sorry vignettes in my mind.

I am shocked, for example, by the early, casual way youngsters take to drugs. It's all made to seem easy and gay and smart, like learning to swim or dance or drive a car. Depend on it, your fourteen-year-old child knows more about pot and meth and LSD than his parents know.

Miss Hall, who is now eighteen and cured, began her drug experiments at thirteen. Here is a sample entry from her diary: "Our class took a field trip to a museum today and Keith, Doug and I were riding about two feet higher than all the others due to some hash we brought, along with my little water pipe. We had ourselves a good stone right on the bus."

Fortunately, Pamela had a wise, loving mother—though it took her some time to discover her daughter's addiction. After the initial shock, she sent her freaked-out little daughter to a sanitarium, then put her in the care of a Swiss family. She also wrote to her regularly, loving, reassuring letters that make you cry.

"I view drugs now as something senseless and a waste," writes Pamela.

She also suggests a way to combat the growing use of drugs by the very young. "Parents need to give their kids more of a close-knit family life. If parents could somehow make their homes more open to discussions and if they could encourage an aura of trust, perhaps it would help."

Funny, isn't that what we old-fashioned, buttoned-down bourgeois types have been saying all along?

My favorite clergyman, the Reverend Sydney Smith (1771–1845), took an eminently sensible view of the hereafter. Hell, to his mind, was 1,000 years of tough mutton or a little eternity of family dinners. And heaven, he said, was "eating *pâté de foie gras* to the sound of trumpets."

I'll take Smith's heaven any day. And I promise not to make a fuss if the feathered choir mutes that trumpet. But an updated hell, to most of us, would offer greater tortures than tough mutton. For example: *Can you imagine 1,000 years of airline food?*

Steel yourself and think about it: an eternity of "roast beef" carved from the dry rot of old wood. Dehydrated potatoes simmered in library paste. Foam rubber croissants. Plastic *poulet à la crème,* and don't ask what's in the crème.

Remembering the specialties of pie-in-the-sky cuisine brings to mind a pretty stewardess who asked the elderly gentleman across from me if he had enjoyed his dinner. "The butter was nice," said he.

I have often been tempted to pack a box lunch before a domestic flight. (Foreign airlines respect the pleasures of the table, even if the table is a lap tray, subject to sudden turbulence.) Not having packed a lunch, there have been moments when I've thought of stepping briskly into the plane's galley and announcing, "I'd like to make a small omelet, if you don't mind. . . ."

Those jaunty little sky hops, so busy defrosting the stuffed pork chops, would be signaling for an emergency landing before I'd finished my request. On American aircraft, you don't cook, you *thaw.*

Once I confided this ambition to a traveling companion who was wont to shake his head over my constant urge to feed the hungry. "Stay out of the galley," he begged. "You'll end up making omelets for everybody."

No doubt I would have, too. But I am haunted by the prospect of going to a restaurant someday and finding the food so ghastly that I demand to see the kitchen and proceed to whip up a dinner my escort and I can digest.

This day will soon be upon us if present restaurant trends continue unchecked. All forecasts are glum. Barbara Norman, a distinguished culinary expert, predicts that all but a few restaurants eventually will be serving airline-style dinners. Almost no cooking will be done on the premises. Instead, the restaurant will buy "a packaged menu of frozen or freeze-dried 'chef-ready' foods from a conglomerate center and merely add the finishing touches."

Microwave cooking and reheating will replace the slow, savory, old-fashioned ways. Disposable dinnerware will make dishwashing obsolete. (But don't ask that the plates be hot! If you do, they'll melt!)

Miss Norman interviewed a number of restaurateurs, all of whom assured her that *haute cuisine,* with its emphasis on fresh ingredients and fine sauces, was virtually dead already. People simply do not demand good food anymore. They want "informality, quick service, amusing decor and . . . all-the-steak-you-can-eat-for-$5.

An advertisement in a restaurant trade journal carries the caption "We'll help your chef pull a fast one on your customers." You'd better believe it.

This indifference to good food is surprising in view of the culinary renaissance that is supposed to have taken place in America over the past decade. Gourmet shops are thriving. Gourmet cookbooks sell like the hot cakes you never can find in the index. Imported delicacies, such as pâté, caviar, snails, fine cheeses and confitures are available in the plainest groceries, not to mention department stores. Women talk about food at parties and send each other recipes in the mail. Brides who can't cook—and who don't specify the full *batterie de cuisine* as wedding gifts—are looked upon as unequal to the role of woman and wife.

If Americans could learn to care about the goodness of food and the well-being of their bodies, they'd harass their local bistros and hotels the way Ralph Nader harasses General Motors. But they're timid. Or they don't care enough. And the paradox puzzles Philippa Pullar, whose book *Consuming Passions* I am now reading for the second time.

While cookbooks and exotic foods sell well, she notes, women go on thawing little pies and adding water to the powdered potatoes. Surveys show that most women read cookbooks purely from curiosity, writes Miss Pullar, the same way they read about the landscape of the moon.

The environmentalists should join in the fight for better food. When the aroma of good cooking no longer fills the air at six o'clock, we are a doomed race. One way we can guarantee the blessed continuity of that aroma is to send back to the kitchen every dish that is ill-cooked, oversalted, barely warm or in any way unpalatable. Tell the chef to recycle it via the disposal and send you two poached eggs.

Now, in the summertime city, we sadly note the sunless pleasures of tired people.

One of these is the window-shopping stroll in the early evening along Madison Avenue or Fifth. The city's roar is silent now. The pavements are cool, the push and shove are gone. People walk slowly, expectantly, past the gauntly beautiful mannequins in the bold, bare gowns, past the shiny luggage and the good bone china, the books and the pictures and the hideous night-lit banks with the clean-up squad swabbing down the plastic plants.

Out-of-town visitors used to find special delight in these evening promenades. You could tell them by their white shoes, their cries of "Oh, look!" But now they're staying in their hotel rooms after dark, immobilized by the tales of our muggers and holdup men. They're also repelled by the grilles and gates and heavy mesh protecting the glass that protects the shop treasures.

"People who have come here on a holiday sit in the lounge or the lobby all evening," a hotel man reports. "The phrase you keep hearing is, 'I hope I get home alive!' "

Such is the name and fame of Fun City.

There have always been, we old residents like to think, areas of New York where anybody can stroll without hazard to life, limb or wallet. But now I'm not so sure. Now that I have actually seen with my own eyes the hustlers doing their hustling on Madison Avenue in the fifties at 10 P.M., I'm ready to concede that Babylon is falling, is falling, that great city!

Watching these ladies of the evening—and what a misnomer that is!—ply their trade is not an uplifting experience. If their presence should be coolly shrugged off as one more token of urban blight and the new morality, very well, *you* shrug it off. I am offended, but my heart breaks for the girls reduced to such commerce and for the vanished New York of soft summer nights when some unseen watchman kept the city safe.

The girls I saw working Madison Avenue in their little hot pants were brazen and swift. The pair preceding us closed in on a nice, neat middle-aged man carrying a briefcase. Even to an unpracticed eye he didn't seem a likely "John." It took him the space of a block to persuade the girls that they'd tapped the wrong chap.

People who go out in the evening more than I do say that East Side prostitutes usually cruise in open cars. Sometimes they work in pairs on Park Avenue. A well-known artist who was accosted recently ordered the girls in sharp tones to be gone. In a trice something hot and searing struck the side of his face. Acid. It missed his eyes, but he will have scars.

There have been other stories, some reported in the papers, of men being attacked by the rougher sort of prostitute who works the West Side. A visiting Italian businessman was stabbed to death a few blocks from the Hilton Hotel. A West German diplomat was badly beaten. These are ugly stories. But one wonders if this form of street crime will diminish if the mayor's task force, now studying the feasibility of legalized prostitution in New York, recommends municipal brothels with registered inspected girls. The experiences of other cities suggest that this is not the answer.

The reasoning behind legalized prostitution would seem to be economic as well as social. If off-track betting fulfills its promise, the city will be taking in $5,000,000 a month by next June. By 1973, according to one estimate, legalized betting should enrich the city by $75,000,000 a year.

According to Dr. Charles Winick, a sociologist who has made a long study of prostitution, legal brothels do not reduce the streetwalking and other forms of illegal prostitution. Hamburg, for example, set up an Eros Center staffed with 136 girls. Outside the center, the city's 4,700 known prostitutes continued their trade.

In Nevada almost anybody can open a brothel provided it's not on a business street or within 400 yards of a church or school. One town, Winnemucca, has 3,000 inhabitants and five brothels. "Police drive by every half-hour in case any customers get rowdy," reports Dr. Winick in his book *The Lively Commerce*. A local minister who denounced harlots lost his pulpit.

Neither in Nevada nor any other spot, Dr. Winick told me, has legal prostitution been a boon to the community. Moreover, when the oldest profession is held in check, there is a falling off in other crimes.

And that reminds me of an article I read a few years ago stating that legalized gambling brought about a significant increase in the kind of disturbance entered in the police blotter as "family trouble." Welfare clients tend to gamble. When they lose, they beat their wives, abuse their children and engage in tavern brawls. Maybe the first duty of a city is to protect people from their natural vices.

Modern poetry has never been my dish of tea. Too fuzzy, too freaky, too disrespectful of the traditions I prefer to honor. But my occasional encounters with the jagged rhythms and ugly ellipses of modern verse have left one searing impression. Today's poets are not world losers and world forsakers. They are critics of life. And that is good.

They see life, Lord love them, in terms of ravaged beauty, broken lives and justice denied. They make poems to the memory of clean water, to Che Guevara, to the black mother kissing the wounds of her rat-bitten baby. They are not concerned, as Eliot was, with objective correlatives and the damp souls of housemaids. They would sooner bite hot iron than gloss a line to make it pretty.

Poets are valuable because they carry a keener sense of man's frailty—and immortality—than do the rest of us. They see deeper, wider, farther. Against hope, they believe in hope. When we cease to listen to our poets we'll grow deaf to our own inner music.

This is why one is always pleased to see poets on page one. And Yevgeny Yevtushenko was there in the New York *Times* recently reminding Soviet society, and ours, that repression has no place in literature or in government. The Stalin style must never return, he said. And poets now have an obligation to attack the forbidden and to face up to reality, past and present.

Yevtushenko was leading up to a dramatic point. It is as relative to our world as to his. It should already be preying upon the conscience of America.

"The day is coming," the poet told a congress of Soviet writers, "when our sons and daughters will grow up and ask us, 'Papa . . . what were you doing at this time?' "

We must prepare ahead, he warned, for that sacred and difficult moment.

Yevtushenko was alluding to the questions young people are beginning to ask their parents about the tortures, the purges, the hate and fear that marked the long reign of Stalin. "Did you not resist the tyranny, Papa?" one hears wide-eyed Dmitri, a schoolboy, asking. "What did you do when your friends were shot?"

That sacred and difficult moment is coming for all of us.

Presto, it's 1990 and there sits a tousled lad of fifteen, face solemn and perplexed under his student lamp. His history book is open to the Savage Sixties. "What really happened in Vietnam, Dad?" he wants to know. "Did we really kill all those civilians? And what did we win, anyway?"

The answers to such questions will, if given honestly, lack even the irony of Old Kaspar's replies to Little Peterkin. In Southey's poem, you will recall, a small boy turned up a polished skull in the garden. "Now tell us about the war," he demands, "and what they killed each other for."

Old Kaspar remembers the country being wasted far and wide and a thousand bodies rotting in the sun. But he cannot tell who won. He can only repeat, over and over, " 'Twas a famous victory."

At least, that was how the battle of Blenheim took its place in history. The Vietnam War will never be shrouded by the false colors of patriotic legend. The blood and the horror cannot be washed away. Our shame is already recorded in the history books of many nations.

And what was papa doing at the time?

If he marched in peace demonstrations, joined the GI coffee-house movement or registered as a conscientious objector, his son may regard him with greater respect than if he did his duty in Vietnam. For Vietnam will always conjure up massacred civilians, defoliated farms, napalmed babies and an army of sadists high on drugs.

That there have been decent men caught up in this war, men of high courage and a sense of mission, are truths history will also record. But such facts fade before the stark atrocities and the coldhearted duplicity of the government that ran the war.

For too long we have had a government that has gone its bloody way in contempt of the will of the people. We have allowed undue power and wealth to accumulate in the wrong hands. And we have bent a too-slavish knee in the direction of that power.

"Man is a toad-eating animal," wrote William Hazlitt. "The

foulest idols are those which are approached with the greatest awe. . . . For one tyrant there are a thousand ready slaves."

We should all be Jacobins, Hazlitt suggests, hating tyrants as fiercely as tyrants hate liberty. The tyranny of the Pentagon, the tyranny of John Mitchell's Justice Department, the tyranny of the policeman drunk with a little authority—let these be the targets of our passion.

"Papa . . . what were you doing at this time?" How blessed the man who can say: "I was fighting for liberty . . . at home. I stirred others to fight. We tried, we cared. And we had a few famous victories."

Anybody for ox-cheek soup? Or a nice bowl of hotchpotch? How long since you've tasted cock-a-leekie or pishpash?

With botulism in the news and some potentially lethal cases of Campbell's soup still at large, I'm for ox-cheek soup and any other kind you simmer and stew on the back burner. In this age one expects to live dangerously—but not at table, thank you. There are lovelier ways to die.

By way of true confession, I'll admit to having used Campbell's consommé in sauces and casseroles for years. It has a fine, robust flavor. It's delicious chilled with a few drops of sherry and a touch of grated lemon peel. As steady fare, however, I find canned soups unappetizing. They're at once too sweet and too salty. And I always imagine I'm tasting globs of the lactic acid, the caramel coloring and other treats we never found in the hotchpotch.

That suspect chicken-vegetable mixture (brewed in a 230,000-can batch!) sounds particularly nasty. If any blend had to be chock-full of botulin, this soup deserves it. And I write not as a foe of the canning industry but as a connoisseur of soups. Out of the Campbell and Bon Vivant calamities may come a positive good: delicious homemade soup for dinner.

The ox-cheek broth cited above can't be found in just any old cookbook. I've never made it, but simply reading the recipe cheers me on a glum day. It's in a tattered old cookery book published in 1799 and picked up for ten shillings at a bookshop in Manchester, England. Naturally, the type is set with that dear, funny long *S* which looks exactly like a modern *f.*

Thus, we read: "Break the bone of an ox-cheek and wafh it in many waters. . . . Throw in a little falt to fetch out the flime . . . and lay the cheek-fide down in the ftewpan. . . ."

If ox-cheek soup is not your fancy, I might just send you *The English Housekeeper*'s recipe for a ftew of ox-palates. On the other hand, I may just save it for my own cookery book.

Because we rejoice so much in progress, it is always assumed that our forebears had a terrible time keeping body and soul together. No frozen food, no ready mixes, no tinned soups. But they managed. Their cookbooks suggest that they set a hearty table. As soon as the meat "went off," they threw it out or they fed it to the dogs. Eggs and cream were in everything. Fish came fresh from the stream, untainted by enzyme detergents. People had no pesticide worries then, and somehow they put up with the pests, perhaps the lesser evil.

Of course nobody of sound mind would exchange today's convenience and comfort for the drudgery of yesteryear. But why can't we keep the comfort and salvage the good home cooking? To smell bread baking in your own house is to know paradise.

And while we're whipping up flummeries and syllabubs and boiling two calf's feet for a bit of jelly (on second thought, we needn't go *that* far), we should all be making a great fuss over the inadequacy of our consumer laws.

The U.S. Public Health Service reported a few years ago that 1,000,000 cases of food poisoning occur annually. Many doctors call this figure conservative. Epidemics of food poisoning have doubled since 1952. Two varieties, salmonella and staphylococcus, are extremely virulent.

For too many years the food lobby has determined public policy on food. Every consumer protection bill to date has been emasculated before passage by the food packagers.

Additives are the chemicals that preserve, tint, coagulate and guarantee you that subtle store-bought taste. There is some evidence that such additives can cause heart disease, birth defects and digestive problems. Additives are particularly vicious in baby foods. Despite the outraged cries of young mothers, most of the additives remain.

The food industry is the largest retail business in America. Total sales stood at $125 billion in 1969. In many respects, the industry serves us well. But its concern with profit has consistently overcome its concern with the consumer's health. A few conglomerate companies control the entire food spectrum.

The canners, Ralph Nader says, have steadfastly opposed disclosing full information of contents on labels. As a result, "nearly two-thirds of all chemicals now placed in foods do not appear on the labels." One wonders, could some of these chemicals combine to make the canned soup (or whatever) a more hospitable culture for bacteria?

Perhaps the answer is no. I'm an unfrocked chemist at best. But they're the nicest kind, if you like the taste of honest food.

All of us at times economize in the wrong places. We feel virtuous, but the virtue never fails to cost us dearly.

A tense, upward-striving young man buys a gaudy new car and gives up the vacation he desperately needs. A month later he is in the hospital. "Utter exhaustion," says his doctor. "Needs a vacation immediately."

A working girl pinches pennies by paring her food budget. Less protein and fancy fruit, she decides, more pasta. It's uncanny how quickly she sees results: more dollars in her savings account, also an extra inch in the flitch, splotchy skin and chronic fatigue. She visits her doctor. Then she buys an expensive assortment of iron and vitamin pills. The pinched pennies are gone. She feels damaged—and for a while she is.

A foolish economy—*that's* the hobgoblin of little minds. Economy that destroys is no economy at all. True economy, said Shaw, is the art of making the most of life. He was right. Some individuals—and a few institutions—master this art. Governments, it seems, never do. When governments pinch pennies they always leave bruises on the most vulnerable people.

At the moment, New York, like so many great cities, is pinching pennies by curtailing cultural life. Libraries and museums are operating on a part-time schedule. Art exhibitions are being cut back, certain library and art gallery wings may close permanently. Where admission once was free, a ticket will now cost a dollar. This sort of economy lays a lash upon the city's most vulnerable residents—teachers, students, intellectuals and artists. Above all these, it punishes children.

Unless the city juggles its funds—a device not unheard of at City Hall—the New York Public Library will be forced to close its science and technology division and its research library of the performing arts. The library has a $1,200,000 deficit. It has already trimmed its services to the minimum and begun closing its doors on weekends. Once open seventy-five hours a week, the city's branch libraries are now open forty. This is a shame and a disgrace.

A city that does not value its books and its arts is a city the watchman keepeth in vain. The barbarians are no longer at the gates, they're at City Hall.

We all know, without being reminded, that the city is hard-pressed for funds. But if Mayor Lindsay can find $24,000,000 for the remodeling of Yankee Stadium, he surely can find $1,200,000 to cover the public library's current deficit. Are baseball fans more precious than people who read books and visit picture galleries? If they are, then we're on our way back to the Dark Ages. May the Lord preserve us a few monks to guard the treasures.

People who know more about sports than I do—that's any smart kid of ten or twelve—say that baseball is a dying game. Rebuilding Yankee Stadium in pink marble with an astrodome won't revive a long-gone pastime. Some other game, I have no doubt, will rise to replace baseball. But there can be no replacement in a civilized society for books and pictures. If our young people lose the habit of visiting libraries and museums, they will grow up unfinished, deprived citizens, and the city will be the poorer.

Under optimum conditions, life in New York is brutal, abrasive and mean. Works of art are a comfort in such adversity. Access to books, by any decent scale of values, is more vital than access to sports.

As a cultivated man, Mayor John Lindsay has always taken a benevolent interest in the city's cultural life. But to place Yankee Stadium above New York's great galleries and museums is to place himself alongside that boorish English king who called *The Decline and Fall of the Roman Empire* "another damned thick square book." He capped this with the immortal line, "Scribble, scribble, scribble! Eh, Mr. Gibbon?"

Randall Jarrell, a fine poet who died tragically a few years ago, left some touching lines on "Children Selecting Books in a Library." He was moved by "the child's head, bent to the book-covered shelves." He noted the child's pace—"slow and sidelong and food-gathering"—among the books. A true and lovely figure of speech.

His final advice: "Read meanwhile . . . hunt among the shelves, as dogs do grasses/ And find one cure for Everychild's diseases/ Beginning: Once upon a time there was. . . ."

There's a doctor down in Texas who predicts that man may one day live to be 200—even 300—years old. I'm not sure the idea has charm.

Still, Dr. C. W. Hall, a dreamy chap who directs the artificial organs program of the Southwest Research Institute, looks ahead to the day when we'll be celebrating 175th wedding anniversaries and wishing our youngest grandson would settle down now that he's well past 100.

Old age, assuming we're all going to live 200 years, won't start until we're at least 165 and, presumably, eligible for Social Security. This also means we can postpone our entry into a nursing home until we're getting on toward 170. And having just read Ralph Nader's new report on how America cares for its aged, no delay in entering a nursing home can be quite long enough.

It is said that any civilization can be judged by the way it cares for its elderly. By that standard, we are a land of brutes and barbarians. The Eskimos, putting the old folks out to die on an ice floe, were probably more humane.

It seems that all the inequities of life bear down hardest on the elderly. In *Old Age: The Last Segregation*, Nader points them out. "Consumer fraud, inflation, fixed pensions, street crime, absence of mass transit, spiraling rents and housing costs, swelling medical and drug bills and the virtual end of the extended family unit. . . ."

And you want to live to be 200? Listen to what life is like in the old folks' home.

Another study of nursing homes says that 25 percent of the inmates die during their first three months of residency. In such cases, one may regard death as an almost deliberate act of will, a release from the agony of bad food, thieving attendants and indignities too intimate, too horrible even to describe.

In our obsession with youth and progress, we have allowed nursing homes to become dumping grounds for the aged and infirm. Three-quarters of these homes, the Nader report states, do not meet government standards. Nevertheless, the government endows them with $1 billion a year. Since 90 percent of the homes are privately owned, somebody is making a wicked profit in operating these foul way stations to death.

This most heartbreaking of all the Nader reports was researched and compiled by a group of college girls, six of them not long out of Miss Porter's School in Farmington. To gain firsthand knowledge of how the aged are treated, these gently bred young ladies went to work in nursing homes. They were keen-eyed, easily shocked and kept careful diaries.

Among the diary items: "The colonel tried to tip me 25 cents for taking him to the bathroom."

The girls also noted that the food was abominable, the nurses often brutal and that the physical therapist, due every Tuesday, never came.

"There does not seem to be any rehabilitation program," says another diary entry. "One man, totally bedridden, never even wore clothes. He sat up to eat and then went right back to bed."

For the elderly who are accustomed to bathing every day and wearing clean clothes, nursing homes offer the final indignity—a bath once a week and steady attrition of their wardrobes by thieving attendants and laundries with a bad habit of "losing" half the garments sent.

Another book, *Home Life*, tells a touching story of how important it is for the aged to be clothed and ambulatory. The hospital wings have a way of removing all tokens of a patient's mobile life. Shoes are taken and all clothing goes to a storeroom. Authors Dorothy Rabinowitz and Yedida Nielsen offer this pitiful story:

> One old man who had somehow kept hold of some of his clothes
> put them on each morning over his pajamas. As soon as he was

dressed he left his bed. Having nowhere else to go, he stood for hours against the wall of the reception room outside his ward. Each day he reported there after the morning meal, dressed with tie around his bare neck and jacket over pajamas, hat on his head and cane in hand. He leaned against the wall observing traffic . . . like a man waiting for a bus.

In most homes there are no activities beyond watching TV. Patients are given massive doses of tranquilizers ("Cheaper than hiring nurses," as the administrators say). Food poisoning is not uncommon, since the homes buy substandard poultry and meat, as well as damaged canned goods. There are nurses and aides who slap and push patients, tie them to their beds and steal their meager possessions when they fall into their drugged sleep. Virtually all nursing homes, says the Nader report, are guilty of pharmaceutical overkill.

The remedy: More stringent codes, more inspectors, withholding of funds from homes that do not comply. Since the director sets the tone for the home he should be licensed—after passing strict examinations.

Do you suffer from futuriasis?

It's the scourge of the '70's, the *Wall Street Journal* recently advised us, and everybody from Henry Kissinger to your scowling cab driver has a touch of it. The primary symptom would seem to be a tearing anxiety about what tomorrow will bring.

In short, are we nearer famine, pestilence and horrible death than we dare to think? If so, what can we do about it—now?

For young people the answer to anxiety is a rejection of the society they see as responsible for the problems. Back to nature, back to the land, back to the simple life, helped by hash, casual sex and a regular remittance from the anxious folks back home in suburbia.

Interestingly, a good many older people are also fleeing the automated, polluted, bedeviled world we have evolved in the hope of sweetening life for our posterity. A new culture, a life-style that recalls our pioneer heritage, is putting down deep roots.

It may look preposterous to city folk—all that churning and weaving and stomping on grapes—but it has caught the fancy of people who have been too long in city pent. Only problem is that going back to the land requires cunning and stamina and skills one cannot learn anywhere but on the land—the hard way.

The intensity of this back-to-nature movement was borne in upon me yesterday as I held the Whole Earth in my hands. Specifically, *The Last Whole Earth Catalog*. It weighs almost as much as the Manhattan telephone book. And it contains the pure culture of America's disenchantment with twentieth-century progress and all its nagging worry about the future.

A page devoted to shortwave radio equipment features this testimonial to "ham operators." It begins ominously: "When this country falls apart, all that portable equipment and electronics knowledge and all those established nets are going to be *the* tools to stay alive and co-ordinate with your friends."

The Last Whole Earth Catalog tells you where to buy all the things that a bourgeois city dweller hardly knew existed. You can order a sack of whole wheat from Deaf Smith County, Texas, for only $4. You can raise your own barley and make Tibetan barley bread (recipe offered by catalog). There are instructions for making adobe brick out of powdered molasses and bunker oil. There are instructions for capturing a colony of bees. ("Smear honey on the landing strip.") And, this being the New Culture, there are instructions for getting the most out of your hashish pipe and getting over a bum trip on LSD.

One learns a great deal browsing through the 448 pages of *The Last Whole Earth*. ("Last" because the publisher had a small nervous breakdown and is bored with the whole earth and all its fruits.) I never knew that when buying geese—"Genuine Canadian honkers!"—one must buy a pair because they mate for life. I never knew that you could make scented candles in your own kitchen and a real geodesic dome in your own backyard. Reading the catalog makes city life seem rather pallid. How do you know you're a Real Person until you've mastered gracious living in a tree house?

An important feature of the Whole Earth book is a compendium of all the important how-to books for amateur homesteaders. *The Impoverished Student's Book of Cookery, Drinkery and Housekeepery* sounds like cutesy college humor, but it's full of sound advice. So, one imagines, are *The Bug Book, Simplified Carpentry Estimating, Creative Glass Blowing* and *How to Get by Without Money.*

Certain products carry testimonials from contented users. "I cured my warts with a Swiss army knife and voodoo," is a fair sample.

As editorial "filler," the catalog stuns us now and then with a slingshot of philosophy. "You don't have to take dope to do things," we're advised. And think about this: "Someday the world will be ready to follow any man who feels good." So ready now it scares you.

Do you see yourself as a damsel with a dulcimer? You can buy a lovely dulcimer strung on an oak frame for $200. Like to migrate to Alaska? First, write for *Jobs in Alaska,* Box 1565, Anchorage, Alaska. Enclose $2. Never mind packing your black tie.

Bargains are everywhere. Instructions for a do-it-yourself burial for $50 are set forth on page 225. The undertakers' lobby won't like it. That's its great charm.

You can order Vietnam combat boots for $9.95 and a snake bite kit for $3. If you'd like to dramatize the dangers of overpopulation, there are suggestions for holding a weekend "starve-in" in your town. "Persons with kidney trouble or other ailments should skip this token famine and wait for the real thing," says the catalog. Remember that.

Oh, it's a lovely strange book. Strange because it looks on certain pages like a relic from the past . . . and it's actually a manifesto for the future.

It's the tiny, tossed-away items in the papers that haunt me. The single sentences that lay bare a heart, a history, a way of life.

For three weeks now I have brooded over the disclosure that one of our astronauts, a recent moon voyager, has only five books in his home. *Five.* Not counting the telephone book.

"It's incredible . . . a house with five books," I murmured from deep inside the New York *Times.*

"Not incredible at all," said my realistic listener. "You heard those boys describe what's up there on the moon. They're *map* readers."

When you're that far from home, I expect it's nice to know how to read a map. Our astronauts are clever enough in the studies that will prosper their journeys into the cosmos. They've obviously read a great many training manuals. They know an igneous rock when they see one. But I'm persuaded that their vision of the moon, despite having been there, is infinitely poorer than that of men whose inward eye has beheld a thousand strange landscapes. Visions ranging from the fantasies of Hieronymus Bosch to Coleridge's Kubla Khan.

As someone once said—in quite another context—"And what should they know of England who only England know?" And what do they know of lunar mountains and dead seas who have traveled no realms of gold while sitting snug at home?

The astronauts, like too many of their fellow Americans, will never qualify for membership in the clerisy. And that's a pity. What's the good of being literate if one doesn't read books?

More of the Same

I love that fine archaic word "clerisy." It has been well defined by Robertson Davies, the Canadian critic and novelist. It refers, he says, to people "who read for pleasure and with some pretension of taste."

The clerisy does not include people who read how-to books and maps. Nor to those fastidious types who will read a book only if it's (1) a best seller, (2) dirty and (3) a gift from a friend who will insistently demand, "Howja like that book I gave you?"

Reading is an intensely personal pleasure. As the clerisy shrinks in size, we who read for pleasure find our delight diminished. There are too few to share our excitement in a new discovery or our disenchantment when an old favorite hits a clinker. I miss the world in which I came of age, where people exchanged books and offered strong opinions about them. A special joy goes out of novel reading, for example, when one is unable to say, "Oh, didn't you just love the part where. . . ."

As a reader, I miss the company of what a lending library lady used to call, with bloodcurdling archness, "the booksy folk." But as one of the booksy folk, I was pleased to discover that a new literary cult has sprung up. Its idol is Sylvia Plath, the brilliant poet and novelist who died by her own hand at thirty. She was not the sort of figure in life to inspire any but the objective admiration of critics and poetry lovers who understood her technique.

Sylvia, as the cultists call her, was a plain girl with two children, an estranged husband and few friends when she turned on the gas in 1964. Now she has taken her place alongside Katherine Mansfield, Virginia Woolf and other female writers who suffered greatly and died too soon.

Sylvia Plath's novel *The Bell Jar* seemed to me ill-formed, studiously smart but, in its final episodes, heartbreaking. At twenty Sylvia had attempted suicide. All the details are here, sharp as the razor blades she used to carry in her purse. Her description of mental illness throbs with a pain too deep for sound or foam. She makes you *feel* the electric shock treatment and hear the "whe-ee-ee-ee" shrilling through the air with a blue light.

"With each flash a great jolt drubbed me till I thought my

bones would break and the sap fly out of me like a split plant. I wondered what terrible thing it was that I had done."

In a recent issue of the *New American Review*, Sylvia's friend the poet who signs himself (infuriatingly) A. Alvarez describes Sylvia's last days in London. Clearly, she did not mean the final suicide try to succeed. She timed it to coincide with the arrival of a housemaid. But the maid could not get into her flat. She also left her doctor's name and number in clear view beside her body.

"Her calculations went wrong," writes A. Alvarez, "and she lost." Out of her mistake, he believes, the myth, the cult have grown.

"I don't think she would have found it much to her taste," this account goes on, "since it is a myth of the poet to be a sacrificial victim, offering herself up for the sake of her art."

One can weep for poor Sylvia Plath, so young and so gifted. But nobody has died in vain who inspires a great body of Americans to read a novel and poetry for pleasure, thus enrolling themselves in that special dying elite, the clerisy. An elite not likely to be graced—alas!—by an astronaut.

"Distrust," wrote Nietzsche, "all those in whom the desire to punish is strong."

Distrust the prison guards, swinging their "nigger sticks" as they saunter down the steel-barred corridors.

Distrust the warden who casts a prisoner into "the box"—a stripped, solitary cell—for minor infractions of petty rules.

Distrust the system that calls itself "correctional" when its function historically has been the systematic degradation of those entrusted to its care.

Finally, distrust the governor who coolly turns away when des-

perate men cry for help—turns away even when told that his
sudden appearance in the prison yard might save hundreds of
lives. A great fortune buys a man many treasures, but courage
and compassion are beyond purchase.

The tragic events at Attica State Prison are a bloody testament
to the shrewdness of old Nietzsche. It is never he who is without
sin who casts the first stone.

"All men would be tyrants if they but could," Abigail Adams
once wrote to John. In prisons and in politics, men can be and
are.

Our prison population is brutalized and dehumanized. When
the men under the lash can bear the pain no longer, we damn
them for "stirring up trouble." And the governor orders the
storm troopers loosed with guns and tear gas. It's barbarous! The
psychiatrists who say our sick society uses criminals, crying "Cru-
cify him!" to relieve our own inner guilts, are merely confirming
the wisdom of Nietzsche.

The entire prison system seems to be grounded in the worst
sort of mealy-mouthed hypocrisy. It begins with calling a grim,
maximum-security prison a "correctional facility" and the club-
swinging guards "security officers." It ends with a serious young
pathologist telling the press that he performed autopsies on the
dead hostages and that *all* had died of police bullet wounds, not
convict stabbings. Nine men, shot down in the name of the sover-
eign State of New York to preserve the perfect tranquillity of the
correctional facility.

If the insurrection at Attica has served no other purpose, it has
certainly separated the good guys from the bad. I do not refer
simply to those involved in the riot scene.

Of course, one will long remember certain TV images. The
grave concern of William Kunstler begging for a little more time.
The shattered look of columnist Tom Wicker as he left the
prison. And the stories of inmates who had saved the lives of hostages by covering them with their own bodies, thereby sacrificing
themselves.

But there are other memories less exalting to the human spirit.

Judge Samuel Liebowitz saying of convicts on *The David Frost Show*, "They're all a lot of psychopaths!" And David Susskind telling Dick Cavett that the "criminals" were not to be pitied and that they should have settled down calmly after the warden played a little taped speech promising reforms. Would David Susskind have settled down? Not bloody likely!

The men had had too many promises. They had negotiated peaceably as long as they could. Yesterday, at the Fortune Society, I read the manifesto issued by the Attica inmates in July. It was a deeply touching document.

"There is not a strike of any kind to protest these demands," this document stated. "We are trying to do this in a democratic fashion. We feel there is no need to dramatize our demands."

Eventually, of course, there was a terrible need. But the "observers" who kept the long prison vigil seem convinced that the final drama, bathing the stage in blood, could have been averted.

While visiting the Fortune Society—a struggling group dedicated to helping ex-convicts—I spoke with two young men recently discharged from Attica. One was Al Cruz, a soft-voiced Puerto Rican, quick, neat and well spoken. Talking with him, the thought came: "This man was surely loved as a child . . . what went wrong?" It was drugs, of course. Drugs, followed by armed robbery, followed by Attica.

What hurt most in prison? "The little things," said Al. Only one shower a week.

(Al worked in the metal shop where the thermometer climbed to 120.) He dreamed of showers. ("You just can't make a nice suds with the cold water in your cell.") It was the hot tea with the evening meal when every man thirsted for a cold drink. It was the $5.25-a-month allowance and the confiscation of a good part of the parcels sent from home.

Was there physical brutality? John (no last name because his new boss knows nothing of his record) joined us to describe how five guards delighted in beating the one prisoner they were "escorting" to solitary.

"But there's a new law now that says you have to have a mat-

248

tress in solitary," smiled John. "And now they let you read. It's a little better." It took a lot of outside pressure to bring about these modest reforms. But the major "crimes of punishment" go on, breaking human spirits, destroying men who might so easily be reclaimed.

The whole system is rotten, and if it isn't changed we'll have Attica riots all across the land.

Our tax laws, as we who bear them know, are written to punish the poor and pardon the rich. All concessions, all loopholes, all rebates are reserved for them as has. The working class pays a higher percentage of its earnings to Internal Revenue than the man whose mortal passage is cushioned by dividends, rents or the wheeling and dealing that brings in "capital gains."

Of all the inequities visited upon salaried workers, this one is the harshest. Someday one would like to see a Taxpayers Protective Association, with a militant membership of millions and spearheaded by someone like Ralph Nader. If the oil and gas lobbies can pressure Congress into maintaining the preposterous depletion allowance, a lobby of honest working citizens should be able to equalize the tax laws.

But until we achieve that citizens' lobby, Americans carrying particularly unjust burdens must "associate and demand." It's the only way. And it's the way we ceased being a put-upon British fief and became a free nation.

One group that's badly discriminated against is working mothers. Female voices are now being raised demanding that the working mother be allowed to deduct the cost of child care.

Agitation for such a law started several years ago but was opposed by the House Ways and Means Committee. Leading the opposition was a Congressman, now passed to his reward, who said that a tax break for working mothers would lead to extravagance and self-indulgence.

Why, asked the late Representative Noah Mason—a Republican, of course—should the government come to the aid of a woman who is working "to buy a $750 fur coat her husband can't afford?"

Why, indeed? Any Congressman who gives a churlish answer to that question should also tell us why 21 Americans with incomes in excess of $1,000,000 paid no income tax at all in 1968. And how about the 155 with incomes over $200,000 who also paid no tax? And how about the dandy tax breaks for people who clip coupons and collect rents?

There are extremely rich people in this country who pay less than 5 percent of their income in taxes. But there are 2,500,000 with incomes below $6,000 who pay 14 percent, a total of about $100,000,000 a year. Most of them, it is safe to assume, do not own $750 coats, be they cloth, fur or feathers.

It ought to shame our House of Representatives that we are the only industrialized nation in the world that does not underwrite some sort of day care for the children of working mothers.

A mother of three who earns, say, $87.50 a week frequently pays $27.50 to a part-time baby-sitter. Or a similar amount to a day-care center that must charge a small fee or close its doors.

To the fishy eye of a penny-pinching Congressman, baby-sitters and mothers' helpers are a frivolous indulgence. Not a legitimate deduction like the $40 "business lunch" for two that's a way of life on Madison Avenue.

Racing thoroughbred horses is a deductible expense. So is raising prize bulls. So is running a farm or a flower shop or an art gallery at a deliberate loss. But paying out a third of one's salary to a baby-sitter, because one cannot exist without the remaining two-thirds, is an illegitimate expense.

If you are a woman sitting all day in a straight-backed chair beside a metal desk, typing "Dear Sir" over and over (and wondering, "Is Johnny having his orange juice now?") you are nobody the House Ways and Means Committee is going to lose sleep over. Nor do most Senators care. After all, you're hardly in a position to contribute $50,000 to any legislator's campaign.

In a society whose basic decencies are being steadily eroded by social inequities, women are still denied status in the market-place. They are put down, precisely as blacks, former convicts and ex-mental patients are put down, whenever they try to better themselves.

Some people believe that Women's Liberation is going to solve these problems. It has the potential to do so but seems more likely to squander its substance in fighting for the right to drink in men's saloons, the right to pilot commercial planes and the right to flaunt the lesbianism that afflicts too many members.

No, the reform of our tax laws requires the pressure of all working citizens. And the time is long past due.

In sorrow the poor bring forth children. And in hunger and shame the children mature and multiply. Thus is the culture of poverty—not to mention the affliction of crime—passed on, generation after generation.

In recent years, a good many social planners have come around to the view, once considered heresy, that the cycle of poverty can be broken only by a radical intervention of the state in the rearing and shaping of the child.

A bill providing a vast program of health service and day care for both the welfare poor and the working poor has passed the House Education and Labor Committee. Its eventual effect would be a dramatic reduction in welfare costs, a significant drop in the crime rate and a great leap forward for our entire society.

The aim of this bill would be to do for the children of the poor those things their parents cannot do. One provision, opposed by the administration, guarantees free day-care and health services to families living below the "low living standard" level of $6,900 a year for an urban family of four. Like Head Start, this project would permit millions of small children to see, for the very first time, an orange, a doll, a doctor, dentist.

Unless the Neanderthals in the House defeat the bill or the President vetoes it, we shall see a new era unfolding. The possibilities are grand and tender and good for us all. Children who might have entered first grade stunted in growth, brains damaged from malnutrition and able to speak only a few basic phrases would instead be launched with almost as many blessings as children from prosperous homes.

Because the purse strings of Congress are in the hands of rural Southerners and conservatives, this enlightened legislation is bound to stir anguished debate. As we all remember from the famous hearings on hunger, there are small-minded, mean-spirited men in Congress who will fight to the death any measure that promises to lift the poor out of their wretchedness. This is particularly true if the poor happen to be black. Their reasoning, never acknowledged but tacitly understood, is simply, "Give those people free vittles and more schoolin' than they're fit for, and next thing you know they'll be votin' and holdin' office."

Exactly. And they'll be going off relief in Harlem and Watts and taking their place in the labor force. "And gettin' real uppity and takin' good jobs away from white folks," broods the small-town conservative from the North, a breed almost as obdurate and vicious as the rural Southerner. I say "almost" because the Yankee farmer's fear of the blacks is somewhat less irrational, if only by reason of geography.

To deny assistance to hungry, deprived children is not only barbarous, it's shortsighted, politically and financially.

When President Nixon asked about the cost of a food aid program, the budget bureau came up with a cost-benefit ratio. To give each poor child decent minimal nutrition would cost the government $475 per year. But it would cost $1,516 per year to care for that same child grown to the status of sickly welfare adult.

There is ample precedent, as well as an aching need, for the state to take over certain responsibilities in the rearing of poor children.

Traditionally, the state has always provided shelters and foster homes for children whose parents were dead, separated, mentally ill or otherwise unfit. The courts have not hesitated to place "difficult children" in reformatories and the notoriously misnamed training schools, where young boys are corrupted sexually by their elders and given apprentice training in crime.

Writing of Mississippi's Child Development Group, a project destroyed by that state's representatives, journalist and social worker Pat Watters said this: "What invariably impresses visitors is the confident bearing and bright-faced demeanor of the Head Start children. This miracle seems to have been wrought by no more than the application of undiluted 'progressive education,' a commentary on the mediocre norms of most Southern education."

John Kenneth Galbraith proposed a few years ago that the hundred lowest-income areas in the country be designated special education districts. Special efforts would be made in these areas to feed hungry children, to offer incentives for staying in school, to involve parents more directly in the teaching of their young.

Dr. Galbraith failed to win acceptance for the plan in 1963. Today the need is immeasurably more acute. But hopes are dim. We shall have to change the makeup of Congress before we can save our children.

P.S.: President Nixon vetoed the day-care bill. A few weeks later he endorsed a proposal for a space shuttle to the moon. Cost: $6.5 billion. Minimum.

In this business one gets used to being called names. The street argot of the far right no longer shocks: Commie dupe, nigger lover, bleeding heart and traitor, preceded by assorted adjectives all too nasty for tongue or pen. (*My* tongue, *my* pen, anyway.)

But recently there arrived in the mail a new epithet. "You're an ideology snob," said the square, neat script. "Like all liberals, you think that only *your* ideology can save the world."

The lady went on to list the action program she believes liberals are advocating. "Put all blacks on welfare, including prostitutes and addicts. Open the prison gates and let the criminals resume their murder and robbery and rape. . . . Impeach Nixon. . . . Downgrade our flag. . . . Turn Vietnam over to the Communists. . . ." And so on, four pages of hysterical nonsense.

One could write back to the lady explaining that no sensible person, least of all an "ideology snob," subscribes to any of the above notions. But it would be a foolish gesture. The conflicts between liberals and conservatives go deeper than most of us realize. We have different values concerning love, freedom, truth and the perfectibility of man.

The liberal looks at the world affirmatively, believing that man can be liberated and that governments can be humane. He is as opposed to repression of human souls as he is to suppression of news. He abhors hierarchies, harsh authority and the selective justice that punishes the poor and the black.

To those of us holding such views, the life around us confirms our judgment that repression, race prejudice and carefully maintained economic disparities have only worsened the suffering built into our system.

An ideology snob? Yes, I confess it, and that's not easy because

I'm already a food and wine snob, a grammar and diction snob, a monogrammed linen snob and a four-letter-words-are-not-permitted-in-this-house snob. It hardly leaves me time to be snobbish about my ideology.

In any American crisis, people tend to split apart and huddle under the thatch of their prejudices. This is why debate in the political arena is so rancorous. This is why a prison riot rends society in a particularly brutal way. We all fear the passions of those who do not share our prejudices.

It will take years of social planning—and enormous sacrifice—to bind up America's wounds. We have for too long denied ordinary men, particularly the alienated blue-collar class, a connection with the great issues of our time. The schools have failed to educate young people for participation in government. The media, particularly the backward press and radio of the Midwest and Deep South, have failed to inform. Thus, when a crisis comes too many Americans lack the knowledge and the capacity for critical thinking that will solve the problem.

This situation is worsened when the men who hold power move toward a policy of repression. The Nixon administration and, most dangerously, the Justice Department have added new sting to the backlash.

William Pfaff, a former editor of *Commonweal*, writes wisely of this problem in his book *Condemned to Freedom*.

"What is crucial is that the values of the governing elites remain democratic," he writes, ". . . that they remain constantly attentive to the fact that they are custodians of the easily shattered compact the people have made with one another—an agreement to live at peace with one another."

On the basis of its moral values, its response to poverty and injustice, it may be said that our governing elite hardly deserves the right to govern, let alone the status of elitism.

"Much is asked of the elite, intellectually and morally," Pfaff continues.

We should quickly add that much is asked, morally and intellectually, of the ordinary citizen in these times. Given a public horror such as the riot at Attica State Prison, the citizen's first offering should be his compassion for all the hapless souls involved.

Shocked by such a tragedy, citizens' groups should be forming everywhere demanding the reform of the entire penal system. It might be helpful if we instituted something like the English "prison visitor" system. Volunteers from the outside world should be permitted to come inside the walls to teach, counsel, bring books and records, conduct group therapy and, in general, prepare the prisoner for his eventual return to society.

Jails ought to be clean, decent and healthy, as well as secure. The prisoner should be shown how to rehabilitate himself. Penal discipline should be firm but fair. Aggressions should be channeled into useful work and study. Prisoners whose pathology suggests incurable viciousness should be segregated from the young, the intelligent, the salvageable. Above all, a "correctional facility" should correct.

If such an ideology is snobbish, so be it. Let's all be snobs together and save the world.

In the great cities of America, the long, dark night of the jungle has closed in.

We live, all of us, behind a symbolic barbed wire of "security precautions," but nobody feels secure. Nothing reassures us. Not the triple locks and chains, not the burglar alarm or the guard dog with the bared teeth and burning eyes.

There's no place to hide, and there's no guarantee you'll be alive tomorrow. You can forget about the revolver in the glove compartment and the mugging whistle in the handbag. Nothing helps. A man was safer in the unlit alleys of Hogarth's London when throats were cut as casually as slops were thrown from windows. It was the way of the world.

It hurts to remember that there once was a time, even in neighborhoods of low repute, when a citizen simply assumed the goodwill of his fellow men and walked unafraid at any hour. There was a time when a woman could safely walk abroad, armed only with her innocence and dignity.

One sighs for the lost grace of life, for the decencies that used to hold society together. Remember Montaigne's theory as to why his château was never robbed or pillaged? Read it now and envy the sixteenth-century seigneur.

"Perhaps the ease with which my house can be attacked," he wrote, "is one of the reasons why it has escaped the violence of our civil wars. . . . I made the conquest of my house cowardly and base. It is closed to no one who knocks. . . . I have no sentinels but the stars."

No sentinels but the stars were watching on West End Avenue when a young French student, here on a brief visit, was shot in the neck and paralyzed for life. Shot *after* he had handed over his wallet. (He has since died.)

It seems at times that we are no longer dealing with young hoodlums and thieves but with the criminally insane. We are living in the Age of Murder. More police with more guns is not the answer. The kind of violence we are now experiencing tells us that the mind and heart, the very blood cells of our society are sick. The institutions that hold civilization together are failing. Too many boys and girls are growing up savage, sadistic, choked with hate. Society fails them when they are small and vulnerable. Suddenly they are strong and swift, they have guns and knives. They even the score with society.

Besides the overt violence at every hand, we live in a climate of death wishes. Something perverse and bitter in people makes fantasies of death, sets traps for the unwary, thirsts for blood.

In recent months, a story has been going about wishing death upon Frank Sinatra. He has been reported ill with terminal cancer. In Memorial Hospital here in New York, in Los Angeles, in

New Haven. That he was recently seen in Athens dining with a pretty girl and feeling fine will come as a disappointment to all the devoted ghouls who would rather read that he'd just had his larynx removed and would never sing again.

It's impossible to contemplate the criminal climate of the inner city today without crying "Why?" Where did we go wrong? Why must we live in fear?

In a broad sense, one can say that the crime flourishes because poverty flourishes. We have failed to care for the aching, terrible needs of our poor, particularly our black poor. Congress has failed, our bureaucracy has failed, the capitalist system has failed. Such are the generalities, all subject to challenge.

What sort of people commit the crimes that make our streets unsafe? When the summer of love in Haight-Ashbury was followed by a summer of violence—with the beats and the bikers, the hippies and the hoodies—turning the once respectable area into a foul ghetto, a psychiatrist, Dr. Ernest Dernberg, made a clinical study of these youthful sociopaths. Most were seriously disturbed, he found, and had suffered severe damage in childhood. They had poor self-images and little sense of guilt. They built their self-esteem through drugs or acts of violence. Some could not be called runaways because they'd never had a home to run away from.

In the past ten years, child abuse has risen 500 percent. So has drug abuse. I've no statistics on street crime, but the rise must be enormous. If we cannot adapt our young—and most criminals are under twenty-five—to our society, must we alter society to suit the young? If so, the society is clearly doomed.

Perhaps Arthur Koestler is right. We are slipping down the evolutionary scale, back to the "old brain." The crocodile under our skulls, as he calls it, is becoming dominant. Koestler believes a mental stabilizer, a pill to restore reason, is the only answer. But who would administer the pill, once we developed it? And would the crocodile brains take it? Probably not.

More of the Same

"A bill," wrote Betty MacDonald in her memoir of the Depression, "is a thing that comes in a windowed envelope and causes men to pull in their lips and turn the oil burner down to 60 degrees and women to look shifty eyed and say, 'Someone must have been charging on my account.' "

Those of us who live on the social frontier between capitalism and disaster are familiar with windowed-envelope trauma. We can enumerate the little luxuries that have vanished from our lives. If the President's new economic game plan doesn't work, we can shortly begin enumerating the little necessities.

In August, we all hoped that the wage-price freeze might cushion hard times just enough to dull the hard edge of privation. Of course, nothing dramatic or even significant has resulted, though some splendid claims have been made by Treasury Secretary John Connally.

But hope springs eternal. Judgment is suspended for a while. It is only when the President faces the television cameras to make everything perfectly clear that doubt, like a sly gray rat, begins nibbling at the mind once more.

As the President was explaining to the nation, in his This-is-for-your-own-good voice, just what benefits would accrue from Phase 2 of his economic game plan, the thought kept intruding, "How long since Richard Nixon has lost sleep over a windowed envelope in the mail?"

Does the boy who weighed out the rice and beans in his father's grocery store ever glance at the "situations wanted" columns in the newspaper? Could some old, rusty chords in his being still be touched by the pride and hope—and, yes, the fear

—behind: "BOOKKEEPER, all phases. Bright, capable, nice appearance. Ten years with one company. Will relocate."

Does the solemn student who rose at dawn to drive a truck to the vegetable market understand that his survival in office is now threatened by millions of unemployed youths who can't even find a truck to drive?

If we succeed in cutting inflation by one-half, if we can somehow keep prices and wages under control while profits are maximized and dividends left strictly alone, why 1972 will be not a good but a "great year," Mr. Nixon promised.

A great year, we may deduce, because restoring a glow to the economy is bound to restore Richard Nixon's sagging prestige and reelect him. Thus the new game plan, Phase 2. Now we shall have what might be called "semivoluntary controls." We'll also have guidelines, directives, pay boards, compliance officers and a lot of screaming, raging confusion.

The President said he expects all good Americans to cooperate. He didn't add that cooperation, in this context, means sacrifice, restraint, honor and a boundless faith that all will be well in the best possible of worlds. Like most women, I'm fairly muddleheaded about economic theory. But I know a lot about landlords and car dealers and bankers—and Phase 2 may go down in history as a slight thaw followed by a major disaster.

Without impugning the patriotism of any single group, it simply doesn't seem likely that businessmen are going to lose money, deliberately and with good cheer, to help the President fight inflation. Salaried workers who have been promised raises aren't going to take kindly to the idea of appealing to a wage review board for an "adjustment."

Should the Nixon economy plan fail, the political consequences will be serious for the Republicans. Mr. Nixon will not be returned to office by men in bread lines, or even by that bookkeeper with the nice appearance who's willing to relocate. "In the poverty of the people," wrote Machiavelli, "is the destruction of the Prince."

When times are hard, it ought to be to our advantage to have a man in the White House who remembers the pinch of poverty. But the *nouveau riche* hate to look back. Spending one day in Whittier, California, trying to reconstruct Nixon's boyhood is "suffocating," wrote one of his biographers. Perhaps this is why he has indulged himself in what psychiatrists call therapeutic forgetting. Maybe he has even forgotten the $16,000 fund from well-wishers that almost lost him his place on the 1952 ticket.

There are economists among us who believe that the only solution to our endless cycle of inflation and unemployment will be a changeover to state capitalism. Michael Harrington, among others, has observed that modern capitalism, with its terrible inequities, is destroying the culture, morality and idealism that once made the country great. It's a thought to take your mind off windowed envelopes for a little while.

When the president of the New York City Board of Education suggests that children be assigned to classrooms according to their astrological signs, you begin to suspect that your tax dollars are producing a race of primitives. And someday, when it's their turn to educate, they will give academic credit for rain dancing, fertility rites and advanced witchcraft.

Not since that wild-eyed clergyman in Pennsylvania announced that the world would end on New Year's Eve, 1969, has any presumably educated person made a statement so fatuous as President Isaiah Robinson's pronouncement on the need to consider a child's horoscope in planning his education. One winces at the thought of a faculty meeting debating such questions as "Can a nine-year-old Libran with a reading block achieve literacy under a Gemini teacher?"

I choose the sign of Gemini for this hypothetical debate because the only astrology book I can find says that Geminis are nervous, neurotic perfectionists. The same ancient wisdom presumably lies under the statement that Taureans—that's me—run to fat and have a genius for handling money. Being chronically underweight and overdrawn, I can only find this hilarious. But it's not hilarious to think of this mumbo-jumbo setting standards for the education of small children.

Mr. Robinson's remarks on the value of astrology in public education bring to mind William Hazlitt's observation on the methods of certain professors whose aim is to make each pupil "as great a blockhead as himself."

Were the illiterate parents of a public school child to demand consideration of the child's birth sign in assigning his teachers, we'd try to be understanding. We'd explain that astrology was, at best, a pseudo-science, a myth devised by the ancients who could arrive at no other explanation for the whims of fate. But when a superintendent of schools takes horoscopes seriously, we are headed back to the caves.

To drive out superstition and replace it with reason is all but impossible. A panel of the most distinguished astronomers and mathematicians in the land could present an all-day demonstration, giving solid proof that astrology was rubbish . . . and it's doubtful that they would convince Isaiah Robinson or any other true believer. When a myth offers comfort, when it adds color and mystery to otherwise drab lives, naturally the myth dies hard.

Psychologists have noted that certain personalities are particularly prone to a belief in the occult. Rigid, authoritarian types, for example. And people with a touch of paranoia, who suspect that malign forces beyond their control are to blame for their "bad luck" or their character disorders. One might even go so far as to say that implicit faith in horoscopes or witchcraft or spiritualism is, in itself, a character disorder. It does not augur well for our society that faith in all this occult rubbish is steadily growing.

I have learned from experience, however, that it is futile to argue astrology with anyone who lives by what she (it's usually a she) fancies to be the irrefutable wisdom of the stargazers. Such beliefs are held viscerally, and they cannot be demolished by logic, reason or a statement from Dr. Harlow Shapley.

The same rigidity in attitude, the same desperate clinging to the myths that comfort may be observed in the realm of politics. You are never going to persuade a John Bircher that the Communist conspiracy in this country owes its menace largely to the propaganda of the FBI. You are never going to convince a hard-hat that one of the major defects in our system is that too many people like himself have been denied the education, the decent wage, the fair tax that should be his automatically in a democratic society. You'll never convince him that the Bill of Rights grants freedom of expression to all, including, in the words of Justice Oliver Wendell Holmes, "freedom for the thought we hate."

Because Americans hold their political convictions so passionately, we are probably crying after the wind when we ponder the effects of television news programs on the mass mind.

The audience that regularly watches TV news and documentaries is basically conservative, surveys show, and to judge from surveys of its reading habits, passive and incurious about the world. One recent survey of viewer response to news programs asked the question "Does the camera lie?" An appalling percentage said yes. Whatever is shown on the screen that does not conform to the a priori judgment of the viewer is rejected more often than not.

In his book *The Image Candidates*, Gene Wyckoff concluded that the "rational import" of what candidates for office said on TV had "very little influence" on the viewers' perception of his image. Minds had been made up in advance and thereby closed to persuasion. They know what's written in the stars.

Writers of fiction have a sweeter time than the rest of us. Their escape hatches never really close. They can slip in and out of reality as they please, smiling at imaginary conversation and forgetting to pay the milk bill.

Creative writers have the further advantage of being able to "work through" their anxieties—to use psychiatry's favorite phrase—by projecting them into a fictional setting. This, perhaps, is why topical novels provide such rich clues to what's bothering the national unconscious.

If you would sample the pure culture of America's current malaise, spend a weekend with some of the new novels, especially those with a political slant. The style may be shrill and commonplace—whoever said polemics had to be brilliant?—but John Doe's dark-of-the-night fears are all there . . . confirming your own.

A novel called *V.P.* will dazzle nobody with its wit and grace. But it will articulate the formless fears many people try to shout down each time they see the incumbent VP setting off on another tour.

Author George Merlis, who is on the staff of ABC News, gives us a Vice President who challenges the renomination of the President. He is able to do so because the country is in a crisis state. There's a small but costly war overseas, there are angry extremists, both left and right, making trouble at home. It all sounds hideously familiar. Then the VP hits upon a "pragmatic" solution.

"My scheme," says the VP, "does not call for turning our backs on those dropouts, those extremists. It calls for *re-educating* them and re-admitting them into society."

Yes, he concedes, you might say the reeducation would take place in concentration camps, "because these centers would *concentrate* society's problems within their fences." So much for effete snobs.

The Nazis, this fictional VP chuckles, gave concentration camps a bad name. But, "Let's look at it this way: What's wrong with society concentrating in one place all antisocial elements?"

Later in Mr. Merlis' novel we see the VP making public a secret report prepared for the President by one of the great foundations. It's on "the mechanism for suspending elections and ruling the government by executive decree."

One point in this emergency program reads: "Army Signal Corps personnel shall be utilized to operate all broadcast facilities. There will be no need to program separately for each television channel and each radio station, though it is recommended all be kept on the air . . . for information programming." So much for know-it-all commentators.

Then there's William Burroughs' book *The Wild Boys*, his most intelligible effort in several years. The time is "the uneasy spring of 1988," and police states have been set up everywhere under the guise of drug control. Adolescent guerrilla armies roam the earth, dousing ordinary citizens with gasoline, looting, killing, destroying.

Pure nightmare, this book, with touches of science fiction and comic book horror. Such sentences as this ultimately defeat Burroughs' purpose, which is to remind us how low we are sinking on humanity's scale. "Glider boys with bows and laser guns," we read, "roller skate boys . . . naked blowgun boys, long hair down their backs, slingshot boys, knife throwers, shaman boys who ride the wind"—these are the creatures who will level the planet and make dust of all our monuments and temples.

I confess I stopped reading *The Wild Boys* when I came to the "warrior ants," a vicious regiment "made up of boys who have lost both hands in battle." Their weapons, if you can bear it, "are screwed into their stumps." By comparison, Burroughs' bearded

Yippees who "rush down a street with hammers breaking every window" are jolly pranksters.

In the same period I have also read *Les Guerrières*, a savage fantasy about an army of Amazons with painted faces and painted legs intent on destroying men. A must for Women's Lib, this one. Author Monique Wittig is a rather special taste, like tattooed breasts or Germaine Greer. There is barbaric beauty and a fierce, driving genius in this book. There is also a great deal of paranoia. If you believe that man has "enslaved you by trickery" and dragged you into the dirt, then Mlle. Wittig is speaking to *you*.

Fashions in romance are ever changing, as we hardly need be told. But I wasn't really prepared for the romance of *Harold and Maude*, as set forth by Colin Higgins. Harold is nineteen, you see, and Maude is eighty. What happens? Well, if you must know, Harold falls in love with Maude, takes her to bed and the next day Maude dies. Happy.

On May 28, next year, a New York couple will celebrate their tenth wedding anniversary with a 1929 bottle of Mouton-Rothschild claret bought recently in London for $7,000. They'll be drinking it in clear violation of puritan America's unwritten sumptuary laws, and they may have terrible hangovers next day. But nobody at their anniversary dinner is likely to forget what sort of liquid refreshment was served.

Still, one may fairly question the wisdom of such an indulgent purchase.

Now, I've nothing against $7,000 wines, provided they're drunk in decent moderation. I'd also find it a novel experience to sip a lordly vintage and enjoy its tender glow without some cliché collector piping up, "It's a naïve domestic Burgundy without any breeding, but I think you'll be amused by its presumption."

We say that a lot around my house because we drink a lot of naïve domestic Burgundy. The line originally appeared in *The New Yorker* under a cartoon by James Thurber. Now it's enshrined in all the standard dictionaries of quotations. It has supplanted, in salon conversation, the question of Omar so cherished by the ruddy old topers in English novels. To wit: "I wonder what the vintners buy/ One half so precious as the goods they sell?"

Offhand, most of us could name a variety of goods—aye, treasures—we'd buy with $7,000, ranging from emerald earrings to tax-free bonds. But would we grow old fortified with the memory of a wine so rich, so dazzling that the earth, for a moment, moved beneath one's feet? Maybe not. Still, if one believes Ernest Hemingway, there are other ways of making the earth move.

In all the literature of wine there is no description of claret more precise, more exquisite than this one in a letter John Keats wrote to his brother in 1819. "I like claret," said the poet. "It fills one's mouth with a gushing freshness, then goes down cool and feverless—then you do not feel it quarreling with your liver. No, it is rather a peacemaker and lies as quiet as it did in the grape . . . and the more ethereal part of it mounts into the brain . . . not like a bully in a bad-house looking for his trull . . . but rather walks like Aladdin, about his enchanted palace, so gently you do not feel his step."

There. If that jeroboam of claret purchased at Sotheby's recently doesn't measure up to Keats' description—if, indeed, it has gone to vinegar—we trust Mr. Paul Manno, the purchaser, will complain to the auction gallery and to the Baron Rothschild. He could, one imagines, stop the baron in his tracks with the question I once heard a besotted American ask a waiter on a French ship: "Did you make this with your feet?"

But a man who can afford to pay $7,110.90 for a bottle of wine surely would not be so crude. Still, the thought persists: Did Mr. Manno (an art and antique dealer) get a guarantee with his purchase? Does Mouton-Rothschild '29 travel?

It's possible that Mr. Manno, however grandly he wished to proclaim his love for his wife, may have erred in permitting his public relations man to publicize this purchase. So hard are the times generally that austerity has become chic. We deplore flash and glitter among the rich; it suggests a callousness toward the poor, an insensitivity to the mood of the times.

But there is this salutary potential in the publicizing of Mr. Manno's gift to his wife. People who consider a predinner martini the only stimulant the digestion needs may now be persuaded to abandon gin for the pleasures of table wine. I daresay they'll be healthier for it.

Though wine drinking has risen sharply in recent years, due largely to the average American's zest for aping the customs of foreign lands, there are still millions of Americans who look upon wine every night with dinner as an unbecoming decadence.

As recently as ten years ago, when I used to write pieces on cooking and entertaining for women's magazines, there was a taboo against wine in recipes. Finally it was relaxed to the point where one could specify a dash of sherry in the sauce provided one added parenthetically "(lemon juice may be substituted)." Well, dammit, lemon juice shouldn't be substituted, as I was at pains to point out. But the editors knew their public better than I did. To this day, I still get temperance tracts in the mail from nice old ladies whenever I write about wine.

If the nice old ladies knew the truth, wine is the tonic, the life-enhancing elixir they should be drinking every night. "Take a little wine for thy stomach's sake," wrote Saint Paul. And he was, medically speaking, on solid ground. It's not just that wine maketh glad the heart of man. Wine stimulates the gastric juices, eases the pain of angina, provides iron, vitamin B and other minerals. Louis Pasteur said wine was a more healthful drink than milk, even pasteurized milk. Galen called wine "the nurse of old age."

I still think $7,000 is an outrageous price, even for a jeroboam of Mouton-Rothschild. But I'm in favor of any propaganda that introduces Americans to the rich, subtle pleasures of wine. Even a naïve domestic Burgundy is more civilized than a martini.

There was an ancient, barbarous horror in the photograph. The stance of the girl was older than the sod on which she stood. The picture will haunt us for many days because she was so slight, so limp; lashed to a pole, her head shorn, bowed, bloodied and tarred. Another victim of the current Irish "thrubble."

Martha Doherty is only nineteen. She was savaged by her own people because she was a "soldier's dolly." She loves a lad in the Royal Anglican Regiment, a unit in the despised army of occupation. It's treason in this time of civil commotion even to smile at a British soldier in Northern Ireland. But Martha Doherty has smiled and given her hand, and the good Lord knows what more, and despite the tar and the feathers and the bitter cries of the Bogsiders, Martha married Private John Larter, the enemy of her people.

Romantic Ireland's dead and gone, as Yeats was ever at pains to tell us. ("It's with O'Leary in the grave.") But the marriage of Martha and John suggests the kind of romance the Irish treasure in their lilting ballads. The bridegroom was described by his priest as "sick and worried but determined" and did wed his lass with the shaven head.

It hurts even to think about that wedding with the flowers and the incense and the bride in all her adorning—hairless under the wig and the veil. Because she is nineteen and in love, the ceremony may have washed away Martha Doherty's guilt and sorrow. The Irish have a rare gift for slipping out of dark moods and into laughing nonsense. It's one of their survival secrets.

But what about later? When she is "old and gray and full of sleep and nodding by the fire"—Yeats again—will the memory of black pitch on raw scalp, of brutish hands binding her to the pole still haunt the dreams of Martha Doherty Larter? Probably so. And there will be more girls tarred with the same brush, reviled and scorned in the bloodied streets.

From far across the water, the prolonged civil strife in Northern Ireland is cruel and stupid and exasperating. People with so rich a gift for living, people who know how to sweeten adversity and make moments of grandeur on a shilling or two *ought not* to be enmeshed in so much sorrow and ugliness.

But with the Irish, it seems, there's always a bit of "thrubble." One remembers the first Queen Elizabeth roaring her displeasure over Essex's failure to put down Tyrone's rebellion. (Essex captured one castle, then tried to make a deal with Tyrone.)

When the Puritans closed the theaters of England, one of the reasons adduced was the "unsettled condition" of Ireland.

Since Brian Boru, the Irish have shown themselves to be scrappers. I'm muddled about the origins of the present discontent, but my sympathies are with the Catholics. Any side on which the Reverend Ian Paisley fights establishes itself, in my mind, as wrong. Paisley has been called the George Wallace of Ulster, which may be too gentle a description. One's reflexes recoil from fundamentalist preachers, since the very term connotes bigotry, repression and irrational clinging to outworn dogma.

The Reverend Paisley strikes one as remarkably un-Irish, a kind of genetic sport. He attended Billy Graham's old school, Bob Jones University. This heavily endowed institution has a superb collection of Italian Renaissance paintings and a curriculum that seeks to stomp out science and logic along with the flesh and the devil.

I have never met anyone who attended Bob Jones University, but I once read a hilarious magazine piece by a man who had been kicked out of Bob Jones. His sin was this: When his prayer captain—that's right—came around for 11 P.M. bed check with his little flashlight, the author of this piece was not on his pillow, prayerfully asleep.

With their roistering ways, their quick wit and fine irreverence, the Irish—even the Protestants—must find the Reverend Paisley a great bore. One would hope he gets the kind of knockabout reception he deserves in the streets of Belfast. And how grandly the Irish can curse a man—or a cause or a nation or a cat that's suddenly got in the way.

H. V. Morton's lovely book *In Search of Ireland* captures the character of the people as perfectly as any I've ever read.

"The poet knocked at a door," goes one paragraph, "and before it opened he had time to curse the Celtic twilight, the Gaelic League, the Government, the Opposition and the Holy Roman Empire. He was in good form."

Blessed, lyrical, brooding, wonderful people! May the Lord soon deliver them from their "thrubbles." Meantime, I shall continue to weep silent tears for that battered bride, bald as an egg on her wedding night. This in Ireland where Yeats saw "A woman of so shining a loveliness/ That men threshed corn at midnight by a tress."

Vindication should be sweet. But one is always embarrassed to write, "Well, now, weren't we saying precisely *that* just the other day?"

That sort of thing always strikes me as a bit too smirky and self-preening. Nevertheless, I cannot help remembering all the scurrilous letters that came in last winter when I referred to the militants of Women's Lib as "castrating females." They wanted my head on a platter. They were so vexed and so anxious to proclaim the delights of their teeming beds that I was sorry I ever used that clinical phrase.

But recently my eye fell upon a newspaper headline: LINKS WOMEN'S LIB AND IMPOTENCE. In brief, doctors are reporting a significant rise in impotency among men. And the booted, braless girls on the barricades are being held responsible.

A normally aggressive male can stand up to the challenge of women who take karate lessons and spit out four-letter words to men who doff their hats in elevators. "But the more passive male eventually becomes impotent because of unconscious fear or hostility toward women," says Dr. B. Lyman Stewart of Los Angeles.

The melancholy fallout from female aggression gets further documentation from an article in a recent *Harper's Bazaar*. Dotson Rader writes in "The Feminization of the American Male" that authoritarian women are causing men to become passive and hostile.

"This hostility," he notes, "prevents a man from becoming whole and results in anti-social and self-destructive behavior."

I know little of Mr. Rader's background save that he's a freelance writer disenchanted with the radical movement. (One of his books is *I Ain't Marchin' Anymore*.) *Harper's Bazaar* establishes him as quirky and immature with one statement: "At 29 he is single and wants to be a cowboy actor."

Well, this would-be cowboy actor believes the American male could do with a lot of toughening. But he's as inconsistent in his way as some of the Women's Lib polemicists.

"What we must do is decrease the pressure on men to compete and master; increase their freedom of spontaneous action and healthy aggression; and end their captivity to women in the early years. . . ."

In short, women have emasculated men by demanding too much of them. It is enormously difficult, Mr. Rader says, "for young men even to survive manhood in the United States."

Student rebellion, crime, family abandonment, school and job failures are all, in Mr. Rader's view, the fault of castrating females.

It's a thesis stated in more scholarly fashion by Dr. Patricia Sexton, a sociologist, in her book *The Feminized Male*. The schools play a decisive role in taming the rough beast in every boy, she believes. Boys are rewarded for the passive, feminine qualities: obedience, conformity, neatness. Mr. Rader suggests that coeducation be deferred until the last year of high school. Both agree that we should have more male teachers. Women tend to force boys into attitudes of docility.

But mama is only half the problem, Mrs. Sexton reminds us. The other half is papa. The absentee father, the ineffectual father who says, "That's your mother's problem" and, of course, the brutal father against whom the dutiful son will take up arms if necessary all work against the boy's self-fulfillment as a man.

No doubt I shall be hearing from Women's Lib again, this time reminding me that impotency was a problem in our society long before Ti-Grace Atkinson denounced heterosexual love as demeaning to women. And there are elements in this masculine failure that have little to do with the current mode in "sexual politics."

Psychiatry stresses that impotency may be caused by man's primitive fear of being "damaged" by the all-devouring earth mother. It is also pointed out that impotency frequently has elements of simple revenge. So has female frigidity.

If men are damaged in their self-esteem, if they are made to feel responsible for all that ails womanhood today, naturally they are not going to fall easily into the role of tender, ardent lovers.

"Give the girls on the barricades another five years and there may be a parade up Fifth Avenue by the Men's Liberation Movement," we wrote last February. That may have been a rash statement then. Today I'm not so sure.

In one of Ionesco's odder comedies, a bickering young couple faced a rather novel problem. There was a corpse, of unknown origin, in their bedroom and he was growing longer every day. Added to that, poison mushrooms were sprouting nastily from the cracks in the walls. This was particularly upsetting to the wife who, for reasons I've forgotten, ran a switchboard in the living room. The only reassuring sound in the house was her gladsome cry, "I'm putting you through! I'm putting you through!"

One day the bedroom door burst open and out popped two enormous cadaverous feet. The feet grew, the mushrooms grew. The couple ultimately solved their problem by pulling the house down around them.

I think of this strange pair every time I look around my house at the stacks of books and magazines. They grow like fungus, and they keep popping out of cupboards like those cadaverous feet. From time to time I dispatch boxes of books to thrift shops, to the Merchant Seamen, to the Fortune Society, to hospitals. I send all fat novels to my sister in the country because she has now read *War and Peace* three times. Books are pressed into the hands of dinner guests. Books go home with the cleaning maid and the elevator man. If the house I live in isn't conversant with the best in modern literature, it's not because I haven't tried.

But this week, as books spilled from every chair, sofa and table, it struck me that my system was all wrong. I should be reading and cherishing more of the new books and clearing the shelves of the old. Did I, a nonbibliophile, really need three editions of *Moby Dick* and five of Thoreau's *Walden*?

No housewife can long resist a chore whose time has come. Accordingly, we are making, the cat and I, a clean sweep of the shelves. I remove the books, she dusts the empty space with her great Persian tail. We both feel virtuous in the manner of small-town librarians setting the stacks to rights.

For my part, I also feel a little sad. For weeding out one's bookshelves is coming face-to-face with one's yesterdays. Books are not simply the sum of the past but the sum of one's own private past. The old adage "Every age hath its book" is true in a deeply personal way. And it is the books of my green youth that stir my deepest sighs.

Here is my old tattered copy of *The Education of Henry Adams*, part of the college library I have never surrendered. In passing such undergraduate marginalia as "SNOB!" or "Awful prig!" I wonder if the Merchant Seamen would find an annotated *Henry Adams* comforting on a long voyage? (Surely they've all read *Moby Dick*.) I decide to keep Henry, as certain details of his life come floating back. His wife's suicide (with photographic chemicals) on a quiet Sunday afternoon. His terrible grief, his efforts to be jaunty on trips abroad with his two nieces.

Elizabeth Stevenson's biography of Adams stands next to the *Education*. And I am grateful, as never before, for my old bad habit of underlining whatever takes my fancy. The past few days have passed in rapture as I have read, steadily and at times incredulously, the passages marked long ago.

It's nice to know that Henry Adams found, after long grief, "a kind of rest in being at last really old, tired and ready for death."

Also marked is a note Adams wrote before his last trip abroad: "Of course, I expect two or three more paralytic strokes before autumn but I might as well have them in Europe as here. I am not made for Boston, Mass., and would rather go to heaven another way."

Here are the Holmes-Pollock letters, two volumes. By volume two both Justice Holmes and Sir Frederick Pollock were pushing ninety. But what spirit, what tough old minds! And Holmes, ever courtly, always closed his letters with "My love to Lady Pollock."

Here is a marked entry in a Pollock letter dated June 8, 1922. "I hope decent Americans understand that when Lloyd George asked W. Randolph Hearst to lunch he may have honestly thought to please the people of the United States by doing honor to an eminent American journalist: for his ignorance is enormous and his information very odd."

Another postscript from Pollock, 1927: "I told you, I think, I don't believe Sacco and Vanzetti's defense was honestly conducted in their interest—tho' I see no reason to think the jury was in fact prejudiced."

Here are the books of youth, books read "in the dead calm of ignorance and faith." Here are some of the novels—how quaint this seems—that startled me with their obscenities, and I was over twenty-one when I read them. Here is the best of Hemingway, a writer Mr. Justice Holmes didn't much fancy.

Here are the shelves of laughter, dear Ruth McKenney, Perelman, Ogden Nash, Betty MacDonald. And Will Cuppy who used to write me such funny letters. The seamen and the prisoners might love these books, too. But they'll have to wait until my will goes to probate. For the time being, the book stacks will have to go on growing—like that poor dead man's terrible feet.

Blame it on the gray morning skies outside my window. Or the bleak climate of the heart in those numbly automatic moments that precede the benison of hot coffee, the blast of vulgar cheer from the radio.

Anyway, there was the New York *Times* obituary page and on it the name of a woman I never met and then, before my eyes, a sudden stinging mist. And the thought: "She was so alive in my mind. She cannot be dead!"

Why do we mourn the passing of a person we have never known in the flesh? Perhaps because we have known him (or her) so intimately in spirit. Perhaps because the dead one's vision of life somehow coincided with and enlarged our own.

There are few authors who bring a lasting richness to our inner lives. But Nan Fairbrother was such an author. And the news of her death in London, at fifty-six, filled my bright kitchen with an aching sorrow.

Nan Fairbrother was a scholar with a sensuous, lyrical appreciation of life. She wrote five books, four of which repose on my shelves so dog-eared and underscored, so fringed with tiny strips of paper as to render them unfit for lending. And that is just as well. They are too intimately mine to withstand a journey out of the house.

Miss Fairbrother had a special genius for setting down the homely joys of country life. But each joy was filtered through a mind so richly stocked, so at home in the gardens and drawing rooms of the past that musings on bird song or compost were raised to high art.

Wearing her learning lightly as a flower, Nan Fairbrother wrote of ancient days and also of her husband, William, a London doctor, and her two boys, John and Peter. Her first book, *An English Year*, described her lonely ordeal as a war wife, making do in a chilly, rotting sixteenth-century farmhouse. It is a kind of commonplace book.

I open *An English Year* at random and read: "The spring has come suddenly as it does at the end of February, on some still evening after rain with the thrushes singing late."

"With the thrushes singing late"—so simple, so lovely. She was that sort of a writer.

"We long to be new-made and radiant in spring," she continues, "not from vanity, but from the need to make a suitable gesture to the immaculate season."

A few pages on she is writing of her small son's "Paul Kleeish drawings," of the proper way to tour the Louvre, of Baudelaire's women ("Dorothée, my favorite . . . I always feel she was cleaner than the rest") and of Oscar Wilde's young men. Then she cautions against judging great men by their private lives.

"For man can exist on three different planes, as an animal, as a human being and as an artist. But when we have decided where he belongs, his existence in the other categories becomes unimportant."

The shadow of the war makes *An English Year* a sad book, however beautiful and wise. Still, it is a finer work than its sequel, *A Cheerful Day*, in which Miss Fairbrother learns to love London, finding pleasure in the way ugly buildings become beautiful in the subtle, shifting light of English skies.

Of all her books, perhaps the one best conveying the pure essence of Fairbrother is *Men and Gardens*. Here is a history, a geography, a treatise on flowers, herbs, love and art. We move, in an airy, all-seeing fashion, from the crude vegetable plots of Saxon serfs to the stately landscapes of nineteenth-century topiary artists. We are shown, without pedantry, how gardens mirror the age, the manners, the morals, the hungers of the men who created them. It is a glorious stroll down a garden path 2,000 years long.

In her next to last book, *The House*, Nan Fairbrother described the joys and agonies of building that "little place in the country." The problems with drains and chimneys and workmen are familiar stuff. As always, it's the sudden excursion into richer realms that takes the fancy. Here are some underscored lines on falling in love:

"The promise is not in other people, it is in ourselves. Encounters are only intensified to love affairs by the force of our own vitality and that is not inexhaustible. . . . Falling in love is an act of creation by the lover . . . and to fall out of love is to die a little."

Miss Fairbrother's latest book, *New Lives, New Landscapes*, arrived from London a few months ago. It is a serious work on ecology, neither poetic nor profound. But it doesn't matter. The other books are there, glowing with one woman's exquisite vision of life. The vision can never die.

"What ails people nowadays, anyway?"

An old question, more terrifying in its implications every day. In an overindulged culture, the sons degenerate from the sire. Tradition molders, discipline declines and morals become a matter of jest. But in our society the degeneration verges on self-destruction.

The hideous damage done the John F. Kennedy Center for the Performing Arts illustrates my point. Tourists—a word that often seems interchangeable with "vandals"—have wreaked such havoc upon this handsome new memorial that the trustees have had to ask Congress for a $1,500,000 emergency appropriation to keep the center open.

According to one account, visitors have stolen pictures off the walls, snipped swatches out of draperies and carpets, stripped crystal chandeliers of their prisms, even pried faucets from bathroom basins.

Ashtrays, china, glassware and silver have been stolen in quantities from the center's restaurant. This suggests that the vandalism cannot be blamed—as it so often is—on rowdy black school children or adult delinquents from the ghetto.

The thieving habits of the prosperous are a troubling phenomenon of our time. C. P. Snow had some astute comments on the problem when he visited New York last year.

"The more affluent a society becomes," he noted, "the more sadistic violence seems to run loose. That's one of the bitter ironies."

The idle affluent tend to become bored at an early age, Lord Snow continued. In England, he said, "it is not the poor who have time to think up sadistic acts."

Tourists, who presumably know better, have stolen virtually everything "reachable and detachable" from the Kennedy Center. They've walked out with plants, posters, paintings, menus and the brass shields from electric outlets. In the appropriation center chairman Roger L. Stevens is seeking, the sum of $227,000 is earmarked for "security," meaning guards and policemen. With 20,000 visitors arriving in a single day (as they did the day after Thanksgiving), the amount may not be sufficient.

Exercising the greatest charity, one cannot call thieving tourists souvenir seekers. They are a new breed in America, irresponsible as apes. In all of them there seems to be a need to destroy beauty and order, to desecrate the shrines and pull down the pillars. The Goths descending upon Rome behaved this way. But they had an excuse: It was their first encounter with civilization.

Pilferage and vandalism cost this country $2 billion a year. Schools are now built without windows because youngsters consider it fine sport to hurl rocks through the plate glass. Each item you buy in a supermarket or a department store costs at least 5 percent more than it would if the stores were not subject to so much pilferage.

One hotel that used to accommodate "the better sort of people" now loses 20,000 towels and 475 Bibles every year. Street-corner telephone booths are rapidly becoming extinct. Vandals not only found a way to steal the coins, they also made off with the glass doors and the telephone books.

What underlies this destructive behavior?

Lord Snow blames the boredom of the affluent. Others say the stealing is done mostly by hostile blacks, resentful that the rich white folks have so much while they are starving on welfare. Drug addiction is also blamed, along with permissiveness, corrupt police, too little love at home and the worsening of relations between angry blacks and the authorities.

Overpopulation might be cited as a cause of vandalism. The abrasions of a crowded life can unsettle reason. We've too many people who cannot be absorbed into the economy. We've a seething, restless subculture that refuses to be educated, refuses to accept the old ethic of hard work and honesty. They see a world run by a smug Establishment and they want in, even if "in" means only a prism snatched from a glittering chandelier.

It is often said that we live in a state of unacknowledged civil war. There are hordes of Americans who, if left to follow their own instincts, would behave exactly as Nazi soldiers behaved in the countries they occupied. Some poison in the air, rising from the cruelties of life today, has invaded their minds.

Storm Jameson, in her superb autobiography *Journey from the North*, describes the behavior of Nazis quartered in the Polish National Museum. "Bored, the soldiers amused themselves by dressing up in the ancient costumes before tearing them to shreds, cut up the Gobelin tapestries to use as blankets, bayonetted the Egyptian mummies, fired with bows and arrows and revolvers at paintings until they hung in ribbons, used Limoges enamels of the 16th century as oven dishes, used and then smashed the old china and glass, pocketed the Greek, Roman and Byzantine coins, and left everywhere . . . those heaps of excrement which are the characteristic German gift to houses in every country they invade."

If visitors passing through the Kennedy Center can leave the great halls in a state of filth and near ruin, can you imagine what they would do if permitted to remain overnight unguarded?

The news that a Phobia Clinic is flourishing in Westchester hardly surprises us. If the state of the national psyche is a true index of need, there should be a phobia clinic in every block, open evenings like laundromats, delicatessens and those seedy storefronts with the beaded curtains and the discreet sign READER & ADVISER.

Never Go Anywhere Without a Pencil

Now, I happen to have been a Reader & Adviser for many years. That is to say, I read a lot and I freely advise anybody who'll pause in his mad folly and just Listen a Minute! That includes President Nixon, the Paris Peace conferees and the man who is supposed to be doing something about my kitchen linoleum.

All phobias are ridiculous and stupid—except to the person who has a phobia. The woman who is too terrified to ride to the second floor in an elevator pities her absurd friend who is terrified of cats. All of us who fancy ourselves phobia-free tend to clap our hands smartly in the presence of the sufferer and say, "Willpower, now! Just tell yourself it's all nonsense."

All phobias, the psychiatry books tell us, begin as free-floating anxieties which then become fixed on one object or situation. The phobia can be dispelled only when the poor soul who's got it understands what lies behind his fear.

I once had a friend whose phobia was escalators. She walked, rode the elevators or stayed firmly on the ground floor. Escalators terrified her, she said, because the mechanism propelling them was invisible. Also, the ascending motion made her dizzy.

Interestingly, this girl who cowered before the escalator once flew through a blizzard in a Piper Cub. She saw no peril in a single-engine plane whose pilot carried a flask and was known to have the Hell's Angel approach to aeronautics. Who knows, she might have conquered her escalator fear had this daring chap consented to pilot her up to the second floor of Bloomingdale's.

In this day of botulism and mercury-poisoned fish, it was fated that Americans would develop food phobias. Health foods are a billion-dollar industry now. What's often overlooked is that these natural, untainted foods with all their locked-in goodness often spoil quickly for the simple reason that they contain none of that nasty spoilage-deterrent. Let the food faddist beware.

A brilliant and estimable woman used to visit my house frequently, bringing with her the most tiresome phobia of all: a fear of germs. This woman drove her husband and children mad with her compulsive scrubbing. Her husband claimed to have origi-

282

nated that old complaint, "You get up in the night for five minutes and when you come back she has changed the sheets and laid out clean pajamas."

We tried, with many a jest, to deter this lady from her all-out germ warfare. She was not amused by my imitation of Lady Macbeth crying, "Out, damned spot!" She was not amused when her husband gave her a beautifully wrapped can of Dutch Cleanser for Christmas. She regularly fired maids because they demurred at shampooing the velvet coat hangers or ironing the dust cloths.

I've always had a special liking for Henny Youngman's mother-in-law who was so tidy she put clean paper under the cuckoo clock every morning. But patience with my germ-phobic friend finally snapped when she used three guest towels in the course of a one-hour visit.

"This has to stop," I murmured, handing her a psychiatric text on phobias and compulsions. I suggested she might like to take it home and study it. She did. Later she told me that "all that nonsense about guilt and toilet-training and compulsive neuroses" didn't apply to her because the case histories in the book dealt with people who are mentally ill. And she, of course, was a heigh-ho, average, normal female except that all the perfumes of Arabia couldn't have sweetened those little hands.

Phobias in our time reflect the tensions of a troubled world. People who have always been terrified of flying are more so now that skyjackers are directing planes to Cuba, Cairo and other stops not on one's ticket. A psychiatrist, Dr. David Hubbard, has made an intensive study of skyjackers and says they are paranoid schizophrenics. Instead of two sky marshals on every plane we probably should have a psychiatrist and a male nurse.

There are phobias behind many of our social failures. It's a racist phobia that makes middle-class residents howl in protest when a low-cost housing project goes up in their neighborhood. It's a youth phobia that turns college-town residents against students. It's a poverty phobia that makes each one of us uneasy about the Nixon price freeze. Mass phobias can be just as destructive as private ones. Maybe we all need to visit the phobia clinic.

Americans are great holiday folk, always blowing out candles, marching in parades and saluting the flag. Besides honoring our noble dead by closing banks and schools, we issue calendars noting such transcendental events as the passage of the Mann Act (June 25, 1910) and the entry of Joan of Arc into Orléans (April 29, 1429). In case you're planning to transport a blonde or crown a prince, there now are two auspicious dates to bear in mind.

The date books in my house are nothing if not complete. We've even got a calendar that makes fun of all other calendars by reminding us that it's Neat Feet Week or Belt a Bartender Day. Also listed are Motivate a Mouse Day and—a time of holy obligation—Straighten Someone Out Day.

Journalists tend to mark this last occasion several times a year. Still, our work is never done.

What sets me to brooding over this mock commemorative business is a growing conviction that Americans, especially young people, have become too detached from the roots that nourish us all. In losing their sense of historical identity, they are forfeiting a certain pride, a steadiness in the face of adversity. A society that marks National Pickle Week is a society that tends to forget the true meaning of the Fourth of July.

This is not a plea for more flag-waving (we've quite enough of that and most of it by Pickle Week patriots). Nor is it a plea for more TV drama about young Abe Lincoln splitting rails and George Washington chopping down that famous cherry tree. In a mature nation the hard facts should be as familiar as the myth. Professional patriots, however, rarely look behind the myths.

284

Watching a recent CBS report on the young Michigan banker and his upward-striving family, the thought struck me that the children, so immured in their "advantages," were ignorant as coyotes.

It's easy to run through the litany of clichés about the grubby materialism of too many Americans. But the malaise afflicting us all would be somewhat eased were we not so rootless—and so disdainful of such roots as exist. Shoddy values, yes. But how now are we ever to restore to young cynics the sense of an heroic American past?

Traveling through France one sees in village after village commemorative stones and plaques whose inscriptions might as well be dripping blood. *"Aux Martyrs de la Barbarie Allemande"* is a common phrase, followed by the name of each citizen killed by German "barbarism."

Another phrase that halts travelers says simply, *"Passant, incline-toi, souviens-toi."* In passing, bow and remember. One does, always.

In the American South, a traveler also feels this aching, proud sense of dead heroes all around, of guns but lately stilled, of a woman alone in a pillared house fingering the leaves of a ghostly soldier's journal.

I once read of an English village whose High Street had a certain rise alongside a crumbling wall at which point old men often made the sign of the cross. If a foreigner asked a villager "Why?" the answer was a rambling tale about a knight who fell among assassins as he was hastening to the Holy Land. Now he lies buried under the slight rise in the walk.

Centuries later the village is having a kind of restoration. Suburban renewal, if you will. The road is widened, the wall demolished and lo! under the rubble—a skeleton in the coat of mail of a Crusader on his way to wrest Jerusalem from the heathen Turks.

American history offers no knights in armor, no holy wars. We cannot renew ourselves by sitting on the ground and telling sad stories of the death of kings. But we can learn to honor such history as we have.

I felt a sad twinge the other day reading a headline in the paper, NO FUSS OVER OLD FRANKLIN. The burden of the story was that President Franklin Pierce's birthday occurred that week—and nobody cared. The man in the street is damned if he knew there ever was a President called Pierce. Worse, the full column setting forth certain details of his life omitted all that was gallant and generous and tragic—and he rates all those fine adjectives.

Franklin Pierce was our only alcoholic President. He died of cirrhosis of the liver after a life of unremitting sorrow. His first two children died in infancy. His third, a boy of eleven, was crushed under the wheels of a locomotive as the horrified parents looked on. One hopes that nobody in the White House ever asked the hungover Commander in Chief, "Sir, why do you drink?" "Why not?" he might have replied.

President Pierce, though his administration was mediocre, deserves to be remembered for more than his drinking habits. He appointed his old college friend Nathaniel Hawthorne American consul in Liverpool, thereby affording him the leisure to write great American novels. Weigh that against Pierce's "mediocrity" and grant it a milligram or so.

All history eventually fades into fable. But before it does, let's tell the youth of America who we are and how we got to where we are.

We live, it seems, not by dogma and creed but by fads, fancies, slogans and verbal twaddle. Such devices may not enrich the mind, but they certainly do pass the time.

A few years ago the fad that passed the time was Fractured

...ry dinner party was sure to dig his
... with unmistakable pride of au-
...rench for "No light in the bath-

... sounding suspiciously like a postcard
... arisian pal Moe Juste, began popping up
... board fences. More howls. But by then the
... ented the game had moved on to a new caper.
... p doll jokes enjoyed a long run and were often hi-
... rs later, though, the only one that comes to mind is
... er-in-law doll. "Wind him up and he does nothing."
... rently, the fad is a merry little game of wild paradoxes, all
... olving Good News and Bad News. It's the most quotable
game of all because it demands a sense of irony, an understanding of black comedy and, most important, total irreverence.

If one had to define the form of this game it might be called
"antithetical parallelism"—at least, by students of rhetoric it
might. The bad news mocks the good, parodies it or demolishes
it. Naturally, the game lends itself wickedly to politics. The best
players are cynics, stiletto wits and silly girls who like to laugh.
The game takes on richness and gaiety as we move up the intellectual scale. Unlike the half-witted "Knock-knock-who's-
there?" of years ago, Good/Bad News demands worldly knowledge as well as humor.

The news game was the subject of a recent competition in *New
York* magazine, a chic, glossy weekly loved by the "in" crowd. It
may be a trend that the single most duplicated entry was the
Good News/Bad News announcement: "John Lindsay will no
longer be mayor of New York/ He's running for President."

An amusing variation had John Lindsay giving his staff the
good news: "I'm going to run for President. . . . Now, the bad
news. So is Paul Newman."

The jest that won first prize for one Germaine Sande—and
rightly so—has Prince Charming saying to Cinderella: "Good
News! The glass slipper fits you perfectly. Bad News: I just found
this big toe in the grass. . . ."

A touch of this mocking game seems to have crept i
salon conversation. Only the other day I heard a prope
"My son-in-law was in the advertising business and do
But now he's a social worker in Alabama and doing goo

A friend who makes great sport of my old-fashioned h
flinging open the dining-room and kitchen windows after d
to dispel the stale cooking odors arrived the other day with
news. "Somebody has invented a gadget that completely eli
nates auto exhaust," said he. Then the bad news. "The gadg
gives off stale cooking odors."

While the Good News game is in vogue, I expect I'll continue
to scan the front page every day with our two categories firmly in
mind. And for weeks to come I'll be reminded of another entry in
the *New York* contest. Good News: President Nixon is planning to
visit China. Bad News: He's coming back." A snide joke, yes, but
that, to mint you a smart new phrase, is all part of the game.

I may not be up to the dazzling level of Mary Anne Madden's
New York competition, but I have had a lovely time inventing
some good/bad news pronouncements of my own.

Good News: Ralph Nader has been made president of General
Motors. Bad News: He has just recalled all common stock.

Booking agent to ladies of the DAR: "Bad news: Martha
Mitchell will be unable to judge your Yankee Doodle Drummer
Boy contest next Saturday. Good news: I got you Jane Fonda in-
stead."

NASA executive to Betty Friedan: "Good news! We have just
named you our first woman astronaut. Better news: And you'll
be going on the first solo rocket to Mars!"

Rental agent to tenant: "Good news! Your rent is being rolled
back 15 percent. Bad news! Your shift on the elevator will be Friday, Saturday and Sunday."

Young bureaucrat to wife: "Good news, darling, I've been
mentioned for a very big government job." Wife: "Bad news,
darling, there are two FBI men upstairs reading our old love letters."

Hairdresser to Representative Bella Abzug: "Good news. Mr.

Claude can set your hair now." Bella: "Bad news. I'm keeping my hat on. Will he mind?"

Here's a snippet from a recurring nightmare: A voice on the telephone says, "Good news! Agnew is positively not going to run in '72." Bad news: "He's going to replace Justice William O. Douglas on the Supreme Court."

It's a marvelous game—if you can keep your mind off politics.

In one of his caustic little essays on the Decline of Everything, Malcolm Muggeridge confides his dreamiest ambitions: 1) to accompany William Shakespeare back to Stratford and 2) to show Jesus Christ around the Vatican.

In the same spirit I, too, set out on make-believe journeys. In one of them I am escorting a pair of history's great gourmands— say Brillat-Savarin and Alexandre Dumas—up and down the aisles of a gaudy, blinding, acre-wide, all-American supermarket.

Incredulous, they sample the homogenized, fortified, concentrated, unspoilable foods on sale. They bite into the finger-lickin' precooked chicken. They nibble the foam rubber bread and the box-ripened peaches, hard as the cobbles of Lyon. Dutifully, they taste it all: "Soups powdered in plastic bags/ Steaks polished and wooden/ Fish cutlets like Arctic crags/ Air-tight pudden."

The verse is from *Punch* (from the droll pen of J. B. Boothroyd) and the description is sound. The "air-tight pudden" tastes of laundry starch, and anybody who buys a frozen fish from a grocery locker is a fool.

The high chemical content of our food is bound to dismay the palates of men bred to fresher, simpler tastes. Nobody put riboflavin into the consommé when Dumas *père* was writing his *Grand Dictionnaire de Cuisine.* And nobody added water, horse meat or chicken fat to the hot dogs, and not simply because there were no hot dogs.

It is good to hear that food stores will soon be obliged to post an all-over price index where customers can see it. But it would serve an equally noble purpose were the government to require a full statement on every label and every meat tag telling us precisely what chemicals, what padding, what ersatz ingredients were contained therein.

I was dismayed the other day by a news dispatch telling of the ways federal food inspectors interpreted federal guidelines. To say that the rules are bent is to indulge in understatement.

Did you know, for example, that a carton of eggs containing four substandard eggs is still a Grade AA carton? Hot dogs and the ever-suspicious viands called "luncheon meats" can contain, the guidebook says, 30 percent fat. (Much too much, Dumas would instantly protest.) The meats usually contain more than that before the inspectors say "No, no."

A chicken containing 13 percent water is approved for sale by the government. Sometimes chickens are passed despite a much higher water content. "The General Accounting Office," says the AP piece, "has estimated that a 1% increase in the water content of poultry costs consumers $32 million a year."

In a Madison Avenue gourmet shop the other day I bought some red currant jelly. The color, held up to the light, was a rich ruby and lovely. The jelly had a cloying, sticky taste, not unlike the backs of postage stamps. I looked at the label, expecting to find such ingredients as pectin, sugar, artificial coloring. There wasn't a word. Not a clue as to why this currant jelly was so nasty.

We all owe a vote of thanks to the consumers' groups currently bringing a suit to force manufacturers to publish all official complaints against their products. We are too meek, too sheeplike when it comes to complaining of bad food. Thus we are cheated, and in a way that strikes at our very survival.

Another of my fantasies would involve taking a great chef from the past—Escoffier or Carême—to an American hamburger bar.

To MacDonald's, let's say, where the computerized recipe calls for ten hamburgers to the pound. *Mon Dieu!* Can you imagine a Frenchman's reaction to such supremely insulting morsels?

We hear from time to time that Americans are in the midst of a culinary revolution—that what TV calls "gourmet food" (and pronounces "gorrmet") is now commonplace on most American tables. Aside from the prevalence of pizza (most of it ghastly) and a rage for fondue and *quiche lorraine,* I can't say I've noticed the revolution. Nor has restaurant fare improved to any lip-smacking degree.

In most American cities it is difficult to buy the delicacies, the special foods that are available in New York and San Francisco. The custom butcher, the greengrocer with his boxes of winter grapes from Belgian hothouses and the open-air market are all casualties of the age of convenience. Someday our great restaurants will have airplane-style kitchens where precooked, prefrozen foods are thawed by infrared coils.

In her book *The Happy Mediocrity,* Elaine Kendall mourns the passing of fine food from the American table. "The bespoke meal, like the bespoke suit or shoe, seems destined to become a special privilege of the quirky few," she writes. And there's another national tragedy, right there, unless one belongs to the quirky few. And I'm saving my pennies to join.

1972

Time for a Change

. . . This was the year the Nixons walked along the Great Wall of China and the President said one would have to conclude that this was indeed a Great Wall. . . . California's Supreme Court threw out the death penalty, saying it degraded and dehumanized all who participated in it. . . . Clifford Irving, lately of Ibiza, conned McGraw Hill out of $750,000 with a bogus autobiography of Howard Hughes. . . . A new nation, Bangladesh, was born out of Pakistan in blood and horror. . . . The Anderson Papers, revealing the President's devious support of Pakistan during this unpleasantness, created almost as much to-do as last year's Pentagon Papers.

John Mitchell resigned as Attorney General and a thousand spotlights went out on Martha. "I'm furious," said Martha.

Father Dan Berrigan was released from Danbury Prison as Father Phil went on trial, with six others, in Harrisburg, Pennsylvania, charged with conspiring to kidnap Henry Kissinger. . . . The Presidential primaries got underway with school busing the big issue. . . . And *The Godfather* finally reached the screen, with Mafia leaders in a pout because they weren't asked to the black-tie opening.

An indiscreet lobbyist named Dita Beard showed us how big business made out under the Nixon administration. Apparently it made out just fine, but for a price—in this case a $400,000 contribution to the GOP convention kitty. . . . J. Edgar Hoover passed on to a directorship up yonder.

As always, the horns blew, the sirens screamed. The wild bells rang out to the wild sky. Old-timers in paper hats sang *Auld Lang Syne*. But, more markedly than ever, it is a sad kind of joy that welcomes in the New Year.

Recent history has conditioned us to pray a lot but to expect no favors from God. Nor, indeed, from anybody else in positions of power.

If we greet 1972 with trepidation, it is owing to the simple truth that 1971 was a killer. A year of blood and tears, of broken promises and hard times. A year in which the American system continued to degrade the many and exalt the few. A year that saw low cunning in high places and small, mean men appointed to seats of honor.

And now the old year has ended. And the ordinary man, the decent, slightly shabby citizen who ultimately pays for all wars and all disasters, can only shrug and hope that 1972 will be a little brighter, a little kinder.

We are still dumping tons of bombs on North Vietnam. But now we are calling such murderous forays "protective reaction strikes." Moreover, the White House is letting it be known that the President personally ordered the latest protective reaction strike, as if it were another deed for the Golden Book.

"The realm has gone to wrack," as Tennyson said of Camelot. Unemployment continues to rise, along with the cost-of-living index. Every social welfare bill that crosses the President's desk is vetoed with mealy-mouthed pieties about the need for more individual enterprise, more old-fashioned integrity. Day-care centers, for example, might damage that inviolate American institution, the family.

Time for a Change

To view a New Year with fear nibbling the heart like a nervous mouse used to be considered neurotic. You were "projecting" onto a larger sphere the sorrows of your own narrow life. Only the blind and the dull complained that the streets were dark, observed Emerson. "To the illuminated mind, the whole world burns and sparkles with light."

Well, maybe it burned and sparkled in 1841, when young Emerson was keeping his journal. But the world has grown bloodier, and a major casualty has been American innocence. We're worldly-wise now the way youngsters in the ghetto are streetwise. Such wisdom constitutes armor of a sleazy sort, but it is not making us a better people.

The bitterest irony of the final month of a bitter year was the beamish report the White House sent forth advising the world of President Nixon's achievements in '71. He came out firmly for curing cancer, putting welfare recipients to work and giving tax relief to the rich. In the immortal words of Lieutenant Calley, the achievements add up to "no big deal." But the White House publicists would like us to believe they do. And some people assuredly will.

The wife of an officer who is either dead or languishing in a North Vietnamese prison contributed a bleak little essay to the New York *Times* this week. "I have been married for 10 Christmases," she wrote. "This is the fifth year of separation. . . . I see no end. I cannot rejoice in the birth of the Son of God. My son has no father."

"We finally have in sight the just peace we are seeking," said President Nixon in 1970. He also said in the course of his 1968 campaign, "Let me give you the promise of the future. . . . Prosperity without war, progress without inflation."

No, we are not in a mellow, mince-pie mood as the New Year begins. "As yesterday was, so tomorrow will be." And don't ask, "How could it be?" The answer is *there* in the papers every single day. Evil abroad in the land begets more evil—1972 could be worse precisely the way 1971 was worse than 1970.

But something turns our faces ever to the sun. Those who have known love are always confident that love will come again. Americans who have had years of wine and roses can only tell themselves that it will be wine and roses again someday. Not to hope is to die a little.

To keep the picture in focus, there *were* some heartening developments in '71. The newly opened door in China is a hopeful sign. Some economists say that the devaluation of the dollar will help us all, though the average consumer has been living on a devalued dollar for years.

"The sum of life ought to be beautiful when the fractions and particles are so sweet." (Emerson's journal again—and don't ask what I was reading late into the night.) One sees particles of hope if one looks. The real J. Edgar Hoover is now emerging from the folds of the flag and the mists of legend. Martha Mitchell seems to have hung up the phone. Reforms in campaign spending are slowly being accepted. Heroin addiction among the young is said to be declining. The ecologists who would save our planet from slow suicide are finally making an impact. "Dirty movies" are a bit cleaner than they used to be. And fashions are prettier.

Besides all the foregoing, it's best to be sanguine about the New Year because, ready or not, dry-eyed or damp, it's here!

In a small, sedate town in New Jersey there's a brawling woman with a nice sense of history. Arrested, she asked the local constable to indict her as a "common scold." He obliged, under a law not invoked since the 1880's. Mrs. Marian Palundrano now faces three years in prison and a $1,000 fine. Not without guile, she has requested the old Puritan punishment prescribed for scolds—a public dunking.

Time for a Change

In the cozy, conforming world of suburbia, Mrs. Palundrano comes on like Carmen with a rose in her teeth. Her neighbors, giddily involved in the mystique of Washday Miracles, no doubt regard her as an embarrassment. "A woman of the town," not to be encouraged in her scolding.

But are not free spirits to be encouraged wherever we find them? In these times we need all the scolds we can get. One fierce, contentious, high-minded woman with a carrying voice should be present at every public meeting. We'd be better governed with a public scold or two on every city council and town hall board.

Let's send a public scold to every state legislature and at least six to the House of Representatives. There are moments when Bella Abzug can't do it all . . . and the likes of Mrs. Palundrano might help. Under a lash of female tongues, Congress just might be goaded into passing some of the progressive legislation it is forever kicking under the table.

Socially and privately, I confess, scolds are dreadful creatures. Women who raise their voices—*anywhere*—are intolerable. Men have a shuddery distaste for loud women. I well remember a political dinner at which a distinguished gentleman roared down the table at his wife, "Darling, if you can't speak softly, shut the hell UP!" Sound advice.

It took a lot of common scolding to win the vote for women, to ram through laws protecting girls who toiled in death traps like the Triangle Shirtwaist Company. There were common scolds behind the passage of the child labor laws, behind, in fact, most laws promoting social welfare. That's women's work, and one could wish that more women were engaged in it.

Until Dorothea Dix and her glorious band of battle-axes cried "No!", the insane were chained to a ring in the floor and fed garbage. To many menfolk, as well as "nice ladies," such women as Susan B. Anthony and Margaret Sanger were common scolds. But for their scolding women's liberation would have come a slower, sorrier journey.

In our own time, it may be said that the legalization of abortion owes much to the common scolds. Some radical groups, such as the Red Stockings who gave vivid, intimate testimony at open meetings, were the shock troops of the crusade.

Women's Lib would be nowhere today without its public scolds, who shall here be nameless. The movement might have collapsed in the orgy of exhibitionism that launched it had there not been a raffish, uninhibited scold or two, doggedly pushing for equality everywhere, including McSorley's Saloon and the Supreme Court.

It may also be said—and I confess to having said it often—that the liberation of women might have gone forward with greater dignity and rallied more men to the cheering stands had the common scolds not scolded so much. But that's a matter of conjecture, and you'll have to take it up with Betty Friedan.

Whatever happens to Mrs. Palundrano, I hope she finds a socially productive outlet for her energy. Being a common scold without a cause just won't do. It's a waste of energy, a dissipation of one's primal force. Somebody should put Mrs. Palundrano through a course of "consciousness-raising." Then let her go scold where she can do some good.

No doubt I'll be hearing from Nice People who believe common scolds belong in jail, pointing out to me all the damage a brawling virago can do. American history has suffered its scolds with a shudder. There was Mary Todd Lincoln screaming at her gaunt, put-upon husband until he gently threatened to have her confined.

Another White House scold was Mrs. Harding, whose tantrums lasted far into the night, punctuated by, "Just remember that it was me who made you, Warren Harding!"

Carry Nation, our undisputed public scold number one, not only smashed up saloons with her hatchet, she tore cigars out of men's mouths, draped shawls over nude statues and inveighed against corsets, plumed hats and apple dumplings with brandy sauce. "She did as much physical damage as a small army," says one historian.

Carry Nation's life was not without its sad ironies. Her second husband was blind drunk at their wedding. And her only daughter grew up alcoholic. Both mother and daughter were eventually judged insane. But the Anti-Saloon League lived on.

Another of my favorite scolds from the past is Dr. Mary Walker, the first woman to wear men's trousers. She also wore a stovepipe hat and a wing collar and carried a cane. She was forever being thrown out of men's rooms and ladies' rooms.

Her talent as a scold was so highly developed that when she, the only woman Army doctor, was captured by the Confederates during the Civil War, they kept her a few weeks, then gave her back. Common scolding, like every other female art, must be artful.

Hardly a Republican in Greater New York let last week pass without sending me the results of the Sexiest Man in America poll conducted by a local radio station. The winner, you see, was Spiro Agnew. (SPIRO *AGNEW??????*) He won over such established lady-killers as John Lindsay (winner of Sexiest Man vote in England last year), Paul Newman, Joe Namath, Dean Martin, Tom Jones and Burt Reynolds. Not an easy victory, we must admit.

All these polls, some old instinct tells me, were shaped by the fine hand of press agents. How else explain some of the raggletaggle gypsy girls who bob up regularly on the Best-Dressed List? But I doubt that GOP press agents are rigging ballots at a New York radio station. What I suspect is that some dedicated Republican secretaries counted the votes at that radio station. I may be wrong. If I am, I apologize, though not to Mr. Agnew.

As the primary season approaches, it's curious how often "sex appeal" is cited in a candidate's favor. Ten years ago we spoke of charisma (Kennedy had it, Nixon didn't). Or brains or integrity or legislative records. Now it's sex appeal, and I'm not sure this is progress, politically speaking.

Getting back to Mr. Agnew, I'll concede that he is beautifully tailored, that he carries himself well and smiles nicely. Squinty eyes and a bit much chinny-chin-chin would be minus points in a male beauty contest. Still, he is what one of his admirers told me he was in her angry letter—"an impressive figure of a man." But a "glorious Greek," as so many readers claim? Well, I'll take the Praxiteles' Hermes. *He's* still sexy after 2,500 years.

It is commonly said of President Kennedy that he had great magnetism for women. But postelection surveys showed that Nixon carried the female vote.

Among the Democrats now eyeing the Presidency, John Lindsay is probably the handsomest. His are qualities women find irresistible: He's tall, graceful, with an easy kind of elegance. Senator McGovern is handsome and appealing until he opens his mouth. Something in his prairie twang, his ministerial manner dispels—for me, at least—all sex appeal. My down-East grandmother used to laugh helplessly at a neighbor who had what we called a "way out West voice." In private, he probably laughed at her Yankee speech.

Still, it's more than likely that Lincoln had a Western twang. Certainly Eisenhower was a voice from the plains. But, despite the tangled syntax, it was an authoritative voice. Indeed, it lingers in memory as tough and warm in timbre, very much like Clark Gable's.

Senator Muskie may look like Jim Nabors in some photographs, but his voice is superb. He may be the first "intimate orator" in American politics. He is always talking to *you.*

What makes a candidate—or, indeed, any man—sexy to women? That depends, naturally, on the fantasies and early impressions of each woman.

Once at a dinner party I expressed a preference for tall, lean, handsome men with blue eyes. "Ach, so," said an elderly psychiatrist in the group. "That was your father, no?" That was my father, yes, but I can cite a dozen attractive, sexy men who have none of those attributes. Not one of them, however, smokes cigars, wears short socks, flashes his teeth at every passing mirror or speaks in obscenities.

One flat assertion I will make. I have never met a conservative with sex appeal. Never. Men who grouse about welfare spending and foreign aid and help for ghetto children are always the wallet fumblers when the dinner check arrives. Always. Their spirits are small in ways that suggest cold nights in the boudoir.

Now, there may be right-wing conservatives somewhere in this great land who are warm-blooded, greathearted, kind and gentle. But you find me one and—to quote my tall, blue-eyed father —I'll make you a watch. Men who are warmhearted and tender with women, men who have enough security in their own persons to care about others, tend to be liberal in politics, ardent in love.

Sex appeal, in the final analysis, is a quality of spirit as well as flesh. And I guess that's why I could never vote for Spiro Agnew in the sex appeal poll.

I don't go to the movies much anymore. I shock too easily, cry too easily and usually get seated behind a loving couple whose nuzzled heads have a combined wing span of five feet.

Besides all that, the theaters are overheated and the souped-up sound track leaves my ears ringing like an unanswered burglar alarm.

All the foregoing, of course, is rationalization. The real reason I don't go to the movies anymore is that the violence on the screen fills me with pain and disgust.

Brutality and sadism have never struck me as the wine and song of a jolly evening. I also wonder: What sort of fantasy life is this to offer our young? Then I remember that brutality and sadism are hardly fantasies nowadays. They're the stuff of life in every American city.

I have not seen *A Clockwork Orange*—reported to be the most violent, most pornographic film on view anywhere—nor do I plan to see it. The book was loathsome enough. (I say that with sorrow, having long admired Anthony Burgess' rich, plummy prose.) The mindless acclaim for films of this genre is consistent with the antihumanitarian ethos that rules us today. We're becoming a tough, scurvy lot, it seems, and our culture simply mirrors us as we are.

It's comforting to know that there are pockets of resistance, however. I was reassured by Pauline Kael's review of *A Clockwork Orange* in a recent *New Yorker*.

"At the movies, we are gradually being conditioned to accept violence," Miss Kael wrote. "The directors used to say they were showing us its real face and how ugly it was in order to sensitize us to its horrors. You don't have to be very keen to see that they are now desensitizing us. They are saying that everyone is brutal, and that the heroes must be as brutal as the villains or they turn into fools."

Well, I'll drink to that summation, despite a heart heavy with the knowledge that they just don't make heroes like Jimmy Stewart used to play. To tune in the old late shows on television is to meet a strange race of beautiful, innocent people who might be from another galaxy. For one thing, they wear elaborate night clothes and they only *kiss*.

No one ever has to look far for a mass of statistics proving the United States the most violent country in the world. We're undisputed champions at murder and rape. There are 90,000,000 firearms in civilian hands, including 24,000,000 handguns. Small boys, encouraged to play with guns, grow up to applaud films like *A Clockwork Orange*.

Recently a friend who shares my feelings that the American Rifle Association and its gun buffs constitute the most vicious lobby in Washington sent me a plastic novelty toy. It was a blue handgun in a white holster, and protruding from the gun was a tiny toothbrush! In a violent land, indoctrination can't start too early.

The gun toters say that violence flourishes because we are a permissive society, because our cops are crooked or because we no longer keep the blacks "in their place." These reasons are as specious as my rationale for not going to the movies.

If we face the truth, it is this: Violence flourishes in this country precisely as the poppy flourishes in Turkey. The soil and climate are ideal. There are people to nurture the growth, take pride in the harvest and resist all efforts to turn over the earth and make a fresh start.

We need no more horrifying proof of how violence corrupts than the story of how we fought for the "hearts and minds" of the peasants of Vietnam.

The correspondents who say there were a dozen My Lais and millions of needless civilian deaths are not liars. In his book *The American Way of Violence*, Alphonse Pinkney reports that civilian casualties in Vietnam have exceeded military casualties three to one. Among the dead: at least 250,000 children. A million more may be burned or maimed for life.

Another shocking story, in a recent *Saturday Review*, tells of the "fragging," or murder, of 45 U.S. Army officers—by their own men! These figures are exclusive of the uncounted fraggings by weapons other than grenades, such as rifles or knives.

Fragging, according to Eugene Linden, is a kind of intra-army guerrilla warfare. It is part of the morality we have exported to Southeast Asia, part of the world of hate, fear, heroin, racism and acute boredom.

Many of the fraggings—only 10 percent of which reach the military courts—are "passionless and unprovoked," according to a court psychiatrist. The same words apply to some of our street crimes. Again, few cases reach the courts.

Some observers, like Professor Pinkney, call our violence "the result of society's having broken faith with the people." For too many Americans, life is brutal, ugly and without hope. Violence has become an accepted means of demanding social change. This, in turn, begets more violence. Real life being what it is, you wonder why anybody would go to the movies to see blood and filth and misery.

Oh, I try, I really do, but I cannot keep a straight face when addressed as Miz.

But in my smiles there is confusion. I never know whether to reply, "Yessir, massa" or "Dat's not me, boss."

This "Miz" business may be the one feminine mistake that will bring a touch of humor to the Women's Liberation Movement. For there's no dodging the fact that "Miz," which is the way Gloria Steinem says we are to pronounce our new designation of Ms., is a regional and colloquial expression with racist overtones. Fortunately, it has also become archaic, surviving chiefly in novels where black children are pickaninnies and the common affirmative is sho-nuff.

Naturally, the women who are fighting for female equality did not intend the term Ms. to be comical. Nor, let it be stressed, were they conscious of the antebellum connotation in the pronunciation "Miz." But most people who use it invariably follow up with some tiresome banality in Down South dialect. ("Birthin' babies is easy, Miz Scarlett. . . .")

The original motive behind the designation "Ms." was to erase the distinction between the married "Mrs." and the single "Miss." The message has taken rather a long time to get through. To my eye, "Ms." has always been shorthand for a Latin term, *manu scriptum*. Echoing the sentiments of many a woman, "I do not wish to be addressed as 'Manuscript Van Horne.'" It's bad enough in this age of illiteracy that hundreds of people are under the impression that "Van" is my middle name.

Time for a Change

"Ms.," in any case, just won't do. I have a married name, which I like to see preceded by "Mrs." And a professional, maiden name which may correctly be preceded by either. But call me Miz and you're currying favor with the wrong missus.

In defense of the new designation "Ms.," Women's Lib says that if "Mister" gives no clue to a man's matrimonial condition, why should not women be permitted the same noncommittal label? The argument has a certain validity, particularly if you're a legally married lady on the prowl. But proof that confusion beclouds this latest edict from the liberation front is found in the oddly addressed envelopes we're all getting these days—*i.e.*, Ms. John Doe. Now, that isn't what the "Libbies" had in mind at all.

One of the criticisms leveled against Women's Lib is that it tries too hard to be unwomanly. It is also charged with a lack of humor. But there's something endearingly funny—and wonderfully womanish—about this "Miz" business. It reminds me of Lucy Baines Johnson changing her name to "Luci" and getting into a snit if anybody wrote "Lucy."

I will concede that Women's Liberation has come a long way since the girls first came to public attention by picketing the Miss America contest in Atlantic City.

After an embarrassing beginning marked by vulgar public display and a militant emphasis on lesbianism, the movement has gained dignity and momentum. Sex inequality *has* had a punishing effect on women, and it was time a strong feminist movement was launched. These belated respects are somewhat begrudging because there is much in the movement that I still find repellent. The "sweaty virility" I objected to originally is still there, though not as conspicuously. There is also a dissipation of energy on meaningless goals that will do nothing to advance the root cause which is equal rights and higher status for women.

The right to put a foot on the rail at McSorley's saloon seems to me beside the point, if the point is getting women into better jobs and out of the kitchen eight hours a day. Worse, to make a public issue of the "right" to invade all-male pubs and clubs gives the movement a bad name.

307

It also strikes me that in this year, 1972, women have surely won "the right to control their own bodies." They have the pill, legal abortion, easy divorce and domestic relations courts where delinquent fathers are made to pay their rightful share of child support. That battle is over. Now, if the liberation of women is to go forward, let them concentrate on those matters which will lift women to a higher level in our society. The "female slavery" they constantly complain of is best alleviated by more education for women and equal pay for equal work.

Though the movement has shown a heartening progress in the political field (don't underestimate that Women's Caucus), it still strikes me that there's too much of what might be called the George Sand syndrome in the membership. Madame Dudevant (who took the pen name George Sand) wore male attire, including a top hat, smoked cigars and liked to be addressed as *Mon Frère*. She had scores of lovers (including Chopin) but once wrote to a friend that, after ten years of reflection, she had concluded that no woman would ever find happiness through love and marriage.

For the average, normal woman, this sort of reasoning is sheer madness. Women's Lib has much important work to do. Some of us may object to being called Miz, but we're in agreement with the higher aims. These aims will never be realized, however, if the movement wastes its substance in storming saloons and altering the conventions of address.

It has been a long time coming but it had to come.

Before this administration had held its first prayer breakfast, old political hands were predicting scandal ahead. All those stiff collars and hearty handshakes would be washed out with their dirty linen, it was said. And the reasons adduced for this prediction were not the usual ones of party spite.

Few men are wise enough or good enough to be entrusted with great power. After studying the character of the men around the President, and after hearing the sources of his enormous campaign funds, we knew that the failures of the Nixon years would be chiefly moral failures. Perhaps that is why some of us took to quoting—too often, I'll concede—Thomas Jefferson's remark, "I tremble for my country when I reflect that God is just."

Since January, 1969, people who believe that a public office is a public trust have despaired of this country more than once. In terms of freedom, honor and truth, this democracy, idealized by the captive peoples of the earth, is closer to Orwell's *1984* than most of us care to admit. When 1984 does come, with Big Brother in total charge, we who predicted it will be in the first tumbrels.

The current uproar over the ITT "gift" of $400,000 to the upcoming GOP convention (allegedly in exchange for a Justice Department promise to drop an antitrust action) came as no shock to some of us. It's the sort of scandal we expected to break, in various forms, a long time ago. This is a government of back-room deals, of intimidation, lies and unhealthy respect for the "business ethic," which is no ethic at all.

The flashback technique by which we all relive our sins and omissions produces a sense of hurt pride and betrayal when we apply it to the Nixon administration: Haynsworth and Carswell, Dr. John Knowles, the humbling of Robert Finch and subsequent demoralization of HEW; the law-and-order fanatics in the Justice Department; the incursions into Cambodia, the stepped-up bombing; Army surveillance; the deification of J. Edgar Hoover; the President of the United States calling student protesters "bums" as four of them lie in a Kent, Ohio, morgue awaiting their parents and a quick burial.

All administrations become the lengthened shadow of one man—the man at the top. The men closest to Mr. Nixon, with the glittering exception of Dr. Henry Kissinger, seem to have been chosen to reinforce the defects in his own character. Can

you imagine Ramsey Clark performing the duties that have de-
volved upon John Mitchell? As history vividly shows us, repressive policies are always carried out by men with a natural apti-
tude for the task.

It is difficult at times to keep the President in clear focus. The
zigs and zags in his policies are unsettling. We are moved to extremes of pride and outrage.

The Richard Nixon who journeyed to Peking cut a splendid
figure on our TV screens. We admired his earnestness, his boyish
desire to please, his courteous interest in all that his hosts set before him. Back home, however, we read that William Rehnquist
does not disqualify himself in Supreme Court cases with which he
is deeply familiar (in consequence of his Justice Department
post), and we tremble again with Thomas Jefferson.

It seems fairly clear that Richard Kleindienst has not been
serving truth, justice or honor in his response to queries about the
ITT case. That a man of this stripe is the President's choice for
Attorney General gives one a deep feeling of unease. (This feeling
can be deepened to a kind of panic by reading of various Kleindienst capers in Richard Harris' fine book *Justice.* One would like
to send a marked copy to every single U.S. Senator who will be
voting on the Kleindienst nomination.)

In one of his campaign speeches, the late Senator Robert Kennedy lamented the irresponsible use of power and said our problem was to persuade men of power to live *for* the public rather
than *off* the public. It's a thought for the White House to ponder.

Given men who use power in sly, malevolent ways, you inevitably have a government of men haunted by fears. Looming largest is the fear of being found out. Fear that exposure will break
up the power game, drop them back to the grubby obscurity
whence they came.

This underlying fear explains the Agnew attacks on the media,
the Army's surveillance of peace groups, the starving of public
TV lest it question the status quo, the Gestapo projects carried
out by the FBI. It explains why the Pentagon Papers and the so-

called Anderson Papers have provoked desperate counter-measures.

When the government must defend itself against its own best citizens by subpoenaing reporters' notes and TV news films, we know we are governed by small, craven men. Men who have much to hide, much to fear. They also have much to lose. In this election year there is the growing—and blessed—possibility they will lose.

In the luckless lands where the candle of freedom has guttered out and a dictatorship prevails, nobody ever needs to ask, "What did the premier—or the junta or the generalissimo—do first, once he'd seized power?"

In Spain, Czechoslovakia, Hungary, Cuba, Greece, the answer is the same. "He put the press, radio and television under government control." After that, the rest was easy.

"The people never give up their liberties," wrote Edmund Burke, "save under some delusion."

The delusion usually is that the man occupying the governmental palace knows what's good for the country. And liberties have a way of vanishing by stealth, always in the guise of some act of beneficence.

Another Edmund—Muskie of Maine—has brought the threat to our liberties into immediate focus. "Whether the administration acts with the velvet glove of Herb Klein or the mailed fist of Spiro Agnew, the intent is the same. The intent is to limit access to information."

Even Hubert Humphrey, whose liberalism has been tarnished in recent years, has declared forthrightly that "The administration is waging a guerrilla war against the news media in a brazen campaign to subvert the First Amendment through blatant intimidation. . . ."

For three years now we have seen network news departments wilt before steady, insidious pressures from the White House, the FCC, the Justice Department and Congressional committees. Reporters have been subpoenaed, their notebooks and tapes confiscated. Local stations have been bludgeoned into canceling network news and documentary programs.

In the past year, CBS has dropped its Tuesday night documentary hour, ABC has virtually ceased all documentary production (save for one recent and very good study of the right to privacy). NBC has canceled *First Tuesday* and its fine White Paper series. And Westinghouse Broadcasting now has no weekday programs devoted to news.

Even more depressing, five stations, according to the latest Columbia University Survey of Broadcast Journalism, have abolished their news departments altogether. Eleven percent reported that they had cut back time commitments to news and public affairs.

Given these melancholy facts, a viewer would like to feel that he still has a window on the world via public broadcasting. Despite some thundering blunders and a self-conscious overplaying to the black community, public broadcasting has begun to claim a respectable share of the national audience. A compelling reason for the attention we pay public broadcasting is that it has, most of the time, refused to lick the boots of the administration or the Establishment. With public funding, plus foundation grants, it has striven to remain above the pressures bedeviling networks.

But now public broadcasting, and all who have been grateful for its presence, has an enemy who promises to be tougher, more reactionary and a great deal more influential. His name is Dr. Clay T. Whitehead—known to his pals as Tom—and he is director of the newly created White House Office of Telecommunications.

Dr. Whitehead goes beyond Klein's velvet glove and Agnew's

mailed fist. He has President Nixon's hatchet. In the words of FCC Commissioner Nicholas Johnson, "Tom Whitehead is scaring the holy bejesus out of the industry."

Nobody doubts that Tom Whitehead is speaking for the President when he states, "There is real question as to whether public television . . . should be carrying public affairs, news commentary and that kind of thing."

The commercial networks, continued this astonishing statement (made to broadcasters gathered in Miami not long ago), are doing such a fine job that there's no need for "alternate programming."

There was no need in Nazi Germany, either. And there will be no need here in another four years, if the administration keeps to the course it has set.

Even so fond a friend of Republicanism as Allen Drury has commented on Mr. Nixon's hatred and fear of the press. A voice on my local Channel 13 (PBS) the other evening suggested that the new postal rates, which will raise the cost of second-class mail—chiefly newspapers and magazines—142 percent over five years, is a punitive, repressive measure. With the rates, many publications will go under.

Besides stating that public broadcasting should omit news and commentary, Dr. Whitehead is also opposed to the Fairness Doctrine, which obliges a station to grant equal time to opposing parties.

What is most chilling about the presence of a White House Office of Telecommunications is that it could be followed, this month or next, by a White House Office of Press Communications. As Thomas Jefferson warned, the freedom of the press "cannot be limited without being lost." Under Richard Nixon, it is being limited a little more each day.